WITHDRAWN

HUMAN NATURE AND MANAGEMENT

HUMAN NATURE
AND MANAGEMENT

THE APPLICATIONS OF PSYCHOLOGY
TO EXECUTIVE LEADERSHIP

BY

ORDWAY TEAD

Lecturer in Personnel Administration
Columbia University

[Do not discard, of historical interest]

FIRST EDITION

MᶜGRAW-HILL BOOK COMPANY, INC.
NEW YORK: 370 SEVENTH AVENUE
LONDON: 6 & 8 BOUVERIE ST., E. C. 4
1929

THE MAPLE PRESS COMPANY, YORK, PA.

DEDICATED
TO
C. M. T.

PREFACE

This book tells how to use psychology in managerial work. In order to do that, it has been necessary to begin with a popular but scientifically sound statement of the outlines of the science of human nature. At best, psychology is not the most easy reading. It does, however, seem an essential introduction, since if one is to apply psychological principles intelligently, he should be familiar with their general statement.

The reader is, therefore, warned against becoming discouraged early in the book. For, beginning with Chap. XI, he will be rewarded by finding the practical applications and suggestions which it is one purpose of the book to supply.

Three purposes have been held in view: first, to set forth the essentials of modern psychology and show the point of view it implies toward problems of human relations; second, to help the reader to improve the conduct of his own mental life; and, third, to show concretely the methods and procedures which are psychologically sound in the management of people.

In the first ten chapters are presented the outlines of psychology, with the more controversial issues subordinated. The treatment is deliberately selective and the selection of topics is governed by the desire to explain those aspects of behavior which have direct relation to executive problems.

These same chapters also include material which should be suggestive as to how to put one's mind in order as a conduct-controlling instrument.

The balance of the book explains the applications of psychological knowledge to specific executive tasks. These have been drawn largely from the actual experiences in recent years of thoughtful and progressive managers.

The book should be of use to all executives who have to deal with people. The vocabulary is largely industrial; but the point of view and methods advocated are equally applicable in offices, banks, stores, government departments, hospitals, social agencies, and all other organizations where people must work in groups under leadership.

The book is also designed as a text for college courses in "industrial psychology" and for corporation executive training courses on "man management."

In a sense, this book is a further development of the psychological phases of the subject of managing people already treated in more general administrative terms in the text by Dr. Henry C. Metcalf and myself in "Personnel Administration—Its Principles and Practice" (2d Ed., 1926). It is hoped that it can be used as a complementary text to that.

Such a book is inevitably a composite product, and I have tried to acknowledge in the footnotes my indebtedness to other writers for specific suggestions. In the introductory statement of psychological principles, I am particularly indebted to Woodworth's "Psychology, A Study of Mental Life" and Dewey's "Human Nature and Conduct." Not alone, however, these authors but also scores of students and executives should be thanked for their substantial aid.

To my wife I am indebted for editorial labors which have helped greatly to clarify the text.

O. T.

New York, N. Y.
May, 1929

CONTENTS

ix

CHAPTER X

HUMAN NATURE AND MANAGEMENT

CHAPTER I

CAN PSYCHOLOGY AID IN MANAGEMENT?

The manager of a coal mine recently installed a mechanical coal loader and put it in charge of a technical-college graduate and three assistants. At first, production went well and they turned out 90 tons a day, which was satisfactory as compared with other mines. But the manager believed that, under the favorable mining conditions they enjoyed, more could be done. Meanwhile, the machine operator was having trouble with his men. When anything went wrong with the loader, he would become angry and abusive. Soon the attitude of his crew had changed from indifference to open hostility. The cost of operation and repairs increased, and a thoroughly unsatisfactory condition prevailed.

The manager decided to introduce a second mechanical loader. But this time he went about the choice of the head operator with great care. He selected a man known for his ability to get on with people and win their support. His three assistants were chosen with equal care. As soon as the training period was over, the production from the second loader rose to 100 tons a day. The gang leader had interested his men in the work, in the machine, in the output. Breakdowns were rare; there was a marked pride on the part of all four men in the results which they were achieving. The installation was an unqualified success, and by the judicious use of rivalry with the other gang an additional spur had been added.

1

Seeing this, the manager shifted the head operator of the first loader to other work, put in another man, and took over two of the men from the second team to help improve the situation on the first.   After a little, the result was that both gangs were producing well and without personal frictions or inefficiencies.

Here was an instance where a manager thought through an important problem of handling human beings in a sensible way. Perhaps without any recourse to formal psychological knowledge he did the psychologically sound thing.   He might, however, have been able to help arrest the defects of the first gang boss if he had known what to do and how to do it.   To suppose that this boss was hopeless as a director of men is contrary to the facts which come to attention constantly as a result of the intensive training which companies are now giving to minor executives.

Many will say that the common sense of the manager and of the head operator of the second machine was all they needed. But the fact that they might have done far more, that they might have improved the other head operator, that the good sense which was common to them is not necessarily common to all executives—these possibilities lend color to the view that a more systematic knowledge of human nature would have been an excellent addition to their equipment.

It is precisely this more systematic view which the science of psychology aims to supply.   It aims to take the common sense of experience and see what scientifically lies behind it, see to what extent experiment and experience, in fact, confirm it.   More than that, it aims to add to that fund of common sense by the uncommon method of experiment, of scientific inquiry into the laws of human motivation, into the innate characteristics of people, into the typical patterns of behavior.

But does psychology offer anything which any ordinarily intelligent executive does not know already?   Is it only saying in the cumbersome language of science what one knows from experience?

It would, of course, be foolish to make the simple and obvious complicated—to make words of four syllables grow where words of one syllable grew before. But if there is ever to be a science of human behavior, there must be a precise vocabulary. As new facts, forces, and laws are identified they must be named in an accurate way. If that terminology becomes somewhat specialized, it is, in reality, only in the interest of clearer understanding. And to refuse to cope with the new and strange words involved is, in fact, to ignore the subtleties and refinements of the difficult subject matter, which is human nature. Also, there will be, of course, in a science of human nature a corroboration of many facts and truths already known. It would be odd, indeed, if the random accumulation of experience and observation through the centuries had not yielded some important knowledge concerning human nature. Yet, as I believe this book will show, such a random collection can never prove so illuminating nor so constructive as can the more organized pursuit of knowledge under the guidance of the scientific method. Already, such study, in addition to confirming some familiar truths, has shown how to develop new insight and generate new human power in many new ways.

One has also to remember that common sense is by no means uniform or convincing in its results. Its dictates to some people are that strict autocratic discipline gives best results. It has told others that a discipline obtained by rules imposed from within the group is best. Common sense tells some executives that discharge is a function of the management alone. It tells others that its most satisfactory results are achieved where management shares the function with the workers themselves. Is group conference with foremen and rank and file a waste of time or an educational medium of great value? Is the demand of workers for security as to their basic livelihood one which will sap initiative, or does it represent the prior condition of displaying initiative?

On questions like these, common sense has ruled the day with confused and contradictory results. Yet they are the questions regarding which scientific study about human motives and the mainsprings of behavior has already yielded some definite and positive conclusions. No; so-called "common sense" has had its groping way in such matters long enough. It is time now for the tested methods of a science to be drawn upon in order to see how we can direct human organizations of all sorts most harmoniously and happily for all involved. The science which can do this is psychology. And the promise it holds is almost infinite in range.

Will the Use of Psychology Involve Exploitation?—A more serious objection to the value of psychology comes from those who have watched the uses of psychology when applied in the fields of selling and advertising and have misgivings about the danger of manipulating and exploiting people against their wills. If, as psychologists claim, a working knowledge of their science increases the possibility of *predicting* and *controlling* behavior, is there not a likelihood that managers will use psychology to strengthen their control over the behavior of their subordinates? Is not exploitation of corporate groups by clever leaders under such conditions almost inevitable?

The answer is, clearly, Yes. It will be relatively easy for the adroit executive to take some of the methods here discussed and use them with advantage to himself. He can do certain things with incentives or training or publicity or with the manipulation of the purposes of those he desires to influence; and he can get results. The real question is, Does he get results which *permanently* affect in a helpful way the behavior and desires of those he leads? Does he by the use of a device taken here and a method drawn there get what he really wants? And this question can be answered only after one asks the further question, What does he really want?

The answer is easy to state in a phrase; but it is hard to convey as a truth. The underlying psychological result which the manager *should* be striving for is *such a modification in the desires and purposes both of those being managed and of himself that, over a period of time, what he wants and what they want comes to be much the same.* What he really wants is minds and energies permanently committed to furthering an agreed aim in a cooperative way. He wants to develop a motivation or urge to action in his group which *of itself spontaneously generates from within their efforts to get the results sought.* He wants a situation in which cooperation has become the natural and dominant mood and method of his group.

In order to do that, he further wants, if he did but know it, to discover, adopt and popularize those aims or purposes for his organization which are sufficiently wide and inclusive in their appeal to attract the support of his other executives and the rank and file. If all the purposes which control him in running his organization are intrinsically narrow, limited and in essence selfish, they can never attract for long the support of his staff. If they include aims which reckon with the natural and developing desires, aspirations and interests of his group, that group's loyalty can sooner or later be won.

In other words, he may try exploitation—which means using others for purposes to which they are not consciously a willing party—and may seem to succeed temporarily. But far from succeeding in a long-time way and carrying on over a period of years, his exploitative use of psychology will bring its own defeat. If this point does not carry conviction at the moment, I urge the reader to suspend judgment until he has read further. For the underlying contention of this entire volume is that modern psychology points unmistakably to this conclusion: that *the true means of permanently influencing others lie in the direction of fostering conditions in which people in and through their own inner desires come to seek the results which the leader also comes to desire.*

I can illustrate this principle by reference to the problem of morale building. Every executive wants good morale in his organization. That is, he wants a positive zeal for action in behalf of a known and worthy purpose. Many managers have believed that they could improve morale by various separate devices such as annual picnics, athletic events, evening recreational provisions, prize contests for suggestions, group insurance, and endless other expedients. It is easy to recite a variety of methods which temporarily may benefit morale. But a permanent underlying enthusiasm which does not have to be constantly fed with new excitements and inducements is sought in vain in these directions *unless* something basic is also done to be sure that the members of the organization (1) know what its purposes are; (2) find those purposes congenial to themselves; and, therefore, (3) find themselves willing and eager to espouse those purposes as their own and *seek to realize them as a natural fulfillment of their own personal sense of self-realization and self-satisfaction.*

In securing morale, in sustaining interest or exercising leadership—in all the creative tasks discussed in this book—the question of the purposes for which the action is sought is the "milk of the coconut." In the absence of a consciously articulate answer to this entire question, any fundamental and permanent success with the devices mentioned here will not be achieved. I can say with little fear of contradiction that it is only in those organizations where this problem of consciously formulating, modifying, and sharing corporate purposes has been explicitly considered that the best results are being obtained from the use of the hundred and one detailed measures for morale building.

The aspects of the problem on which the manager must, therefore, seek an answer are: What are purposes? Who formulates them? What are the purposes of my organization? Are they calculated to receive the support of the workers? How must they be modified so that a sharing of them by the workers will surely take place? Chapter X is devoted to an extensive discussion of these very questions.

This truth can be stated in another way. *The activities which people do well, faithfully, and persistently and which give them that vital sense of spontaneous generation from within are those prompted by a realization that they themselves are getting a sense of self-fulfillment from them.* In order to know what self-fulfillment means we shall have to examine the nature of the self and of the kinds of urges which we all naturally follow. But that the sources of influence lie in harmonizing the efforts of the leader with these urges of the led quite as much as in harmonizing the efforts of the led with the wishes of the leader is a fact which is one of the profound secrets of executive power.

In short, what can be done to minimize conflicts of aim, increase understanding, nourish enthusiasm, and make human relations between management and managed both kindly and effective depends only partially on procedure and a great deal upon what ends and aims are activating the groups involved.

It may be objected that such an emphasis on the conscious motivation involves a misreading of the facts about human nature because it involves an overemphasis on the part played by conscious motives in behavior. The best answer to this objection is to admit its soundness. Some of the day-to-day activity of all of us does grow out of motives of which we are not at the time clearly aware. All motives are not consciously phrased when being followed. But in respect to rather long-maintained activities, there are usually fairly definite and conscious purposes in mind. And when we come, as we do in considering problems of executive direction, to consider what the executive wants people to do, we are clearly dealing with the problem of the rôle of explicit purposes. The problem becomes one of discovering what purposes can get agreement from the groups in the organization and what conditions of the industrial environment can influence and prompt human beings into conduct in line with these purposes.

How to Apply Psychology.—A useful distinction is often drawn between the *tools* of management and the *art* of management. The application to concrete situations of the many methods here described is, indeed, an art requiring the utmost skill. People will differ in their aptness in applying psychological knowledge and in their speed of improvement; but that they can improve *by taking thought* experience has bountifully illustrated. There is, of course, a great difference among people in regard to that almost intuitive sense of what will go with others and what people's responses will probably be. Whether or not this sense is educable, I do not venture to say.

But it surely is possible to make suggestions as to how one may improve his use of a knowledge of human nature. It is true, for example, that if unsuccessful experiences of human contact are studied by an individual *after* they have occurred, the reason for the failure will frequently appear. And an understanding basis will be supplied which can be used to prevent the recurrence of ineptitude in a similar situation.

Every executive must, of course, make his own applications of psychological knowledge. No one can help him at the point of his going activity. Also, that activity itself in order to be psychologically effective must be relieved as far as possible of an evident sense of conscious intent. The best art will conceal its use of art by having become, through study and practice, so saturated in natural artistic technique that it flows forth spontaneously. The frame of mind, the underlying attitude, should be so well assimilated that it increasingly gives rise to adept performance.

People are quick to detect artifice or self-consciousness in human dealings. It is supremely necessary that on the job and face to face with individuals and groups, executives should *be themselves, be natural, spontaneous and sincere*. If the fruits of a given way of handling a problem are unsatisfactory, the time for critical reflection and for discovering better ways to proceed is *afterward*. Planning, constructing approaches and lines of attack on problems, and subsequent evaluation of what has happened—these are for one's private office. In action, a straightforward and unstudied attitude is imperative.

At the moment of directive effort, the executive must be a sympathetic and understanding human being and not an introspective psychologist. If he can show himself in his human dealings to be a "regular fellow," there is then the strongest likelihood that he can use his psychological knowledge to add a cubit to his stature.

CHAPTER II

THE PSYCHOLOGICAL POINT OF VIEW

Problems in *human* engineering will
receive the same genius the last century gave to engineering in more material forms.
—THOMAS A. EDISON.

What is Psychology?—Psychology has been defined as "the
science of the conscious and near-conscious activities of living
individuals." It is the "science of human behavior in its relation
to and dependence upon mental processes."

In other words, it is the science which seeks to find out how and
why individuals and groups act as they do, the respects in which
they are similar and in which they are different, the ways in
which they are influenced by their surroundings. It is concerned
with the understanding, the prediction, and the control of human
conduct. It seeks light on the original nature of people, on their
acquired traits, on the way in which they acquire them, on the
resulting modifications in human nature—on the relation of
human nature to human nurture.

The psychological point of view is that point of view which
seeks out the cause and effect relations in behavior and assumes
for purposes of scientific study that there *is* a cause, or causes, for
the behavior which goes on from birth to death.

What is Behavior?—The things which are studied in pursuing
this science are largely actions, conduct, behavior. In formal
language, behavior may be defined as a function or derivative
of a person's adjustment to his environment. It is a response
to the succession of stimuli which confront the individual as
life itself moves on. The stimuli are of many kinds—bodily
changes, ideas, the demands of other people, the objects of the

9

natural world. Because human beings have a certain awareness about their behavior, the inner (subjective) effects just as much as the outer (objective) results constitute part of the behavior to be studied. Behavior is at once a physical and a mental fact. It is at once a personal and a social fact. It is the response of the individual's whole organism to the total situation in which it momentarily is.

Behavior is thus at once a function of the human structure and of its surroundings. To conceive of it as causally related to one alone is to see only half the truth. It is the resultant of the interaction of organism and environment and is brought about by the effort of the individual to secure a working adjustment or harmony between himself and that environment.

Because it is the whole person's reaction to the whole situation, it is exceedingly complex and exceedingly fluid. The individual is never wholly the same in experiencing any apparently identical situation a second time. And no situation however apparently identical ever recurs in complete sameness. Every moment each person and the entire range of influences which surround him are changing by a process of give and take. Not only is every situation always changing into another and different one, but also the response of individuals is not merely to the total prior behavior but to the current relationship as a whole. In behavior, it has been said, the response is to the relating. This means something which is at the same time simple and profound, obvious and yet always being forgotten.

As a concrete illustration of this truth, take the case of a factory which in a period of business depression has faced the necessity of a reduction in wage rates. The management, following the familiar procedure in such cases, posts a notice of a revised scale of wages to take effect at once. The employees seeing this announcement decide to strike; and only with difficulty are they finally brought to delay such action until after a direct conference between them and the manager has been held. There the manager explains the reasons for the reduction. But he is faced not simply with discontented employees plus adverse business conditions. He confronts, also, employees whose confidence in him has been definitely lessened by his conduct. He himself has been responsible for changing one important element in the whole situation—the employees' trust in his judgment and fairness. And he has that additional factor to reckon with thereafter if he is to deal with the situation in its true complexity. The employees on their side are confronted at the meeting by a manager who is changed, in part, from the man they dealt with before the strike threat. The fact of the strike threat plus the facts about the depression have created reactions in him which make him a less simple and less familiar person to deal with than formerly.

Grasp of this reality of changed and changing attitudes on both sides is vital to any true understanding of the evolving total situation. The response of both parties is, in fact, always to a new relationship between them. And only as those affected realize this do they keep realistically up to date in their minds with the real nature of the situation with which they are dealing. Otherwise, there is always danger of a serious discrepancy's growing up between the situation in fact and their understanding of it.

If, throughout the subsequent chapters, the evolving and dynamic nature of situations and of people's relation to them is not repeatedly stressed as it should be, that is not because its importance is being forgotten. It is rather because by giving this vital aspect of the truth about understanding human affairs early and emphatic mention, I mean to put this idea forward as coloring the entire view of behavior here presented. Constantly in need of rediscovering in the mind and conduct of every individual, and of executives in particular, is this truth that *the world one faces as well as the one who is facing the world are both continuously affected by the interrelation which all experience implies, in such a way that a continuous study of going events is required if one is to be sure that he is coping with contemporary reality and not the reality of past moments or days.*

The psychology of the evolving situation is the effort, immensely necessary, to get the raw facts of experience as it moves on and the verbal formulations of understanding as it gropes along behind, to be as much more nearly simultaneous as is possible. And this can only begin to come about when people are deliberately aware of the danger, are conscious that they live in a moving world, and are striving to keep up with it.

What is Human Nature?—In defining behavior, the emphasis has been upon the outward manifestation of inward states. Another view of the subject matter to be studied is obtained if we try to see what human nature means.

Historically, human nature has been viewed in a variety of ways and it is useful to identify some of these because their influence has by no means ceased and the view which modern psychology suggests is seen in sharper contrast in relation to them.

There has been, for example, the view that people always seek pleasure and avoid pain. In this view, everything depends on one's definition of pleasure, since plenty of examples of people's courting pain could be cited—martyrs, mothers, warriors, explorers, and others. Pleasure is in this theory confused with happiness, and the complex sources of happiness are ignored. The modern view is that what is called the "feeling-tone" of pleasantness or unpleasantness accompanies every activity and acts as somewhat of a guide in helping the individual to evaluate his experience.

There has been the religious view, conveniently called "calvinistic," which held human nature to be "fallen" and evil, and claimed that only by repentance and conversion could it be "redeemed" and made worthy. The influence of this negative view has been great and extremely pernicious, because it looked so largely outside the individual in a supernatural direction for the sources of personal power and development.

The notion of the "economic man" has also had its influence among certain groups. This view was that people always acted to advance their economic interests, that money was the supreme motivator. Here, again, the explanation is too simple to be a general one. Money motives are usually secondary; people want money because they want other things which can be procured with it.

Another current school of psychology would reduce all motives to two—self-preservation and sex. The simplicity of this explanation seemingly belies the facts, although its very simplicity attracts many. Unquestionably, people show a strong tendency toward actions regarded as self-preservative; but in the fervor of war or of religious agitation they certainly do not. And in another sense, self-preservative considerations underlie almost all activity and this thus becomes too sweeping an explanation to be illuminating. Pervasive as are the influence and power of sex motives, it is easy to rest a too great burden of explanation upon them.

But what difference does it make what view of human nature is held by people, since they go on living and loving and dying just the same? The answer is that in the long run it makes all the difference in the world. One's notion about the nature of motives makes a difference in educational policy and methods; in ethical and religious standards and observances; in the purposes which people cherish; in the whole significance and value that one sees in life. Indeed, I hope to show that the modern psychological view of human nature provides a background for the understanding and control of practical conduct which is helpful and constructive and, at many points, in startling contrast with the behavior implications of older views.

What, then, is this modern view? This entire book aims to be the answer to that question. But let me attempt to summarize at once, in advance of elaboration, the picture of human nature which modern psychology suggests. No one phrase can aptly characterize it. Rather does one find that a number of words recur in efforts at exposition and give the newer emphasis. Such words as "growth," "change," "emergence," "desire," "purpose," "conflict," "development"—these suggest how attention is now fastened on qualities of the human organism which reveal a dynamic and unfolding self.

Human nature is conceived as growing from within—generating normally and spontaneously ways of acting and of responding to situations which are implicit in the fact of being human and being alive. Sensory, emotional, and reflective powers and capacities are inherent in human beings. They act and experience and learn not alone through outside pressure but because to act is to live; and the will to live, to be, to register as a distinct and unique factor in the world is born with us. Out of this urge of human beings to live come learning, the building up of habits, the choice of activities from among conflicting alternatives. The habits themselves come to have their own propulsive power. Yet they, in turn, come into conflict with each other and in some way individuals find themselves deliberating, evaluating, judging, and choosing as between the seemingly possible alternatives.

In the modern view, the entire range of human desires and impulses is equally worthy and significant. The notion of "lower" or "higher" in human nature is not conceived in any absolute way. The forces which at the moment and in the light of the entire situation contribute to effective living, growth, power, and vitality are the forces to follow. Each situation requires discreet handling in order to be made to contribute truly to life; but the judgment to be exercised is a matter for individual decision in the light of his own promptings and training.

Also, the central fact of desire and of the striving after specific purposes suggests how characteristic is the outreaching quality of life. Awareness increases, desires grow, power to achieve does or does not develop depending on the choices and habits of the individual. No one stands still. Life is fluid; and it is always either progressing or degenerating from the point of view of one's use of individual capacity.

The rôle of deliberation in making selections from among possible lines of activity should, finally, not be minimized. Great store is here set upon the potential uses of reason in helping to forward the emerging processes. How individuals may be helped to wise choices will be considered more fully on later pages. But this sense of the significance of mind should be made part of this introductory picture.

In a word, human nature is now seen as a plastic, dynamic, growing, outreaching, desiring thing which responds eagerly to its surroundings, which experiments, experiences, chooses, evaluates results, and struggles always on to more satisfactions and wider reaches of experience.

These almost cursory suggestions about human nature—intentionally not systematic—are designed only to suggest that human nature is the name given to the bundle of qualities which prompt people to the infinite variety of actions they carry through. It is the name for the totality of motives, numerous, contradictory, and often mutually exclusive in action, which constitute the electric current, so to speak, which charges the human being into aliveness and continuing activity.

He who would be wise in dealing with human nature will find that a few large categories or types of motive tend, in general, to explain the big trends in the normal areas of behavior. But a great complexity of lesser drives, habits, and conflicts enter in to dictate the details of hourly activity. What some of these big influences are which enter as substantial modifiers of human nature will presently be considered.

Can Human Nature Change?—"You can't change human nature" has been repeated so often that the sense in which this is true, if at all, deserves consideration. If the term "human nature" is used to mean the sum of inherent and acquired characteristics as they are exhibited in conduct, then human nature *does* change and develop both in the life of the individual and in the life of the race. But if it is used in a narrower sense to mean the underlying inborn traits present in the human nervous system in the absence of special training, then human nature apparently does not change. The child of 6000 B.C. and of 1929 A.D. could both be taught by the application of the same methods of pedagogy. Suggestion works now as then; and imitativeness. Attention is subject to the same laws, and interest is maintained in the same way.

If this were not so, how would any science of psychology be possible? Psychology can be a science because it is possible to formulate a certain few laws about human responses which prove, in fact, to hold true continuously and from one country and age to another. This factor of universality and permorence in human traits in this restricted sense is not a reason for discouragement; rather the contrary. It argues that, once people really understand their own natures and the laws governing them, they can work in harmony with these laws to forward the processes of human nature most effectively and rapidly. It means that man by understanding the underlying laws of behavior can "strive in the same direction as the blind evolutionary forces which were moulding his planet æons before his appearance; that his task is not to oppose but to crown the natural order; to transform it to a better, not by taking a new direction, but by accelerating and intensifying the old."[1]

The reason why human nature is seemingly able to function on more complex levels of civilization from century to century is not that there is any change in the nervous mechanism, brain, or germ plasm of individuals. It is because the social heritage, the cultural surroundings into which people are born, can be assimilated and appropriated for use during infancy and thus become the effective possession of all who have the good fortune to be the heirs of a given age. The inherent differences between the children of Periclean Greece, of imperial Rome, of contemporary New York, and of the Marquesas Islands of the last century are negligible. The variations in normal response which appear are the result of the manners, customs, traditions and habits dictated by the prevailing culture.

The Relation of Body and Mind.—While there is no need to indulge here in the metaphysics of the age-old problem of the relation of body and mind, it is necessary that some assumption on this point be made and adhered to. It is the assumption of this book that there is in some way a constant interaction and interdependency between what are commonly spoken of as the physical and the mental facts and forces. This interaction is conceived of as continuously reciprocal. The mind is always affecting the body by the flow of its successive awarenesses, and the body is always affecting these awarenesses by the way in which it is functioning.

Any mention of this subject at once raises a question as to the points of view and conclusions of the different schools of psychology. I have no desire to give a false sense of simplicity as to the subject matter or the methods of this admittedly young science. The aim is rather to choose out of the findings and teachings of the different schools those truths and facts on which they concur or those in any one school which throw new and important light on the nature of mental life and behavior. A choice of material is made in an effort to follow the reasonable consensus of modern views without extreme devotion to any one. The following quotation seems to state the present issues and a way of viewing them which is sensible and intelligible.

The consistent interpretation of mental phenomena as conduct in the process of being formed, and the interpretation of every mental state as incomplete action, will assist to some extent in unifying the several schools of psychology which are now talking totally different languages. The structuralist and the functionalist devote themselves to mental states as such, the behaviorist confines himself to behavior that can be physically seen and measured, the psychiatrist is primarily interested in the subconscious sources of queer conduct.

The content of these three main types of psychological inquiry constitutes, according to our present interpretation, the three phases of a continuum. Conduct would be thought of as starting in the obscure sources of the inner self which psychiatrists are studying. These sources become impulses as introspectively known to the conscious self. They are now studied by the academic schools of psychology as though they were more or less distinct entities. These impulses, as consciously known, would be thought of as conflicts which are being decided while the contestants are still unexpressed in conduct. The behavior and the cessation of behavior that accompanies satisfaction would be thought of not as the exclusive and only possible subject matter for psychology but rather as the biological objectives for which mind does its work. In a certain sense, our interpretation is behavioristic, because behavior is the centre about which the mental antecedents are interpreted, and yet behavior is, after all, only a means to an end in the satisfactions that we seek. Psychology starts with the unrest of the inner self, and it completes its discovery in the contentment of the inner self. Only with such an interpretation can human psychology be considered to be human. With it, also, we are able to follow with genuine interest the medical, psychological, and behavioristic studies that throw light on the causal factors in human conduct.[2]

The Physical Basis of Behavior.—Underlying and conditioning all his conscious mental activities are the physical bases of man's behavior. Man is, in the first instance, a "physicochemical engine." He is producing, converting, and giving off energy. And the creation and liberation of that energy in the human organism entail the operation of a muscular, a digestive, a nervous, and a glandular system. The interworking of these systems affects the tone of the entire organism. Any attempt to understand it without reckoning with the effects of these physicochemical reactions is obviously superficial. Current knowledge in this field, although far from complete, offers considerable aid. The science of physiology contains much of this information, and a good general text in this subject should be read by every student.[3] Knowledge of the relation of the glands to behavior is, however, still in its infancy. Indeed, it is impossible to say much more than that it is now known that the glands *do* influence conduct on occasion.[4]

The structure of the brain and of the nervous system and the manner of its functionings are briefly described in most psychology texts and can be studied to advantage.[5]

Someone has aptly suggested the organic relation of man to the rest of the animal world by calling him "a domesticated higher mammal." The evolutionary view of human structure and nature implied in this phrase is accepted in this study and unquestionably suggests a point of view which is helpful. A study of origins and beginnings is often illuminating as to the present nature of a problem. And if one remembers that the process of domestication is necessarily a slow one, that basic wants of food, sex, and shelter are shared by man with the rest of the animal world, that these must be his prime concern as they are of the animals, one is in a frame of mind to be much more discerning, realistic and patient about the frailities and fumblings of human beings. Indeed, in the life of the world and of living organisms, the length of the history of mankind is as an inch in relation to a mile. Humanity is young. Why be surprised and discouraged if it manifests the shortcomings of youth?

To the same effect, a recent writer[6] points out that one can usefully think of the human mind as being, *in a way*, the result of the building of four strata one upon the other—the animal mind, the savage mind, the child mind, and the civilized mind, the last a thin veneer covering the rest.

The industrial environment and, in fact, the environment of any kind of large-scale organization, provides a new and unaccustomed medium for action. It imposes burdens, restrictions, and disciplines unknown even a few generations ago. Man came out of an agricultural, a hunting, a village background where human needs and desires were capable of simple and direct satisfaction. The adaptations required for modern living are, to say the least, drastic. Particularly where, due to international or even interstate migrations, people of agricultural communities (as, for example, from eastern Europe or Negroes from southern plantations) are suddenly thrust into the midst of urban industrial centers, it is obvious that the behavior problems presented will be formidable.

The central thought to be carried away from this mention of the physical basis of conduct is that human nature is greatly limited in its possibilities by the strength and vigor of the physical organism. Man is far less an angel fallen from heaven than he is a poor, bewildered, struggling, aspiring creature out of the clay. And he must perforce keep his efforts at all times realistically connected with the animal needs and desires which prompt him to survival. Whatever efforts at realizing his aspirations may be undertaken—and their name is legion—if they do not build on a basis of providing for his requirements as a physical organism, they are fated to short life.

CHAPTER III

THE INBORN TENDENCIES TO ACTION

A warning should be offered before any attempt is made to discuss the constituent elements in human nature as they are usually divided, named, and analyzed in the psychology textbooks. Such dissection is inevitable and is valuable in forwarding understanding. *But it will be of genuine use only as the reader bears in mind throughout his study of the parts, that it is parts he is considering and that as parts they are falsifications of human nature which is a whole and which always is seen in action as a whole and as related to a specific set of surrounding factors in an always changing and evolving succession of total situations.*

In talking of such separable aspects as tendencies to action, emotions, attention, learning and the rest, much of practical value emerges. But it has always to be applied in full view of the obvious fact that human nature is a complex working together of all these and other elements. However, much the psychologist may talk of elements of human nature, the executive has always to deal with individuals as total personalities. And his knowledge of psychology will be only bookish pedantry if it is not the source of concrete illumination in revealing the motives at work in particular cases. It is this vitalized working understanding and interpretive power which it is my aim to foster in this book by keeping whole people and actual situations in mind as constantly as possible.

If the reader will, therefore, have this warning in mind, he will see the next few chapters not as discussions of separate and chopped-off unrealities, but as shafts from a searchlight playing on one object from many angles.

Consideration of the native and unlearned traits of human beings and of the traits they acquire during infancy and adolescence leads at once to definitions on which the psychologists themselves find agreement difficult.

The usual approach has been to start with what are called *reflexes* as the simplest behavior manifestations. Examples of these are sneezing, laughing when tickled, and the winking of the eye. These are inborn responses which require only the proper stimulus to call them forth. But they help little to explain the more complex activities which one is anxious to understand.

The idea of *instincts* has been another assumption which is now much less generally held than formerly. But because the word is still widely met in psychological writing, it is useful to define it. An instinct is a native impulse directed toward the execution of certain movements and the accomplishment of certain results (Woodworth). It is an inherited combination of of reflexes which has been integrated by the central nervous system so as to cause an external activity of the organism which usually characterizes a whole species and is usually adaptive (Parmelee). It is a combination of explicit congenital responses unfolding serially under appropriate stimulation (Watson). Instinct prompts to action which is without foresight as to ends or previous education in performance (James).

The essence of the idea is that an instinct supplies the general pattern of a behavior trend which tends to result when the right stimuli are encountered—a tendency to act in specified ways that is inherent in the nature of the organism when placed in a specified kind of situation.

Whether there are many or few such unlearned traits is a question. Fortunately, however, there is little disagreement on the fact that in the course of individual growth there are manifested certain broad types of response to typical situations which are reasonably universal. At what precise point in the individual life they appear is, for practical purposes, less important than the fact that they *do* appear. Not that they give rise to sharply divisible units of behavior which can be isolated as evidences of one instinct or another like bones in the study of anatomy. But rather that they identify general tendencies to act along certain lines at what, for the individual, are appropriate times.

Without going further, therefore, into the academic controversy on the subject, it is proposed here to discuss briefly a few broad *tendencies to action* which adult conduct discloses. They are certainly not instinctive in the restricted sense of being explicit responses; they are highly adaptive, modifiable, and modified when observed. Nevertheless, they are so general in human conduct as to offer a helpful clue to the understanding of much behavior. They are propulsive in character—that is, they provide the drive, the power, the source of much individual action—and thus, in the analysis of motivation, they are significant.

The characteristics which will be here discussed, not as instincts but as general desires or general *tendencies to action*, are self-assertiveness, submissiveness, manipulativeness, curiosity, sex, parental desire, pugnacity, the play desire, and gregariousness. I offer no defense for either the inclusion of any of these tendencies or the exclusion of others, beyond the practical thought that a discussion of these nine traits proves to be specially illuminating in explaining a great deal of what people do. Neither their origins nor their adequacy as complete explanations are at the moment under scrutiny.[1]

Self-assertiveness.—This characteristic is placed first because I agree with those who contend that this is one of the strongest and most pervasive of underlying tendencies. The yearning for a sense of individual worthwhileness, for the chance to register effectively, to demonstrate to oneself and to those whose regard one seeks that one *is somebody*, this is a well-nigh universal trait.[2]

This self-regarding sentiment leads one to seek to dominate others, to demonstrate one's superiority over them in some particular direction in order to avoid being too completely dominated, to seek applause—in short, to manifest personal power in any way possible. Typical channels for its expression are found in the home, in one's working environment, in social life, in civic life. And if satisfactory expression is not found in one of these, it is sought the more urgently in one or more of the other outlets.

If, for example, the working environment provides no outlet, the individual will tend to ignore this as a medium for self-expression and will seek elsewhere for an outlet for his desire to be somebody. Unquestionably, much of the unresponsiveness of manual workers which is imputed to laziness, cussedness, and indifference arises out of their complete failure to find in and through daily work a vital outlet for native interests and talents. To make the conditions favorable and to encourage the exercise of self-registration in and through the individual's working life is one of the real jobs of discerning managers.

Out of the self-assertive tendency seem to develop such emulative characteristics as the desire to excel in all kinds of rivalry, to realize one's ambitions, to protect one's self-pride. And out of a serious thwarting of this tendency seem to arise sulkiness, peevishness, stubbornness, jealousy, and defiance. Those who manifest these distressing tendencies are giving evidence that their self-regard has been wounded in some serious way. Hence, they supply distress signals for the watchful executive, who can then try to help people out of existing maladjustments.

Another revealing fact about the self-assertive trait is that its manifestation is naturally related to the existing attainments of the individual. One's assertiveness is not an absolute fact. It is always relative, always comparative to the attainments of oneself and of those with whom one associates. The man who makes $40 a week and is increased to $50 gets thereby a satisfaction as great as if not greater than that of the man increased from $7,000 to $9,000 a year. Aspirations in the usual case bear a close and definite relation to the present accomplishment of the person. And even when his assertive claims are not stated explicitly, it is usually sound to assume that what the individual wants is closely related to present achievement rather than to some remote but attractive condition which the observer may possibly assume is desired.

This truth throws light on the value of all sorts of competitive projects in industry, on the wisdom of using incentive methods of payment and of published production records, on the relative urgency of the "demands" which organized workers make or threaten to make, on the importance of the claims of a shop committee for extension of the area of its jurisdiction. In every such case, the people affected do not want the earth; they want an effective opportunity to register personal progress *in relation to the point that they have already reached.* In considering claims of employees for improvements of any sort, managers should thus try to get behind the scenes of the employees' thinking and study the base from which that thinking and those new desires take their start. Only so can a true perspective be achieved and a wise judgment reached.

Submissiveness.—Submissiveness is at the other pole away from assertiveness. It is the tendency to subordinate one's self to others, to give up for others, to allow gladly another pilot to take the helm and, for the time at least, guide the ship. The reasons for this attitude may be sincere devotion to another believed more worthy; a sense of temporary expediency; a sense of weariness which makes such resignation sweet and restful; or a real fear of following any other course. Also, what seems like submission may be merely an adaptation to life on a different level of attainment from that of the observer, or a manifestation of inertia, laziness, and willingness to follow the easiest way.

The extent to which submissiveness is desirable depends on the individual case. Certainly, to count upon it as a motivating influence because one assumes the existence of weariness or fear is to count upon a most unstable factor. For both of these can change with conditions and leave a frame of mind in which the normal assertiveness will again come to the front and demand its own. Disciplinary plans of all kinds, and efforts to preserve sharp distinctions of industrial or social status, are unsoundly conceived if they aim to keep people down by intimidation or by overwork and underpayment, which may breed excessive fatigue.

Frequently submissiveness is met where people are devoted to a leader and are keen to follow him. How healthy a situation this may develop depends largely upon the integrity and intelligence of the purposes the leader holds. The wise and high-minded individual will realize the danger of capitalizing too exclusively on such an unstable motive factor as his own popularity. He will try to bring in other less personal motives to sustain and carry forward the relationship. He will see himself as really an educator whose job it is to build upon those submissive motives other desires, purposes, and reasons which are integral to the self-respect and permanently underlying self-assertiveness of his followers. For him to try to build his policies on the submissiveness of others is a program too negative to be sound. He is building on the sand of very shifting desires.

This trait is thus one that is peculiarly in danger of being exploited by a shortsighted or selfish leader. The submission ideally should be to the demands of the situation and the requirements of orderly coordination in a joint enterprise and not to a leader who may have ends of his own he is trying to impose.

Manipulativeness.—The desire to register by being creative in some explicit way appears to be deeply rooted. People do not assert themselves by mere bovine existence. They are because they *do;* and natively they seem to do, in large part, by *making* or constructing things. And they tend to do and make things which give them additional favor in the eyes of others. This doing and making comes in later life to be creative in one of numerous fields. In childhood, it starts with the handling, tearing apart, and building up of material things. And as individuals grow it is often possible to identify as a distinct vocational type those who are preeminently motor minded, who show special skill and get great delight out of work with things. At one level of intelligence and training, such people tend to become craftsmen, and at another level, surgeons and engineers. When a person has marked motor aptitudes, this tendency to constructiveness and physical creativity is balked with great peril. When one's creative urge is in the field of ideas, it goes into the preparation of sales efforts, law briefs, sermons, lectures, executive policies, imaginative writing, and the like. And in these fields, also, it is thwarted with equal danger to the personality.

The desire to create is, in short, a far more powerful impulse than one would be led to believe in view of the frequent attribution of laziness to people. The trouble so often is that people seem lazy because they have not found the kind of outlet which is for them self-realizing. The practical conclusion is that the greatest care should be used in trying to get people into occupations which are for them congenial. For to have one's activity congenial means that the individual's creative drive is expressing itself in a satisfactory way. And no better motive to a specific line of effort is to be found than this profound inner sense that one is creating in a self-expressive way.

Curiosity.—The "monkeying around" which manipulativeness involves on the motor side has its mental parallel in the trial-and-error, questioning, wondering, inquisitive characteristic which is so marked in children and which, in a refined degree, keeps on through life if the efforts in this direction are not thwarted and if the results attained have not been too barren. It is important to give this tendency every reasonable chance to satisfy itself. Its fruit is growth in individual mental grasp and comprehension and, at its higher levels, new inventions, discoveries, and imaginative formulations of all sorts. People are probably by nature much more inquisitive as to the what, why, and how of things than is now apparent among adults, because of the unfavorable training and regimentation that early life and schooling frequently impose upon them.

Sex.—The sex impulse usually prompts individuals to seek the society of members of the other sex and to carry on the various forms of by-play which are associated with sexual activity. The power and pervasiveness of this urge are tremendous, and the extent to which it influences and supplies the energy for all sorts of creative projects is not sufficiently realized. Far from restricting its drive to one narrow set of behavior results, this desire seemingly overflows and surcharges much of life with a vigorous tide of energy and power which yields varied accomplishments.

Much has been wisely said about the desirability of encouraging this liberation and redirection of the sex impulse into wider outlets—a process spoken of as "sublimation." But it is important to realize that usually this liberation is achieved most effectively when at the same time the specific sex expressions are taking place in a wholesome way.

From the managerial standpoint, the concern should be that the whole situation surrounding the workers' life is such as to assure the possibility of a normal sex life. Where there is segregation of the sexes (as, for example, in lumber camps and railroad construction camps), where the local community has a preponderance of one sex in its population, where work is so fatiguing that no reserves of energy are left for the fulfillment of the sex life—in such cases, there is a special managerial responsibility to aid in offsetting an abnormal social situation.

Also, many of the individual behavior problems which give rise to restlessness, depression, neurasthenia, and all sorts of other nervous and mental afflictions and aberrations arise more from subtle sex causes than people ordinarily appreciate. The thwartings, balkings, and disappointments that occur in this connection are a fruitful source of disruption, at one time or another, in the lives of many people.

The question as to whether or not there are real mental and emotional differences between men and women is a vital one for management, since any differences which exist should result in a different way of handling. It has proved exceedingly difficult to reach any scientific conclusions on this point. Certain studies have seemed to show that capacity and behavior are little if at all modified or adversely affected by the fact of functional periodicity in women. Nevertheless, those companies which see fit to allow women employees a sick-leave of one day a month probably act wisely in the interest of sound hygiene.

The characteristic spoken of as "affectability" does seem usually to be stronger in women. By this is meant the emotional responsiveness to situations. If women are more quickly affected, it means that a somewhat different line must be followed in supervising their work. The same direct, blunt, rough-and-ready kind of treatment that men will ordinarily understand will, for this reason, often be resented by women. Also, women tend to create a much more personal relationship to their work than men. This may have its good and its bad phases. But certainly any work motivation which derives wholly from a woman worker's centering of her sex interest on her foreman or employer is not on a permanently sound basis.

Slight though present knowledge is on these basic differences between the sexes, it is nevertheless true that many of the most ardent believers in the "equality of the sexes" ignore the obvious functional differences which exist and which seemingly require special treatment. Take, for example, the problem of the married woman worker, whether a mother or not. The number of such workers is increasing each year and will no doubt increase more rapidly in the future. Employers could in their own interest do much more than at present, in providing a special schedule of working hours for them. Here is a source of willing and effective labor which could be drawn on much more fully if the regular schedule of hours were not required and if half or three-quarters time on a job were arranged. Equality between the sexes does not and should not mean complete uniformity and identity in all the activities undertaken, any more than it does in physical structure and function.

Pugnacity.—The tendency to pugnacity does not mean a desire to fight in the fisticuff sense of personal combat. It means rather the tendency to mobilize reserves of energy to overcome resistance or obstacles in one's way. The baby who "fights" when his hands are tied is more representative of the working of this impulse than the soldier on a modern battlefield. Efforts to escape from restraint, to overcome a moving obstacle, to institute a counterattack, to escape from pain, to defeat a rival (in courtship or otherwise)—these are characteristic manifestations of pugnacity (Thorndike).

Instead of being something to suppress, pugnacity is thus an attribute to utilize. The problem is to get the individual's energy mobilized in a useful, constructive direction. There is undoubtedly an emotional stir and satisfaction in the challenge of combat which raises the individual to fresh levels of awareness and vitality. But that "warlike" activities are the only ones to yield this stimulation is clearly untrue. To provide occasionally in adult life the kind of stimulating combat situation which produces this emotional release is a task to which the shrewd manager will definitely set himself.

The Play Desire.—The play desire prompts to random, purposeless, irresponsible activities which are removed from the responsible and sober setting of the day-to-day requirements of life. For children, play is unconsciously educational; for adults, it is re-creational in the sense that it enables, or should enable, the individual to return to routine tasks with renewed vigor and spirit.

The manager's problem here is to be sure that the scheme of life of his workers includes the kind of relaxation, variety, gaiety, and release which the human organism requires as a relief from its regular habits. Whether or not this implies the provision of a company recreation program is highly doubtful, except, perhaps, in isolated localities where the company is the only organized agency in a small community. To tie up recreation too closely and constantly with one's industrial affiliations is likely to remove the very sense of carefreeness which is the essence of play.

Gregariousness.—By gregariousness is meant the desire of people to seek out and find satisfaction in association with other people. This desire has been usefully characterized as giving the individual comfort in the presence of his fellows, making him fearful of prolonged solitude, making him more highly suggestible to the wishes, emotional states, and beliefs of his fellows (as represented by conventions, fads, styles, etc.), making him more suggestible to the claims of the group's leader, making him want to enjoy activity with and in his group.

This factor of gregariousness is to be understood only as one realizes that the individual is at practically all times as much being acted on as he is acting. A person acting together with others—in a mass meeting, in a committee, in a corporation—takes on usually a quality of sensitiveness and suggestibility which modifies greatly what is spoken of as his "independent judgment." This is a fact to be reckoned with for good or ill. And anyone responsible for the activities of a group of peopl should realize that there is a technique for the legitimate utilizing of this characteristic. Further suggestions on this topic are given in the chapter on organizing group thought and action.

Conclusion.—In short, these several native drives to action are universal in their motivating influence, overlaid though they are by all sorts of learned reactions. To have in mind this picture of the raw stuff out of which more complicated behavior is organized is helpful as a basis for understanding the more elaborate and mixed motivation one typically experiences or witnesses.

What kinds of general activities, what kinds of underlying universal drives to action, are influential in the human organism? What scope for what types of experience must be allowed for and provided for human beings? Does knowledge of these native impulsive promptings supply some definite hints as to life needs that are denied to individuals with grave danger? It is to begin to answer such questions as these that this chapter has been written.

CHAPTER IV

THE USE AND CONTROL OF EMOTIONS

Human nature includes, as well as native tendencies to action, native and unlearned ways of feeling in relation to particular kinds of situations. We are, it seems, driven to action by tensions of feeling which relate in some cases closely to the impulsive drives described in the previous chapter. Their importance in life is great; their use is inevitable and their control is essential.

It is harder to state definitely what emotion is than to discuss what some of the most important emotions are. For the purposes of this study, attention is centered on fear, anger, hate, and love.

An emotion has been defined as the way the body feels when it is prepared to act in a certain way. It is a "stirred-up feeling," the feeling of physical preparedness for a fairly specific type of conduct.

All levels of bodily and mental functioning are involved. There is a feeling of tension which when well marked under strong emotion is decidedly unpleasantly toned; there is a certain narrowing and intensifying of consciousness—one can attend only to those objects or events which are relevant to the emotional state, and these have an unusual value. And there are more or less violent changes in physiological conditions and overt behavior,—a wild heartbeat, blanched face and lips, dry throat, stilled breathing, a "rising" of the hair, dilation of the pupils, wide-opening of the eyes, muscular twitchings and tremblings, and the incipient movements of flight or concealment. So much we can observe in the ordinary way. Recent physiological research has revealed the profound extent and the special significance of the organic changes. Under the stress of fear, or rage, the arterial pressure is increased, the pulse is quickened, the blood-supply to the viscera is lessened and that to the skeletal muscles is increased; sugar, as a source of energy, is thrown into the blood from its storehouse in the liver, digestive processes temporarily cease; and the secretion of "adrenin" by the suprarenal glands is greatly stimulated, with the effect of heightening all the above-mentioned processes, of increasing the ready coagulability of the blood, and of restoring fatigued muscles quickly.   These physiological facts help us to understand why it is that, under the stress of great emotion, people are able to perform unusual feats of strength, agility, or endurance; why, for example, the soldier, in a state of fighting lust and battle exaltation, can ignore a severe abdominal wound or degrees of fatigue that would normally incapacitate him.

It is also made clear to us why milder, but longer continued, emotional states, which are not able to discharge in appropriate reactions, as, *e.g.*, anxiety, worry, and fear, have so evil an effect upon digestion and bodily health generally.   Digestive troubles are very commonly emotional in origin.   Clearly the biological significance of emotion is that it normally reinforces and prepares for the effective functioning of those instinctive reactions with which it is so intimately connected.[1]

An emotion thus constitutes a drive to action.   The organism is in a state of suspense and tension until the act is performed and the emotional state discharged.   The sequence of events in the life of an emotion has been outlined as follows: recognition by the individual of some object or stimulus which is calculated to stir a given emotion; growth of the stirred-up state of the organism, with desire to act in the specific way indicated; activities of a specific sort accompanied by a certain kind of feeling which is the emotion; fulfillment of the desire and satisfactory release of the emotion (or failure to complete the desired activity and a less rapid dissipating and disappearance of the emotion in other directions).

Appealing to the Emotions.—From the practical standpoint, it is illuminating to discuss next certain typical human situations in which emotions are to be seen working at a high pitch of effectiveness.   So often is the phrase "making an appeal to the emotions" used to mean a drawing on sources of power, on motives which are influential in behavior, that a clear understanding of the elements involved and of the process of such an appeal is highly suggestive of its possible uses and dangers.

How, then, does an emotional state come about and keep sustained in, for example, war, the church, a profession, a political party, a college, fraternity, or lodge? Of course, the emotional state is different in relation to these several situations or institutions. But at the moment when the individual is actively functioning in the specific *milieu* of war, church, profession, and the rest, certain definite reenforcements are at work upon him to keep alive his state of preparedness to act in their behalf. The devices employed include the following: slogans (*e.g.*, "rum, Romanism, and rebellion"); symbols (*e.g.*, flags, insignia, sacraments, uniforms); music (*e.g.*, military bands, church organs); mass meetings; familiar clichés (*e.g.*, "mother," "home," "widows and orphans"); dim light (*e.g.*, cathedrals, lodge rooms); the physical presence of the hero or his representative; specific postures (*e.g.* kneeling); posters and pictorial representations; a well built-up sense of the group's history and prestige; certain tones and inflections of the voice (as those used by preachers and orators); a ritual or liturgy frequently repeated; special initiation rites which give a sense of being set apart in a preferred group.

The fact that these have always proved ways of maintaining group consciousness is all in their favor. And whoever has the problem of building up and sustaining in people a united, corporate state of mind will do well to study the methods of all these institutions and consider applying the devices that they have found serviceable.

It may be thought that there is something artificial and cold-blooded in such a suggestion that the experience of institutions with playing upon and capitalizing emotional appeals be applied deliberately in such a new field of human effort as industrial life. But such use is bound to be made sooner or later, if not deliberately then as a wellnigh natural growth, as responding to the human necessity for having people's institutional group life warmed and made attractive by emotional attributes which are sustaining. We do not live by impulse alone, nor by intellect alone. We demand that our important activities share in and partake of a feeling tone which is dynamic and gripping—which means emotionally satisfying.

The only qualifying consideration which may be raised is as to the long-time effectiveness of emotional appeals under conditions where the purposes which any given corporate unit intends to serve *cannot* be defended either to its constituent members or to the rest of society. But *assuming a socially valid corporate objective*, the fact is that all the devices suggested above have proved their worth in a deliberate plan to put unity of purpose and desire into the minds of the members of a group.

This process of "appealing to the emotions" cannot fundamentally be separated, however, from "appealing to the intellect." The danger is always that leaders will come to think in terms of two distinct kinds of appeal set over against each other. A more mistaken view of the psychological facts could not be held. The trouble with so much preaching, teaching, lecturing, and morale-building activity of all kinds is that it tends to assume that the emotional and intellectual elements in the appeal are separable. They are not. They are always two halves of one whole—of the total appeal which is made to the total personality of the individual involved. A teacher who assumes that his problem is to deal with the intellects of his students, that he is not concerned with touching anything but their minds, usually succeeds in touching nothing. What are called "affairs of the mind"—the search for truth, the acquisition of knowledge, critical deliberation upon facts or principles—these cannot go on without some eagerness to act, some feeling of significance in the venture, some state of tension as to the outcome of the activity. The enthusiasm and magnetism of the successful leader and teacher derive as much from his emotions as from his intellect. The contagion of his contact is largely emotional in its essence.

The manager of an industrial enterprise who wants to build up in his workers the kind of emotional state that he sees in a regiment or in a college football team must not confine his efforts to what is usually spoken of as "hurrah boys" stuff. He may use mass meetings, posters on the signboards, a company buttonhole pin, and picnics. But he will fail to get permanently satisfactory results if he fails to give his people some mental stuff on which their emotions may feed. They must, in order to respond to his appeals in any sustained way, have some intellectual appreciation of the history and traditions of his plant, the reputation and uses of its products, the manner in which the business as a whole is conducted, the results of their own individual efforts, the financial outcome of the part that they as individuals will have in sharing in the company's success.

Thus, the really sound appeal to groups of any sort and for any purpose is one *which deliberately balances and combines the emotional and the intellectual elements;* provides the stimuli which demonstrably keep the individual ready to act but also keep him convinced that he wants to act in the direction suggested because he understands it is to his advantage.

The Rôle of the Emotions.—The role of emotions in life is pervasive, positive and vivifying. They give power and body to experience on the feeling side. Their influence is so pronounced and so determining that to understand where they work and how they work is of great value in the work of controlling and broadening individual experience. The emphasis in the following discussion of four frequently encountered emotional states is upon the ways in which they influence behavior or should be made to influence it. The choice of fear, anger, hate, and love is arbitrary only to the extent that these are familiar drives, the prominent rôle of which every executive should know and be able, to some degree, to help control.

Fear.—The rôle of fear in behavior is probably a greater one than even the fearing person himself ordinarily recognizes. For it is now known that fears which are forgotten may still continue to have an influence.

Fear is that stirred-up state of the organism which results when strange or sudden objects present themselves and give rise to efforts at escape. Biologically, fear is a state of preparedness to act in the direction of flight induced by definite activity in the glandular and muscular systems. During fear, attention and thought are characteristically centered on the feared thing and on the urgency of escape. In this sense, fear is inhibitive. A total condition of preoccupation results. A similar condition results under conditions of pain, anger, rage, and hatred. All these emotions lead to action that is effective in a special, limited and temporary way. And with the removal of the existing source of excitement and the return of the higher centers to their normal influence the power of the emotions is greatly lessened.

That is why efforts to move people by appeal to this kind of motive are unsound from the standpoint of those seeking to exert a continuing influence. Fear, hatred, and anger *momentarily* mobilize powerful energies in the individual. But all military experience, for example, has shown that the fires of hatred have to be constantly fed afresh in order to be influential. For anger at the enemy disappears. And in industry fear gives way to a callous indifference, bravado, or carelessness. The morale problem in warring armies has been found to lie in finding *positive* motives like "protecting the fatherland," "making the world safe for democracy," "the war to end war"—ideas and purposes which have a relatively sustained and sustaining quality. And the experience with armies is not unique.

Any corporate body which seeks a steady and glowing response from its members finds that only motives which enlist the whole person bring worthwhile results. Some firms more or less consciously build their labor policy on the theory that men work because of the fear of being fired. "Treat 'em rough and tell 'em nothing" is a slogan which is old-fashioned but still far too popular. Other corporations endeavor definitely to share with their workers knowledge and understanding of the company's objectives and its financial condition. They seek the positive cooperation and enthusiasm of their employees. The divergent results achieved by both types in the last quarter century leave no room for doubt as to which appeal and which motivation is more effective in creating and maintaining loyalty.

Another interesting fact about fear is its effect on the conduct of those in control in those cases where they themselves are afraid of their constituents even though this is a fact they would hardly admit to themselves.

A great deal of the conduct of employers in a state of excitement during a strike illustrates effectively the fact that the executive who is himself afraid is in the worst possible state of mind to take command effectively. He is in a position of what has been called "overcompensation." He usually compensates for his own terror by being a bully, a tyrant, an imposer of cruelties—obstinate, high handed, arbitrary.

Prison experience also supports this view. The typical prison warden or guard of the old school became inhuman and brutalized, not because he was vicious at heart, but because he was in a situation where he had to prove to himself and to his wards that he was not afraid of them. His reign was built on fear and the only way to keep discipline continuously effective was to increase the dose, so to speak, as the victim became hardened and inured to the amount of rough handling he received.

Nineteenth-century prison administration provides the example, *par excellence*, of the evil effects of using the fear motive in the administration of groups of people. The hardening, inhibitive, and deadening results on the personalities, both of keepers and prisoners, constituted one of the major social crimes of that era. This condition is, of course, far from a thing of the past. But the new emphasis in penology is upon a utilizing of constructive, reeducational, restorative, self-discovering appeals which give those affected a chance to develop if they can and will. Whatever may have been the results in specific cases of the rather frantic introduction of measures of self-government in prisons, the principle *if intelligently and patiently applied* represents a great advance and a recognition of the psychologically sound elements in the administration of penal institutions.

This prison illustration has real bearing on an understanding of the industrial problem. For unfortunately, there is all too close an analogy. The regimentation of the reluctant and all but enforced labor of large groups of men, the close supervision of their activities, the rigid discipline enforced, and the bleak physical surroundings—these characteristics of American industrial conditions of the last half of the nineteenth century have been all too comparable to typical prison conditions. They make comparisons of prison- and factory-management problems inevitable even if not completely parallel.

The development of all sorts of plans of employee representation in industry in recent years is the clearest possible acknowledgment of the fact that managers realize that positive appeals are needed to replace the older attitudes of bullying on one side and fearful submission on the other.

Fear motivation undoubtedly still has its place. Safety-first campaigns seem to require a certain amount of this appeal to be effective; and, perhaps, also, propaganda for personal hygiene. But even here, positive educational work must go hand in hand with fear appeals to secure the best results.

The great thing to remember about the utilizing of fear is the marked limitations of its appeal. When there is fear, attention is abnormally centered. Escape from the fear is the major desire of the moment. If, as in industry, it be a complex fact, like fear of unemployment, of discharge, of low income, of a "bawling out" by an irate foreman, the result is a state of mind which is chronically deaf to positive appeals to loyalty, workmanship, and interest in the company. Release from such fears is the first condition of any attempt to build up an attitude of positive helpfulness and cooperative interest. Absence of fear is a condition, even if a negative one, of cultivating genuine morale, because only in its absence can there develop desires and purposes among the worker to realize life, to grow, and to express personality in and through the corporate activities.

The relation to fear as well as to love of the emotions of envy and jealousy should be mentioned because these are both motivations of conduct to be met in the business setting, which may become powerful and difficult to cope with. The two emotions derive from fear that one's status or progress are jeopardized as well as often from a misguided love which may desire to monopolize attention and regard. It is not so easy to offer advice as to how these disturbing feelings can be curbed. But in the life of individuals, executives and rank and file alike, the adverse influence of these emotions should be reckoned with. This means identification of their existence, understanding of their causes by all concerned, and conscious effort to direct such feelings into other more wholesome relations.

Anger and Hatred.—Anger and hatred are emotional states in which the stimulus is that which is strange, thought to be unjust, or thought to be obstructive to one's desires. Here, again, the stirred-up condition centers attention on ways of removing the source of the anger or hatred. The angry or hating person is preoccupied, single-minded, unreflective, uncritical. The desire is to be rid of the opposing object in the quickest and most complete way possible. The trouble, of course, is that in human affairs it is not usually practical to be rid of the object in this complete and drastic way. If, as is typical, the source of anger or hate is another person or persons, the remedy for the situation—a way of action which will prevent recurrence of the aggravating situation or experience—is *not* one which makes removal or obliteration of the offending person feasible. If one could easily and completely get altogether away from the source of the trouble, one would usually be far less disturbed. The reason why one is not usually angry at the weather or at a door or window that will not open is that one's emotion cannot effect any change in these. If the door merely sticks, emotion may help to mobilize energy to force it open. But if it is locked and one does not have the key, anger is in vain. Annoyance or exasperation may be present, but anger or hatred seemingly require a stimulus which is responsible and responsive in relation to the person disturbed.

The point is that what the angry person really wants is a way of acting *which removes the reason for anger.* A foreman finds that a worker has misread a blueprint and has spent a whole morning milling out a quantity of parts which are wrong in dimension. He becomes angry and tells the worker just what he thinks of his ability to read blueprints. He does it in a loud voice which is heard by many other workers in the department. The offending worker is no doubt wrong; but he is also resentful at the tone of voice, at the reflection on his ability, at the fact that other workers are witnessing the reprimand, perhaps, also, at the fact that the instructions on the blueprint were not, in the first place, sufficiently clear. The nature of his reaction will depend on numerous factors. But ordinarily, some of the results will be that he likes the foreman less, that he likes his job less, that he is "sore," sulky, and disgusted. The foreman may have momentarily enjoyed his own anger. But the net result is *the exact opposite of the one he was really seeking*—namely, to be sure that the conditions which fostered the error are removed.

An alternate method of handling the situation would have been for the foreman to realize that the error was unintentional; to realize that perhaps the blueprint was not clear or that even if it was he should have gone over the specifications with the worker (indeed, that he should make it a regular practice so to do when issuing men new blueprints)—to realize, in short, that some measure of blame probably attached to him or to his inspector or assistant and on that basis provide a method of issuing work which would insure against a repetition of such mistakes. This is why it is true that the hater or the angry man may himself be the chief victim of his emotion. It incapacitates him from dealing with his problems in a corrective way.

The New Testament, from which, incidentally, a great deal is to be learned about the psychologically sound kinds of appeals to use and motives to elicit, says that one should love one's enemies and "pray for them that despitefully use you." The reason for this seemingly paradoxical command is not just to require some difficult and superhuman way of action. It is rather that the hating attitude toward people *gets one nowhere in accomplishing what one really wants*—namely, to have them get over being hateful and difficult to get on with. In the abnormal condition of war or in the abnormal disturbance which culminates in murder, the individual seeks to remove the hated object by securing his death.

The true solution, in more normal situations, must be one in which the hated object becomes less hated *because he becomes less hateful,* because some sort of change comes about in the hater or the hated or both. Jesus did not suggest that you love your enemies just to be pleasant or saintly or conspicuous in your reaction. He suggested it because he realized that a loving attitude on the part of the one who now hates would most quickly and successfully lead both himself and the one hated to act in the future toward each other more congenially, harmoniously, and unifiedly as to ends sought. The loving attitude was recommended as the *only one* which gave any assurance of changing the inner desires of both parties so that they could live and work together not only tolerably but also enjoyably.

The insight of this precept is the more fully realized if we try to understand the psychological characteristics of love.

Love.—As a simple emotion, love is primarily sexual in its stimulation. It is distinguished from lust, which is desire to act sexually without any qualifying affection, regard, or interest in the personality of the individual sought. Love, on the other hand, is personal in its source and assumes a sympathy with, affection for, a yearning to be "at one with" the person loved. Love depends for its vitality upon proximity to the one loved. It includes as it develops a desire to help, to protect, to be reciprocally desired, to come into unity of understanding, outlook, and being with the lover. The English language lacks a separate word to convey the larger and less directly sexual sentiment of love. This absence of a different word can, however, serve to call attention to the fact that many of the characteristics of sex love are retained in this stirred-up state when it is non-sexual in character. But recognition of its origin helps to explain its power and influence.

How much the loving attitude preserves characteristics of the simple sex emotion is seen if one considers what it involves. People want to be near those they love, to be like them; to help them; to evoke the same kind of loving response from them; to pursue similar ends and purposes; to understand them. The loving attitude is thus an intensely *active* manifestation. It is not passive nor sentimental, as people are likely to think. One loves as one acts, when one is able by direct, effective, and thoroughly vigorous manifestations to disclose to the loved one the depth and reality of one's regard.

Love is, in its best sense, *a desire for and a preparedness to act in the direction of an intelligently intimate, useful, and sympathetic relationship with others.* It prompts to ways of action calculated to give satisfaction and happiness to those loved and, therefore, by that fact, to one's self, also. One's self is projected into the loved ones; and that which makes them happy makes the lover happy. Love becomes an attitude in which people's motives and desires become integrated, unified, and harmonized, due to the more sensitive growth of understanding, common insight, and delight in common experience.

It is highly significant that the great religions of the world, and Christianity preeminently among them, have given such a large place to the significance and utility of the loving attitude. But love is significant as a psychological fact not because religions exalt it. Religions exalt it because experience and insight have shown that as a motive it is powerful, regenerative, satisfying, self-revealing, and self-developing, in the experiences to which it prompts.

Indeed, people's estimate of so-called "religious" and "ethical" values would be far more defensible and more soundly based if they would realize that principles and precepts are not significant because they are sponsored by a religion or an ethical system but that they are thus sponsored because they have been found to be "good psychology." And the kinds of behavior which religions and ethical systems advise are, in fact, worthy to the degree that a wide consensus of experience over a long time has proved them to be good psychology—that is, proved that they express and satisfy essential and powerful elements in human nature.

If, then, this definition of the loving attitude checks with the realities of human experience, the conclusion may be advanced that the world could do well with more action motivated in this way. The loving attitude, in the last analysis, is the *influencing attitude*. It gives rise alike in the lover and in the loved to a state of the organism in which there exists a heightened degree of susceptability to the wishes of the loving one. Those who love respond to each other; they are ready and open to new advances. That is what makes this state so significant. Love is creative in power—originally on the physical plane, eventually in wider social relations. The extraordinary injuction to love one's enemies shows itself in the light of a real understanding of the loving attitude to be one of the most profound psychological suggestions which has ever been made.

Two familiar passages in the Bible, the so-called Sermon on the Mount (Matt. V) and Paul's famous chapter on "charity" or "love," (I Cor. XIII), go to the very heart of the pervasive problem of how people can best influence their fellows. They suggest that the only way to remove enmity, hate, and other obstructions to cooperative action is not by removing the enemy but *by changing the character of the enemy in the particular respect in which he offends.* He may offend merely by seeming "different" in manners, customs, language, and the like; or by wanting something which you have; or by acting in either a too superior or too inferior way. Whatever the reason for the feeling of hostility, it is important to understand and confront it in any serious effort to remove it.

This analysis suggests, then, the method by which a change in attitude can most effectively be begun—namely, by giving tangible, ungrudging evidence of the sincerity of one's real regard for the offender.

Indeed, here lies the answer to the vital question, How may the loving attitude be induced in others? How does one call forth the state of mind which leads another to be thus amenable? The first requirement is the obvious existence of this attitude in the one who is trying to do the influencing. If a person sees that he is loved, his sense of self-importance is at once touched; his attention is aroused in the direction of the one who does him the honor of giving him special regard. Also, this special regard will manifest itself in actions which are generous and helpful. The one who is loved finds himself in receipt of attentions and kindnesses which the loving one seems peculiarly to know how to make valuable and pleasurable. The sense of understanding and insight which the relationship evidences is highly satisfying to the one loved; and there grows up a strong presumption that his own attitude toward the one who manifests love will become a highly responsive and suggestible one. It is seemingly the normal response to meet another's personal interest with one's own reciprocal interest, to have affection respond to affection. Of course, this reaction is not inevitable; but neither is any emotional reaction. There may always be qualifying factors. But as a tendency it has a presumption in its favor—other things being equal.

The other half of the problem is as to whether one can do anything to make oneself a more actively loving person. This is, in reality, a problem of increasing the range of one's affection without diminishing its intensity in directions that it now takes. It is not a question of caring less for one's family so that one may care more for one's church or lodge or corporate associates. It is a question of discovering what elements in those wider contacts which inevitably accompany one's business or social activities are now preventing them from being more a part of you, from receiving more of your deep regard. These elements may be, for example, mental habits of aloofness or snobbery, prejudices of a racial or personal sort, preconceptions of any kind that hinder an honest evaluation of personal worth in others. Each particular case requires analysis to discover its inhibiting origins.

This requirement is universal, therefore, that where obstructions to this kind of deeper regard appear in relations to one's associates, the inner and all but unconscious reason for them must be hunted down and brought into the light for frank acknowledgment. This is the first step toward their removal. The prejudices and obstructions of this kind which managers discover regarding different racial groups among employees, for example, are an exceedingly important case in point. As long as all Italian fellow workers are only "Dagos" or "Wops"; as long as Slavic workers are only "Hunkies"; as long as Russian Jews are only "Kikes"—just so long will there continue to exist in one's mind certain attitudes which prevent the appearance of a more personal understanding and affectionate interest and concern.

There is a further aspect of the loving attitude and its cultivation which demands increasing recognition. Corporate dealings are not all personal. The members of a board of directors deliberating a personnel policy of vital significance to the rank and file of workers involved in plants spread all over the country, are in danger of not visualizing their problem in terms of personal consequences. A proposal, for example, to shorten hours from 44 to 40 may be an evidence *in policy* of a loving attitude. But the *human* reasons for adopting such a policy usually need dramatizing in a personal way in order to have their full appeal. In some way and by some process of education people in directive work must be made to see that a loving attribute can and should be present in such non-personal dealings. In international relations the problem is the same only larger in scope.

It is by no means impossible to conceive of an extension of this attitude of personal concern to groups with whom personal contact is absent. But one condition of such a widening of the area of human consideration appears to be in the ability of some individuals in posts of leadership to dramatize and make personally vivid the affairs of those dealt with but not present in the flesh. In corporate conduct it would seem that this dramatizing responsibility rests peculiarly with the personnel executive. And this is one of the big reasons why that executive should be of an intellectual and emotional stature that enables him to exert a real influence in the top counsels of his organization.

Love as a Guide.—A loving response to a manifestation of love is not always wisely expressed any more than is the manifestation itself. None of the underlying drives to conduct is necessarily a wise guide to conduct in the sense of helping the individual to judge of the timeliness and expedience of the prompting. A loving mother without intelligence is a notoriously poor guide. She may be overindulgent or careless about discipline. The employer who "has religion" may be guilty of the ill-advised introduction of too paternalistically generous practices in his plant—practices which make the employees think he is "soft" or "easy" or sentimentally indulgent.

An important part of the loving attitude is that *it shall be governed and guided by intelligence,* which means, in part, trying to see all the various consequences of specific loving acts before undertaking them. Intelligently manifested loving means providing the loved one with reasonable opportunities to disclose and unfold his own inner nature. One loves truly when he calls out and expects the development of the qualities in another which make him most himself, most a distinct and free-growing personality—not a second-hand replica of the one who loves.

The intelligent display of love does not yield philanthropy or irrational, impulsive, or exceptional generosity. These are naturally and rightly suspect in a workaday world. Managerial regard for workers, the kind of generous affection that goes to the psychological bottom of things, is shown rather in the exercise of faith in the positive qualities of people. It is shown in *the supplying of opportunities for the rank and file to express themselves, to grow and to live fully in and through the normal corporation activities.*

The loving manager—there is no reason why this phrase should not be a scientifically descriptive one—will be he who is trying *to offer to the people under his direction a share of responsibility for forming and directing the group's activities according to the several capacities of each and a share in molding the group's purposes according to their several insights into the purposes found valuable.*[2] Nothing more and nothing less than this is the outcome of the enlightened motivation of love in industry.

The use of love as a motivating influence will, despite all this explanation, still be felt by some to be ill advised and sentimental. The reason for this frequent reaction is, I think, that, more often than not, a loving attitude is construed as being an uncritical or even a stupid attitude. Indeed, it may be and often is. But it need not be. Just as we saw above that an artificial separation of emotional and intellectual appeals was fatal to the effectiveness of the total appeal, just so we can now say that to try to influence people through affection without the simultaneous exercise of intelligence is equally dangerous. And the converse is also true of the use of intelligence without affection.

The interesting fact is that we have today a social situation which is radically new in essence, which can come greatly to our aid in bringing intelligence and affection simultaneously to bear on all sorts of problems. In the conscious use of the scientific method of research and of scientific knowledge, not only about material but about psychological data, we possess an instrument of unique value. This whole book is in effect an attempt to show how with relation to many problems of human contact in group activities scientific knowledge can point the way to an application of human regard to concrete dealings with people. Psychology aims to tell how individuals do and will react and it thus forearms us, *if we will make intelligent use of our information*, with insight and actual methods that facilitate and make kindly and considerate the contacts between man and man. No longer need people who want to manifest affection do it in stupid ways and thus bring affection itself into question. From now on, the opportunity is at hand to wed love to wisdom with the likelihood of a highly desirable issue in terms of personal and group activity.

Emotions Transitory.—It is a quality of simple emotional attitudes that they are not sustained and long lived. They require repeated stimulation to renew them.

No labor policies or programs which contemplate the cultivation of enthusiasm and cooperative zeal can, for example, be set going and left to run of themselves. Because of the constantly fluid character of people's actions and reactions, because attention is distracted to new matters, because the same stimuli cannot be relied upon to produce identical results under the changed conditions which the initial response to the stimulus has brought, constant attention to the effects of any program is necessary. An organization is basically a grouping of individual impulses, desires, and energies. Because this is so, the creation and renewal of harmonized states of mind, sustained and vitalized by valid emotions, are a *continuing* task.

The Individual's Emotional Life.—The control and sensible direction of the individual's emotional life constitute a problem to which managers should be alive. The executive has the problem not only for others but also for himself. The platitude about being able to rule oneself before trying to rule others is still sound; and any serious emotional instability should be cause for serious self-analysis and efforts at reeducation.

The degree of one's departure from normal is not usually something of which each of us is clearly conscious. Frequently, some emotional instability or maladjustment has become so habitual as to seem inborn.   This makes it valuable occasionally to indulge in a little judicious self-examination on this score.   Watson has helpfully suggested that there are a number of questions which one can put to oneself to help discover the extent of any serious lack of emotional balance.   These are questions relating to:

1. Normality of sensitiveness to emotional stimuli.
    a. Do I show anger on insufficient provocation, or do I pass by all situations without showing anger?
    b. Do I show fear for insufficient reasons, or do I fail to show fear where others ordinarily would?
2. The evenness of the emotional level.
    Do I seem to work at a normal, high, or low emotional level?
3. The normality of the permanent general attitude.
    a. Am I free from inferiority, suspicion, and embarrassment?
    b. Am I free from talkativeness, oversensitiveness, display tendencies?
4. Freedom from unusual outlets of emotional manifestation.
    a. Am I free from such unsocial outlets as biting the nails in public, twitching of eyes or lips and motor tics, drumming with feet or fingers, etc.?
    b. Am I free from rumination and day dreaming, which interfere with other activities?
    c. Do I seek highly exciting emotional situations, talk overmuch about sex matters, or show undue curiosity about details of other people's affairs?[3]

If the results of analysis of self or of others, which are obtained from asking questions such as those, indicate a serious degree of emotional instability, it is, of course, desirable that something be done about it.   One of the first things to do is to try to discover its causes.   It may be due to a compensatory release of one emotion where others are obstructed; or to an unduly excited state of the individual because of too unrestrained emotional expression in every direction; or to fatigue or anxiety.   And how the individual case should be handled will depend on the underlying causes.   Further suggestions for corrective activities along these lines are given in Chap. IX.

Conclusion.—The emotional life is thus seen to be a tremendously significant part of experience.   It is in good measure calculable. It is far-reaching in its influence in life. Deliberate and calculated planning is merited if experience is to be directed with true effectiveness. The use of emotional appeals when set in sensible connection with intellectual appeals is not only justified; it is essential if the springs of behavior are to be tapped at their sources. And so powerful are the emotional elements in the individual's make-up that each one should give some conscious attention to his own problem of a proper balancing and controlling of emotional factors in his inner self. Awareness of the kind of behavior in individuals which are symptomatic of a state of emotional instability and lack of balance thus becomes the first step toward improved control.

CHAPTER V

FORMING AND CHANGING HABITS

Another important way in which people are moved to act is by their habits. Habits move people to action in the sense that, given the setting in which a pattern of usually combined and serialized activities takes place, there is a strong likelihood of the individual's wanting to go through the series again. The very familiarity of the whole organism with the set of reactions required to carry out a habit makes the carrying out a satisfying process. That is why people are said to be "wedded to their habits." A great deal of the ordinary day-to-day conduct of most people is habitual, and the motivating power of the habit-forming and habit-following tendency is an incalculably large factor in helping to explain why all of us do what we do. This tendency is innate and constant. From birth to death each individual is making, unmaking and re-forming habits. To understand this process is to grasp one of the most fundamental facts about behavior.

Indeed, in most behavior, what is to be witnessed is not the operation of a single impulse or emotion. It is the operation of a combination of these, gradually built up and welded together to lead to the carrying on of the necessary habitual activities of routine living—brought together in units called "habits" which come to have the force and drive which create action.

Hence, the definition of "habit" as that force which prompts to activity which contains within itself a certain ordering of its own elements, which is dynamic and projective in quality needing only the right stimulus to set it afoot and which also exercises a subordinate influence even when not obviously dominating a given action.[1]

A number of interesting questions at once arise. How do habits get built up? Is it possible to change habits, and if so how? What happens when people are moved to follow conflicting habits?

First, how do habits get built up? It is a paradox of habit formation and, in fact, of all learning, that the individual cannot perform a habit until he has already performed it. By this is meant that the first successful achievement of the behavior pattern of a habit comes as the result of successive trials in the course of which the right combination of nervous and muscular response is finally hit upon.

Take, for example, the case of a man learning to run a punch press—a series of actions, which quickly become a habit series for the performer. He must be given some idea of the succession of motions required. Someone operates the machine while he watches and while also he has explained to him the interconnection of the parts of the operation—how the machine is put in motion and how the material is handled. When the learner has some conception of the various acts involved, he takes his place at the machine and tries and tries again to get the exact combination of motions required. There comes a point when in a happy moment he performs the series properly. And at that moment his whole organism is slightly aware of a sense of the coordination which exists when the action is properly performed. The first successful combination makes it somewhat easier for a second correct serial grouping of activities to take place later. And out of these gradual, successive, and gropingly correct responses proficiency in the habit is finally built up.

In short, one forms a habit by acquiring through practice a motor and mental grouping of responses which comes to unfold in the anticipated way. Mental habits are no exception to this statement. If one has a habit of thinking, for example, that every executive who chews tobacco is "hard-boiled" and peremptory in dealing with workers, it is because through repeated experience (or through reading which conveys the recorded experience or ideas of others) that association of tobacco chewing and dictatorial conduct has in one's experience been found to be a valid habit of thought. One contrary instance, however, is enough to disturb the habit; and two would raise a real conflict in the individual's mind as to the soundness of the habit pattern under which he was laboring.

How to Change Habits.—How, then, do habits change? Suppose, recurring to the earlier illustration, that a new machine of different design with a different combination of levers and new material is put before the worker. He will, of course, learn the new combination but it will require a repetition of the tiresome trial-and-error effort of motion combinations. He will learn the new way only after he has once successfully done it. His own motor and mental achievement is the prior condition of his change of habit. *He must do it himself.* Obvious as this statement no doubt seems, people often find it hard to realize that this is true of *all* habits. The man who holds the notion that tobacco chewing and being hard boiled go together is not usually changed from it by argument or ridicule or preaching. He is changed only as he encounters *in experience* people with this habit who are not hard boiled.

There is a principle here, vital to an understanding of the true nature of the learning and habit-forming process in general. Learning takes place and habits are formed or re-formed *only when the individual is placed in the setting of a whole situation where the thing to be learned or the habit to be formed is the only satisfactory way out of the dilemma or problem in which the learner finds himself.* The pressure of the situation, the logic of events, the physical conditions confronted—these require and suggest a new way of coping with the facts, quite as much as does the individual's own inner urge. Indeed, these two are reciprocal phases of the same total fact—the fact of an individual in difficulty and distress because of the fact of the perverse, contrary, and thwarting character of some element in his environment. His distress is partly internal in cause, partly due to outside conditions. Both must be coped with.

Take as an example a foreman with a quick temper who is anxious to break himself of this unfortunate habit. One important thing for him to do is to try to see that he keeps himself out of situations where his temper will be roused. This means trying to find out the kind of thing that disturbs his equanimity;

trying to find out if it has to do largely with his own physical condition, like bad digestion, fatigue, or anxiety, or largely with work conditions. There may be a distressing home situation, a poor physique, undiscovered ill health, too much responsibility in relation to his capacity, poor support from other foremen or managers. The remedy is usually to be found not in an arbitrary "exercise of the will," in "counting ten before you speak," in appeals to religious sentiment but *in removing the source of the difficulty which is to be found in some adverse circumstances* that he is daily confronting. He can build up a more normal and wholesome habit of response to events only as he can get help from the course of events and conditions (subjective and objective) which will help to make a normal response the likely one, the one to which his total personality will naturally be prompted. This fact of habits as the resultant of the working together of inner impulsions and auspicious surrounding conditions, neither alone but each working constantly on the other, is one that has profound consequences. Understanding of it will help everyone who deals with people to create the conditions as a result of which changes in habits, outlook, desires, and purposes can be brought about.

The relation of the foreman's own desire to the process of changing the habit is also important. If he has the desire, it will greatly aid the process of change. But the wish alone gets him nowhere. Admiration of some ideally even-tempered individual helps only a little. Aspiration is effective only *as it ties itself up explicitly and definitely to the next steps one must take.* The major problem for him is to discover what to do *right now.* As suggested above, this probably means, in this case, analyzing the complex conditions under which he lives and works and taking the specific steps necessary to correct any adverse influences. Practically, interest should be centered not in the end sought but in what may be called the "means whereby" the building up of a new method of response seems likely.

William James has offered a number of now famous maxims which can profitably be observed by anyone who is confronted with the problem of changing a habit or building up a new one. They are:

    1. Take care to launch yourself with as strong and decided an initiative as possible on the new habit.

    2. Never allow an exception to occur until the new habit is securely rooted in your life.

    3. Seize the first possible opportunity to act on every resolution you make and on every emotional prompting you may experience in the direction of the habits you aspire to gain.

    4. Keep the faculty of effort alive in yourself by a little gratuitous exercise each day.[2]

Conflicts of Habits.—Finally, what happens when people are moved to follow conflicting habits? People are so moved for various reasons. Sometimes habits call in one direction and one's stubborn inborn desires call in another. Sometimes one builds up habits which are at odds with those of others in one's group or with the conventions or laws of society. Sometimes new ideas enter to disturb familiar habits. The fact of conflicts within oneself and between oneself and others is a commonplace. How the individual handles this problem in relation to his own contradictory internal claims will be the only phase of this problem to be treated here. The larger conflicts of individuals with groups and of groups with groups will be discussed later.

Conflicting habits represent conflicting preferences and desires. In order to get a basis for action, some choice must be made. And for the best results, such a choosing process would entail deliberation, in order to arrive at a wise selection. But there is, of course, unreasonable as well as reasonable choice.

The object thought of may simply stimulate some impulse or habit to a pitch of intensity where it is temporarily irresistible . . . it absorbs us, sweeps us off our feet by its own attractive force.[3]

Where this is the case, the line of action which follows an unreasonable choice must face the problem of bringing the best possible issue out of a seemingly bad set of causes.

But choice implies a rehearsal in imagination of probable consequences and an acceptance of that alternative which promises to satisfy the whole person by contributing to his growth and unity. It is the "emergence of a unified preference out of competitive preferences." Activity does not stop to give way to reflection; it is rather turned into mental channels. Thus, it will be seen, even in advance of a more extended discussion of the reasoning process, that reasonableness is not correctly conceived as a quality opposed to desire; it is a "quality of effective relationship among desires." Reason and emotion do not stand over against each other as divergent forces in life. Emotion supplies the stimulus which keeps reflection at work dwelling on relevant and congenial matters, until by the stress it creates it forces the reason to focus on one positive line of procedure and follow it.

Put in another way, the practical problem presented by a conflict of habits or desires is a problem of thinking through a way of action which appears to the individual to give the greatest likelihood of all-around satisfaction, appears likely to bring him again to a state of approximate harmony with his whole situation. How to foster properly the right kind of thought habits, the right kind of deliberation, will be presently considered.

Impulses, Emotions, and Habits as Guides to Conduct.—It is clear that habits by themselves do not offer explicit guideposts as to the right line of conduct to follow, any more than do the other motivators to behavior. The promptings of the several innate and acquired drives to action are often contradictory, mutually exclusive, at war with each other. As guides, these forces are bad guides. Whatever may be true of the wise directive power of such forces in animal life, the complexities of human life and desire are such that the human being must always face far more intricate alternatives. Understanding of the motivating power of the more elemental drives gives only a sense of what may be called the "dynamics" of the problem. Understanding is also necessary of the process by which the warring factions are brought to peace, by which overt action comes out of internal strife and bewilderment.

In order to get a picture of this more complex activity, it is next necessary to present systematically a view of the learning and of the thinking processes; for it is in the functioning of the human learning and thinking activities that the unique element in human behavior is seen—the element which supplies the directive and evaluating influences. Indeed, no executive can get to the bottom of his problem of dealing with people who does not realize clearly that impulses, emotions, and habits, integral as they are to human behavior, do nevertheless require, in order to yield wise actions, the interposition of still other factors. What the individual wants to do and will do depends on his original and acquired drives, of course. But it depends, also, on an evaluating process and on a directive faculty which are strongly modifying forces. And whoever would implicate the motives of the whole man (which is the necessary condition of any permanent influence over conduct) must appeal to and get a response from the individual's deliberative self no less than from his impulsive self.

Can Impulses, Emotions, and Habits Be Modified?—It is implicit in this discussion that impulses, emotions, and habits are modifiable. Also, they vary in intensity from individual to individual. Forces of heredity tend to foster such variety. Without entering into the debate about the relative influence of heredity and environment, the position is here taken that both do exert an influence in conditioning behavior. There is ground for believing that important physical characteristics are transmitted as well as some mental qualities and aptitudes.[4]

Also, the first five years of life play an enormous part in forming the kind of responses which one will later make.

Other modifying influences are the climate, the weather, the age of the person, his racial and cultural background, his special endowments and aptitudes. All of these have to be given weight in efforts at prediction and control. Nothing could be farther from the relative simplicity of a mathematical or chemical formula than the factors active in every individual human equation.

Other ways in which responses are modified are by new combinations of stimuli which may give a different result; or the same stimulus may call forth a new and different response. The introduction of an obstruction and delay between the stimulus and its satisfaction in action may cause further complications.

Psychologists have given the name "conditioned reflex" to the situation where two stimuli together come to call forth a response and then subsequently the response is obtained from one alone. An example of this familiar experience would be the case of a head executive who never came into the shop except to "raise a row" with a foreman. His appearance comes to be regarded as the signal in the plant for trouble and complaint from the head office. Foremen learn to fear his coming and try to go into the far end of their department where he will not notice them. Let this executive come once into the shop *without* a complaint, and the foreman will still try to keep out of sight. His very arrival has come to bring about a reaction of fear, dread, and avoidance.

An interesting suggestion about the wide prevalence of what are essentially conditioned reflexes comes from Professor Folsom[6] in discussing how a great variety of handicapping attitudes come about. People's attitude toward personal relationships differ widely—toward paper work in record keeping, toward the practical use of equipment, toward making quick decisions, toward variety in work. And he points out that these attitudes are largely built up by the conditioning process as a result of adverse experiences rather than as inborn responses. This suggests that both the traits and the responses which they evoke can be reeducated under different conditions where the desired response is clearly linked up with a new and pleasurable accompanying satisfaction. Unquestionably, the assurance of reward in income or status, for example, can often help the individual to change his response and his attitude toward particular activities.

The way in which these several factors do, in fact, work to modify conduct can to a degree be stated in terms of general principles. These are usually referred to as the laws of exercise, frequency, recency, intensity, effect, and the several laws of association. An explanation of the working of these, necessary as it is to an understanding of the habit-forming, habit-changing, and learning processes, will be found in the next chapter.

But before proceeding to this, it is necessary to make at least brief mention of the rôle of the sensory equipment and of the feelings in supplying data for mental activity.

The Sensory Equipment.—In order to have subject matter to learn about and to deal with, people must perceive the phenomena of the outer world; and to do this requires the exercise of their sensory equipment.   The sensory equipment includes the senses of sight, taste, smell, sound, heat, pain, the muscle sense, and, perhaps, others.   These senses function through the stimulation of sense organs, sensory nerves, and certain parts of the brain known as "sensory centers."   A "sensation" may thus be defined as an internal sensory response to the stimulating of one of the sense organs.   These are parts of the body which have high sensitivity to a particular kind of stimulus, as the eye, ear, nose, tongue and pain spots.

The senses do not of themselves supply the individual with *meanings.*   People do not have to learn to hear, see, etc.; that is part of their native equipment.   But they do have to learn the meaning of different kinds of smells, sounds, and the rest. And this recognition of sensory meanings, called "sense perception," comes only through individual experience.

Perception is, thus, the second and derived response to the sensation.   It is knowing the fact rather than readiness to act or desire to act.   Perception of meanings where only a few of the sensory facts are supplied may pass over into the more complex fact of inference and reasoning.   Also, perception may be wrong; wrong conclusions may be drawn from the sensory data with which the individual has to work.   *Illusions* are examples of just such erroneous perceptions.

Things perceived and meanings already established constitute the subject matter of what is spoken of as the "flow of consciousness."   The individual as he becomes conscious of impulsive, emotional or habit promptings is perceiving them.   They take on meanings and become part of the perceptual data with which he thinks.   Thus, they become the subject matter of his deliberation and choice.

Feelings.—Still another characteristic of the human organism is the fact of a background or undercurrent of consciousness—a feeling—which accompanies explicit activity and which gives to an activity a definite *tone.*   The most clearly identified feelings are those of pleasantness and unpleasantness. They are distinguished from sensations and emotions in that they are not in the foreground of the mind, are not localized in origin, and are without special sense organs. Pleasantness and unpleasantness apparently come to have motivating power, just as do the other native traits. "The impulse of pleasantness is directed toward keeping what is pleasant, and of unpleasantness toward getting rid of the unpleasant."[5] What the objects and experiences are from which one finds pleasantness or the opposite varies greatly from person to person. These feelings are partly unlearned, and in their attachment to special experiences they are partly acquired in the sense that they come with experience to be associated with specific activities. Because they are propulsive in character, they are most important to try to understand in the individual case. Natively, for example, people like bright colors, but they often acquire a feeling of pleasantness only with subdued colors. This same holds true of many sensations. One can by training and habituation come to admire music and painting which to the untutored may seem bizarre and ugly.

How much one should be guided by the existence of a pleasurable feeling in another as indicating that the other's course of action is wise it is exceedingly difficult to say. The teacher, for example, has surely to be governed by other facts than the student's momentary sense of pleasantness. "No educational theory," it has been wisely said, "can safely neglect the fact that many a horse unwillingly driven to water finds that it wants to drink."[7] One reason why the so-called pleasure-pain theory of motivation is so inadequate is that there are many experiences in life which people do not know to be pleasurable until *after* they have gone through with them. Usually, also, one condition in which a feeling of pleasantness is present is where there is a conscious striving for self-chosen goals.

Conclusion.—The mechanism of habit formation must be understood by anyone who would order his own living wisely as well as by the executive who has the task of reeducating the habits of others. In order to change habits, there must be the desire to change; there must be some conception obtained of the way the new habit works in action; there must be a studying and manipulating of the supporting conditions of the environment to mold and buttress the working of the individual's mental and nervous adjustments. Habit formation to be effective must utilize always the total evolving situation in both its inner and its outer aspects. And, also, since it implies that as habits are formed people have been learning, it is necessary to discuss the nature of learning next.

The aim thus far has been to present a picture of the characteristics which lie at the root of behavior, of desire and of action. General tendencies to action, emotions, habits, the sensory and perceptual equipment,—these are what the more complex experiences of people are built up from. No dissection of motives can proceed far without the background of a knowledge of these forces and abilities. Of themselves, they do not explain human motives. But they do give clues and hints as to their basic elements. And only as such are they to be understood. Out of the experience to which they prompt, people learn of life, of the obstacles to be coped with, of the adjustments which social living requires. And how that learning takes place and how it can be consciously directed will now be discussed.

CHAPTER VI

THE LEARNING PROCESS

The human characteristics thus far chosen for analysis and definition have been either innate or those more or less unconsciously incorporated into the individual's equipment. The picture as it stands is incomplete because much human learning is more conscious and deliberate. Out of the conflicts, vacillations, and puzzlements of individuals as to what impulsions to follow, there does—at least occasionally—come conduct which is unified, integrated, in line with long-established desires and purposes.

How does this come about? What learning is there more articulate than that required in the habit-forming mechanisms and tendencies?

People do, in fact, profit by experience, do learn from experience and reason from experience as to the ends they want to pursue. They do make choices. Can the learning process by conscious intention offer aid here?

The Learning Process.—The process of learning concerns itself with utilizing past experience to make new experience more easy, intelligible, and useful to the individual. What present experience one has depends, in part, upon what factors in the surroundings gain *attention*. What past experience one uses depends upon the operation of the *laws of learning* mentioned above, and also it depends upon the *memory*. To how good use one puts remembered experience depends upon one's energy and *intelligence*. And how much one finds it possible to learn by mental, as distinct from motor, exploration depends on one's *reasoning ability*, including his *imagination* and his *judgment*. These several factors in the learning process will now be discussed.

Attention.—People have to "pay attention" to what they are doing. And what they will pay attention to has been found to be a far from arbitrary matter. Indeed, there are known to be certain attention-getting qualities in objects and situations which predispose them to engage the normal person's transitory interest. These factors of advantage, as they are called, are (1) change in the stimulus which has a certain degree of suddenness; (2) intensity or strength in the stimulus; (3) its large size; (4) repetition; (5) a striking quality of some sort; (6) a definite form. These are the factors native to the stimulus.

An individual is predisposed to attend, also, if he has acquired a habit of attending, if he has accustomed himself to picking out the relevant items in the environment and watching for them—as, for example, a worker often knows by just listening to his machine whether it is working smoothly. And one attends, also, to those matters which are in line with his present interests, problems, and desires. If one has an interest in personnel work, one tends to pick out and read in papers and magazines items along that line; the accountant's eye is caught by accounting items, etc. If one is in the midst of instituting a pension plan, the mention of the word "pension" will at once attract his attention. If one's heart is set on going to Europe, all matters which relate thereto will get notice.

The problem of securing attention is vital for the executive and teacher. Study must be given both to making attractive the thing to be attended to and getting the person predisposed to attending. Take, for example, the utilizing of departmental bulletin boards in a plant. Unless the whole publicity plan is executed by someone who knows how to gain and hold attention and also how to build up the habit of watching the boards, the notices are as likely as not to remain unread. The advertising profession at its best has much to teach along these lines to everyone interested in influencing others; and the manager who ignores all this in trying to get ideas over to his men is missing a much needed ally.

Of course, more than initial attention has ultimately to be secured. There are three stages in the development of attentiveness. The first is the instinctive, exploratory stage; the second is the period of forced attention where one continues to attend because some outside motive operates, such as fear of punishment or hope of reward; the third is the smooth-running stage of sustained and continued attention due to the fact that a genuine interest has been created. When the third stage is achieved, attention has passed over into *interest*. Interest is thus a condition of continuing, satisfying, self-expressive preoccupation with a subject. And the achieving of this desirable state often requires that one pass through the other two. There may, however, be subjective factors in the make-up or training of the individual which make it possible to get his interest quickly and hold it continuously. An individual with an aptitude for music or numbers or color discrimination is likely to become specially interested in activities requiring expression of these aptitudes. And there seem to be in many people natural tendencies to special interests in (1) material things for their own sake, (2) people and their doings, (3) the physical world and its operation.

Take, now, the case of a worker learning to run a machine. He is likely to pay attention at once to his problem, because it is new and challenging, and his welfare depends upon it. His instructor does not have to urge him to pay attention to business. But after half a day, when progress seems slow and the attainment of skill seems to be a far-off result, the worker's eye wanders and his attention is held only because he realizes that his job depends on sticking at it or because his instructor stands over him. Two weeks later, however, when he has mastered the motions involved, he continues to pay attention and may be definitely interested because the entire process itself has come to be an absorbing one and his personality is expressed in the thoroughness of his workmanship, in the amount of his output, in the economical use of the material, or in some combination of these and other factors.

Generally speaking, attention will be permanent and pass over into interest most readily and effectively if the one who attends does so because of some deep-seated desire or long-time purpose to which the present object or activity clearly contributes. The desire to have his department make a record showing for the week may often keep a worker attending faithfully to his task, when factors of attention in the job itself may have become negligible through familiarity. Again and again, such wider desires and more complex purposes motivate people through uninteresting details and through arduous labors, when less important motives would long since have failed. That is the big reason why ambition to get ahead at one's work is so powerful and frequently so desirable a force. It also helps to explain the importance of morale development as an offset to uninteresting work. The bigger purpose helps to sustain attention at all sorts of routines that have lost every other more spontaneous claim upon attention. Almost any project worth engaging upon will require at one time or another putting one's "nose to the grindstone" in order to get to the stage of sustained interest. And this process of continued application must be reenforced by a larger purpose if results are to be obtained. The executive who tries to get workers' interest in detailed operations without giving them a setting of conditions and terms of employment which will naturally help to build up a sense of personal advantage occurring out of the interest aroused will almost surely get poor results.

The individual, in short, tends to pay attention to those items in his surroundings which attract him because of characteristics in the object that appeal to characteristics in himself. He is able to learn as a result of his attending, because his mind is so constituted that it inevitably makes use of his perceptions in fairly definite ways. These ways of utilizing mental material are spoken of as the "laws of learning."

The Laws of Learning.—The laws of exercise, frequency, recency, intensity, effect, and association by combination help to explain how it is that learning takes effect. It is important at least to state these in the conventional psychological way, because anyone interested in teaching other people (and every executive is so interested) should know the outlines of the process.

The law of exercise says that when a given stimulus arouses a specific response, the likelihood of the same response's taking place again is increased by the exercise or repetition of the event. In short, in order to learn how to do a thing well, keep on doing it.

The law of frequency says that this repetition of the event will be much more likely to be successfully learned if it takes place frequently. A too long time must not intervene between periods of practice; and short and frequent repetitions are probably better than those longer and less frequent.

The law of recency says that success is attained better if the last experience of the act has been fairly recent. Do not let a too long time elapse after learning before repeating the matter to be learned.

The law of intensity says that repetition of the event being learned should be undertaken vigorously, earnestly, and actively.

The law of effect says that repetition of the event is more likely and learning, therefore, more certain where the outcome has been successful. Responses that yield satisfaction are sought after again; those that yield pain or dissatisfaction are not. People build up a great many "negative adaptations"; they refuse to respond to stimuli found, by experience, to be undesirable.

The law of association by combination is important because it says that there is a natural tendency to associate what is in mind with other data which are contiguous or similar both in the environment and in the individual's mind. People tend to learn by relating existing subject matter both subjective and objective to the new condition they confront. The learning of names of things and of people takes place in this way. One comes by association to relate word meanings to word sounds and the sight of the printed word. By association, responses are built up so that one item in experience becomes the signal to the mind for a whole body of experience. One hears a locomotive whistle and conjures up a whole series of pictures, perhaps having to do with traveling, with an accident, with an appointment, with steam engines, etc. One hears a factory or store fire alarm, and at once one is prompted to a definite series of responses which have been built up as normal to this stimulus because fire drills have previously established this association.

It is important to make clear what these so-called "laws" (or descriptions of the way in which certain things happen) are calculated to explain. They are abstract statements about the process by means of which one picks out and builds up out of the constant flux of new and varied experience those experiences which from the individual's point of view will be satisfying enough to repeat, and will merit incorporating into his assembled body of skills, habits, and methods of handling given kinds of problems. A great deal of learning will at once be seen to be the formulating of habits—the performing of series of events sufficiently often, intensively, and attentively so that the entire habit series comes eventually to be suggested and to be performed when the initial stimulus is presented.

A great deal of learning has also to do with the solving of problems, the coping with new situations. Something, for example, goes wrong with a machine. The worker may know how to operate it but never have had to repair it. He looks over the whole mechanism; he "tinkers with it"; he tries this bolt and that lever; he may stand back and think over the various things that might go wrong. Finally, he hits upon the thing that is wrong; he fixes it; the machine works and his problem is solved. He has learned how to repair a certain kind of damage. In this case, his learning has been a combination of "trial and error" on the motor level plus a rehearsal in his mind of possible alternatives and a checking up of these.

This mental rehearsal of alternatives is reasoning. And he may learn by reasoning, no less than by "monkeying around" in the trial-and-error fashion, which is the characteristic animal way of learning, if he can cultivate this process of mental trial in an effective way.

Both methods have their importance and both are typically used. A further word is, therefore, in place here about the meaning and implications of the trial-and-error method, leaving a discussion of reasoning until later. A great many skills, both muscular and mental, are acquired by doing the best one can, getting into trouble, varying the working method, gradually "getting the hang of the thing," and, finally, being successful *without ever knowing until one is successful what the conditions of correct performance are.*

It is in this sense that one never knows how to do a thing until one has done it. It is in this sense that "the one who is doing the learning must do the learning." People live their way into their thinking, Whiting Williams has well said, far more than they think their way into their living. The teacher who remarked that "no one ever told anybody anything" had this phase of the truth in mind.

Real learning is actual ability to handle situations so as to secure a satisfactory outcome; and such ability is acquired largely by the actual experience of handling them. "Learning is learning to use." This point is dwelt upon because people are apt to forget what learning really is, confusing it with that so-called "educational process" in which more or less unwilling students are forcibly required to memorize a lot of miscellaneous information.

In industry, any effort to introduce a new policy or procedure—starting a new plan of payment or incentives, for example, or of employee representation or group insurance—*involves a learning process* on the part of all executives and manual workers affected and a teaching process on the part of the executive leader. All new policies are examples of things which people cannot learn in the real sense by reading standard practice sheets, manuals, bulletin boards, or blueprint specifications. They learn them by the experience of making use of them.

True learning consists in both having and using at the right time the ability to meet a situation in a relevant and effective way. It is thus to be distinguished from *learning about*, which is also valuable and has its place. An executive may have learned all about shop committees from the literature on the subject and from conversation with other informed executives. But only the executive who is able to *utilize* his facts to institute, vitalize, and get results out of his committee can be said to have learned fully. He is educated on the subject of shop committees; the others are only informed. And the wise manager will see to it in relation to innumerable problems that his colleagues and workers *pass beyond the state of being informed to the stage of being adept and skilled in the particular action.*

How closely interdependent these two aspects are perhaps needs emphasis. Other things being equal, the person best informed *can* most quickly become the person most skilled. For, in a practical situation, the man who has access to the greatest body of knowledge about previous experiences is most likely to draw on those experiences to prevent repeating his mistakes. No company with any pretense to good judgment would today embark on employee representation without gaining all possible information about its results elsewhere, and surely some executive should be sufficiently familiar with these results to know when new proposals are running counter to all the best experience. This utilizing of past experience in a critical and selective way is not, of course, simply trial-and-error learning. It includes, also, as an invaluable feature, learning through prior dramatic mental rehearsing of the probable outcome from the use of the several alternatives—which is reasoning.

Another aspect of "learning about" should be mentioned—namely, the necessity of knowing the words which closely name and connote the things, material, or ideas which one wishes to think and talk about. Great differences exist from person to person in the degree of accuracy and clearness with which the individual can express himself on matters he is trying to learn. One of the conspicuous handicaps of people who have not had the advantage of much education is their *inability to say what they mean*. This fact should be appreciated by executives in their dealing with workers. The glib manager or foreman can *verbally* "put it all over" his men when difficulties arise. But that of itself will not alter the workers' underlying attitude toward the problem or situation.

The wise executive will always try to discover what is on the workers' mind and not be so literal in his interpretation of their statements that he merely makes them appear ridiculous or stupid. One of the real values of all sorts of shop conferences, foremen's courses, etc., is the help that they can give *in supplying people with a more accurate grasp of the words they need in order to put their desires and thoughts into understandable form.* In this sense, "learning about" is an indispensable step in the complete learning process.

Just because of the tremendous difficulty of verbalizing and conveying ideas by understandable words, learning through experience occupies a large place in human progress. And this means that the total surrounding situation, the environment, necessarily plays a large part in making the learning experience what it is. In other words, the external setting of a behavior situation is a part of the educational influence. In order best to capitalize on this truth, the executive or teacher should deliberately try to surround the learner with conditions of such a character that the thing he sees to be done becomes the thing he not only has to do but also wants to do. In short, the executive may construct a problem situation in which the stage is so set that the solution commends itself to the one subjected to the experience as the only sensible and desirable way out. This aspect of the good teacher's technique is so important as to merit illustration.

There is, for example, the case of a factory where the foremen were reluctant to give up the hiring function in favor of a centralized employment office. The functionalizing of employment was, in reality, only a part of a whole program of improvement in management methods which the head executive had in mind. He wanted his foremen to concern themselves much more than formerly with improvement in the quality of the product and with reduction of unit costs. He put specific tasks up to them along these lines—tasks which required a great deal of time and consecutive attention to carry out. About a month after putting upon them this program of production improvement, he called them together and asked how it was going. All protested that they had far too much to do and were staying overtime too often. Then, while their minds were full of their predicament (unsolved problem), he suggested that if they would let an employment manager handle hiring, placement, and follow-up of new workers it might save much of their time. In the light of the new situation they were facing, they agreed, and an employment man was hired. The manager used the entire surrounding situation to lead his men *to try willingly* a new policy, a policy which he firmly believed they would also themselves desire as soon as they had experienced the value of it.

This method of learning by being placed in problem situations *takes time*. But all learning takes time if it is to do what it is really designed to—namely, bring about a real, convinced, and permanent change of habit, outlook, or opinion. The important thing is to utilize this method intelligently. A good manager will invite and encourage trials; he will even occasionally allow errors (if they are not too costly), in order that individuals and groups may go through learning experiences in such a way that the changed attitude sought does, in fact, come about. Conceivably, in the case of the manager just mentioned, the wrong conclusion might have been reached by his foremen if the employment manager had, for example, proved grossly incompetent, or if he had allowed them to get the idea that he was stripping them of authority rather than lightening their burden. Only in so far as he was successful in helping them to solve their problem to their own satisfaction was he a party to convincing them that the right solution had been found.

In short, put individuals into a problem situation; guide the process by which *they* consider the ways out and *they* decide to try one likely alternative; stir them by the prompting of a strong desire to get themselves out of a difficulty; then help by suggesting the relative merits of the alternatives which they are considering to show how one particular line of action seems likely best to fulfill their desires; and, finally, get them to try it out. This is the formula for the executive leader who would put his people through an effective learning process.

Another way of summarizing this truth about learning is to say that the outcome of learning can be of three fairly definite sorts. It can be in new habits or skills; in new attitudes or appreciations; or it can be in new knowledge acquired.[1] And the astute executive and teacher will be anxious to decide in advance which kind of learning is necessary to meet the needs of his immediate problem. Emphasis above has been upon learning as skill acquiring and problem solving, because ability to deal with concrete executive situations can be cultivated to a most helpful degree by the use of this method of putting people through experiences. And learning, in the two other senses, can in many instances be a natural derivative of the experience of acquiring a skill or solving a problem.

It is important to make clear how far-reaching are the consequences of this fairly obvious statement that people learn by testing their powers against problems whose solution restores them to equanimity. As will be emphasized later, one of the chief things the executive leader should often be trying to do is to help reshape the purposes of his workers and of his colleagues and often, also, of his executive superiors. This reshaping of purposes is essentially a learning process. And the manner of carrying out the reshaping process is practically identical with the manner of carrying on the learning process just described. People can and will learn new purposes, is the conclusion, if and when they find that the following of old purposes does not yield satisfaction, creates more problems than it solves—in a word, makes for unhappiness.

Learning and Maximum Achievement.—A further fact about learning is that continued performance of an act does not necessarily lead to the greatest speed or ease or economy of motion. Usually, performance gets set on a habit level of moderate intensity. If maximum skill and output are to be obtained, some new and special incentives seem to be necessary; some clear measure of accomplishment is advisable; and some comparison should be possible between past and future performance. Also, there has to be disinterested study (the technique of time and motion study is of great assistance), to see if present working methods and motions are, in fact, the most economical and efficient.

These facts have, of course, a most important bearing on the effort of a manager to raise the general level of performance throughout his organization. The fact that most people most of the time work at far less than their full energy and capacity is now well established. Some excitement is required to get them to bestir themselves out of the normal jog trot of moderate activity. Any effort to tone up the efficiency of an organization requires that people who already think they know how to do their jobs be taught how they can do them better and be supplied with fresh incentives.

The Age of the Learner.—It is impossible to draw sweeping conclusions as to the influence of advancing years on the individual's ability to learn.   If the adult learner is willing, he can, by paying attention, frequently learn more economically than the younger student, because he has found out how to apply himself. He wastes no time; he works with a will; he has an important stake in the outcome.   All these factors predispose toward effective learning.

But readiness to learn is itself a habit and it is one that is likely to decrease in influence as the years go on because of other conflicting habits.   The element of time in adult learning becomes specially important.   For learning whether in the manual or mental field involves, usually, the breaking up of old habits and the gradual setting up of new ones.   What we speak of as "points of view" are largely habitual, and the changing of a person's point of view, which is often what adult learning principally involves, takes time because of the number of long-established thought habits to be changed.

There is also the widely met condition of suspicion and even dread of new ideas and a changed point of view.   Executives and foremen share with the rest of humanity this tendency to refuse to consider ideas solely because they are new.   And this fact acts as a handicap to adult learning in industry.   The more formal and obviously academic is the set-up of plans to foster executive learning, moreover, the more difficult is the process likely to be.   It is a natural matter of self-pride with adults and specially with those in positions of some authority that they *do not need to learn*.   Indeed, the desire to learn is one of the most important aids to adult learning.   Only as a desire may be stimulated in executives and workers to cope better with their special problems, to improve their earning power, to qualify for higher posts and similar important motives will plans be successfully worked out which will result in encouraging learning. The fact that most of the learning required in industry is among adults means only that ingenious methods must be used. The task is not impossible; but a special technique of stimulation and patient encouragement is required.

A few suggestions can be made on this point. The new idea to be learned should at first be made to seem as like the present view held as possible. The points of similarity should be dwelt upon. Also, the successful experience of others with the new idea should be stressed. The fact that the learner is in a real problem situation should be frequently recalled to him. He should also be reminded again and again that only as the new idea really commends itself to him as a result of his own experience should he hold it as true. If this means delaying his acceptance of it till he has had the experience, that should be accepted and understood by all. Also, the learner should in some cases be encouraged to think that the new idea originated with him. There is little room for pride of authorship among executives who are trying to get others to adopt their ideas.

The Uses of Imitation and Suggestion in Learning.—Another manner in which the learning process is initiated grows out of the tendencies of people *to imitate* and *to follow suggestions*. Imitativeness is the tendency to perform an act without any direct, specific and verbal suggestion that he should perform it coming to the individual from outside. Suggestibility is the tendency almost pathetically dominant in many people to do something just because they are told to do it. These tendencies appear as factors in learning, because much of trial and error is learning by imitation of acts which have been observed. The man learning to operate a machine will no doubt for a time imitate the motions which he has seen his instructor make in giving a demonstration. A foreman who in walking through his department picks up waste and scrap and puts it in proper receptacles is doing something which *observed often enough* is likely to influence others to do the same. Or one worker throws the remains of his lunch under a bench and "gets away with it." Eventually, others imitate him and a bad shop practice has been started.

Suggestion is the same kind of force made explicit by actual verbal prompting. People respond especially to the repeated suggestions of those who have prestige in their eyes.   The element of timeliness in suggestions is important.   A hint given when one is in doubt and in suspense about the right line to follow is received more enthusiastically and with more likelihood of acceptance than when there is no indecision.   Also, suggestions often have cumulative power; at first, they are not followed, but by dint of repetition they gain the forefront of a person's attention and are adopted.

There is an extraordinary power in these two tendencies which may, of course, be used for ill or for good.   But in the armory of every real leader's equipment will be these weapons which are accessible for use when he wants to set afoot influences which will eventually result in action.   To "drop a word in his ear" is the figurative way of saying that one has let fall a suggestion in the hope that it may bear fruit in action.

Yet anyone trying to use these forces must realize the equally obvious fact of *counter-suggestibility*.   This is the tendency to follow the opposite line from that suggested.   Let a suggestion come at the wrong moment or from the wrong person or in the wrong tone of voice or be objectionable for some other reason, and the individual is likely to embark on a line of conduct contrary to the one suggested and, perhaps, even contrary to that which he had previously intended to take!   So subtle are the forces at work within us that no one can ever hope to guess rightly all the time in his dealings with others.   Just because the influence of imitation and suggestion involve the uncritical acceptance of new lines of action, they present a danger.   When the object imitated is withdrawn or the force of the suggestion has worn off, the individual may reflect that he was foolish to be so susceptible.   The danger is that no motive integral to himself has been set in motion.   Unless the suggestion to be followed really promises to commend itself in the long run to the judgment of the person, its force becomes progressively weakened as one gets away from its influence.   Do not use suggestion, in short, unless you are reasonably certain that its results will find lasting favor with the one who embraces your idea!

Memory.—The place of memory in the human learning process is vital, because upon this faculty depends a person's ability to draw upon and use past experiences which will help him to handle the present situation in the best possible way. Even in trial-and-error learning, where there is little imaginative rehearsal of possible eventualities, the individual will remember that this trial has been made before without satisfactory outcome. One remembers to try it again or not to try it again, as the case may be.

And in reasoning, memory is indispensable as bringing to mind for critical consideration the subject matter of past experience. That experience, of course, comes from a variety of sources. The information one wishes to recall has been received through one's own past activity, through conversation with those who have told of their experiences, through reading, which is the written record of experience, the judgments, and the imaginings of others. It will thus be seen that to have ready access in memory to a field of data as wide as possible relevant to each type of problem one may confront is indispensable to the quickest learning. The "learning about" mentioned above also depends for its utility upon ability to recall information when it is needed.

How, then, does the memorizing and recalling process take place? Is it possible for the individual to make this process more effective in himself?

There are four steps in the process—called, usually, "memorizing," "retention," "recall," "recognition."

The step of *memorizing* may be facilitated in certain definite ways. One should first study carefully and attentively the item to be remembered with the idea of fixing its general characteristics in mind, of finding out how it is related to what one already knows, its significance and meaning. Also, audible vocal statement to oneself of the thing to be remembered is helpful; the motor activity helps to fix the mental image.

The type of mental activity used in memorizing depends somewhat, also, upon certain mental characteristics, which vary from person to person. People are said to be "motor minded" or "visually minded" or possessed of an "auditory mind," if they find by experience that they hold items in their memories best by muscular activity (as reciting aloud or writing down) or by getting "the look of the thing" in mind (as a picture) or by getting in mind "the way the thing sounds." In actual fact, one makes more or less use of all these different sensory aids, even though one sensory channel of memorizing may be for him more effective than the others. At any rate, some activity not solely "mental" in nature is an immense aid to memorizing.

A too long period of memorizing at one stretch is not advisable; change your occupation and space the periods of memorizing and of repeating the new material. It is better to spend 15 minutes a day at it for 6 days than to spend 60 minutes at one time.

Again, try to memorize the material *as a whole*, even if it seems at the start to be the slower method; the unity of the matter is thus kept more strongly in mind.

The emotional attitude throughout the process is important. Start *confidently* and *interestedly*. Don't learn by rote but be sure you know what it is all about as you proceed. Get some measure of progress to encourage you as you proceed.

Also, realize that the *intention* to learn is an important factor. Be seriously convinced that you want to remember when you start.

Finally, discriminate where possible as to the relative value of the material to be memorized. It may be that, for the purpose in hand, memorizing is unnecessary, that all which is required is remembering where to get the facts and data you want when you want them. Confidence, concentration of attention, the picking out of salient aspects, frequent rehearsing of the remembered matter after it has been memorized—these are crucial points.

One apparently does not "improve the memory" in the sense that this is an instrument to be sharpened with use. Systems of memory training which hold out such hope are not psychologically sound. What one can improve is *the method of memorizing specific things;* the ability to memorize in any other sense than this is apparently not transferable. But if each new problem is taken up and pursued in the ways and with the attitude mentioned above, real improvement may be expected.

Retention is the ability to hold ready for use the matter memorized. It is not an ability which by itself can be cultivated. Much depends on the thoroughness with which the memorizing process has been gone through. Something depends, also, on not letting a too long time elapse after memorizing before successive repetitions of the matter take place. One forgets more quickly and one relearns more slowly if the memorizing has not been thoroughgoing. Woodworth rightly says that the more wide awake the learner the quicker the learning and the slower the forgetting. High-pressure mental effort gives the best results, provided it is directed into high-level observation.[2]

Recall is the process of getting back into mind what has been memorized. Much depends upon the force and clearness of the stimulus which will create an association (by similarity, contiguity, contrast, etc.) that tends to restore the matter. Distraction due to fear, worry, or other preoccupying interests lessens the possibility of recall. Helpful advice on this point seems to be first, to give the stimulus full attention; and, in the second place, if recall is not immediate to drop the matter for a time and then come back to it afresh. Some subsequent experience, while one is still desirous of securing the recall, is more than likely to provide a helpful association which unconsciously but effectively leads the mind by free association back to the recollection of that which formerly could not be recalled.

Recognition is the process of correctly identifying what has been recalled as the recollection one is searching for. This identification comes from a feeling of familiarity with the matter in hand. And one seeks such identification by recalling the setting and context of the newly remembered item and finding that it fits correctly into place. There is apparently no way of improving the power of recognition. Here, again, it depends on the thoroughness with which the item to be recalled has been learned, not by rote and in meaningless isolation, but in its significant setting and inherent relationships.

The conclusion is that there are better and worse ways of memorizing and that attention can usefully be paid to the way one studies and learns. A few additional specific hints as to ways of remembering and using what one reads and studies in books are deferred until the chapter on training methods.

Intelligence.—The factor of intelligence is to be distinguished in relation to the learning and the reasoning process because, in the psychological vocabulary, it stands for an unlearned, inborn trait which shows marked difference in quality from person to person and gives rise to differences in the effectiveness with which they learn and reason.   The special definition thus frequently assigned to intelligence by psychologists is that it is that quality in mental activity which enables the individual to be readily effective in the use he makes of mental data in deriving help for the solution of problems.   It is a combination of ability to remember what one needs, to see its relevance to the existing case, to adapt already learned matter usefully to new situations, and, also, to recognize when a problem is not capable of solution. It is the quality of ingenuity in thinking which cleverly picks out the salient features of a difficulty and of its solution and thereby gets results.

Another definition which usefully summarizes the above is that an individual possesses intelligence in so far as he has learned or can learn to adjust himself to his environment.[3]

A crucial element in intelligence is thus a keen *responsiveness to relationships*.   Take, for example, two men trying to set up a new machine from written instructions which accompany the unassembled parts.   One quickly identifies the parts in hand with the parts mentioned; he sees readily how it is that one part fits into another; he "gets the idea" of the way the whole machine should look and is able to assemble it and make it run without too many mistakes.   The other man has to puzzle over the instructions; he makes many wrong guesses as to which parts join the other; he takes twice as long to do the job.   The former has the quality of intelligence to a much greater degree than the latter.

Obviously, intelligence is a precious possession.   And it is doubly useful if, in addition, one possessed of a ready mind has the virtue of persistence, curiosity, and diligence.   Intelligence, moreover, prevents one from letting persistence overdevelop into stubborn, unyielding, pig-headed efforts. It is one of its values that it discovers the practical limits within which a problem can be solved. Suppose that in putting together a machine the mechanic sees that two key parts are missing. If he is intelligent, he will quickly note their absence and as quickly lay down his tools and wait till they arrive before he attempts to finish the job. To know when a problem cannot be solved or is not worth solving is an indication of intelligence. People differ, also, in the amount of curiosity they have about difficulties. Those with a large native endowment of "wondering" and inquisitiveness have one important element to stimulate the use of intelligence.

One further truth about this valuable quality should be understood. Apparently, it is not susceptible to improvement by training. One is born with as much intelligence as one will ever have. How it is developed and used in early life does, indeed, depend on the individual's home and social surroundings; and differences here can greatly influence the likelihood of intelligence's being displayed. But, bearing in mind this important qualification, experiments seem to show that intelligence is a constant quality through life. Education is, therefore, not calculated to improve it. What education does do, and it is a vital aid in increasing personal efficiency in adjustments, is to supply data for problem solving, to supply inspiration for self-development, to place before the individual the tools of scientific inquiry and rational reflection, to give each one the chance to exercise his intelligence to the full in an advantageous social situation, to provide for cultivating native aptitudes, to supply hints as to how persistence and "stick-to-it-iveness" can be cultivated, to supply motives for the exercise of intelligence on a wider range of behavior problems.

The effectiveness with which one uses the intelligence with which he is endowed is thus very much under human control. A wide area for individual improvement and growth remains possible. But it is the part of realism to know that the native inheritance and constitution determines mental ability in the sense that it "fixes certain limits which the individual cannot pass, no matter how good his environment, and no matter how hard he trains himself."

The relative amount of intelligence which one possesses has been found to be subject to measurement in an approximate kind of way, although the so-called "intelligence tests" are still clumsy instruments the results of which should be applied in practical affairs with the greatest conservatism. The criticism is made, for instance, that the present tests depend more upon the educational and general cultural background and experience of the individual than upon innate capacity. In other words, the tests may not sufficiently isolate the peculiar quality of intelligence. Hence, if too exclusive reliance is put upon them in placing an individual, for example, in a graded training class or in an occupation which makes certain demands upon intelligence, the likelihood of error is still present. Leaders of men and affairs usually score high in such tests. But, as often as not, many individuals who also score high have little power of leadership. Ability to deal effectively with people, with big ideas, and with complex machines requires intelligence; but it also requires other factors of physique, temperament, understanding of people, etc., which are less easy to measure or predict.

Studies of school pupils and college students, of the draft army during the World War, of industrial employees, all indicate that the number of individuals with high intelligence is relatively limited, that the majority of people seemingly have only a modest endowment of it, and that another large minority group has still less. One author claims that the statistical studies to date indicate the following grouping of people in point of intellectual equipment:[4]

Near genius or genius	0.25
Very superior	6.75
Superior	13.00
Normal or average	60.00
Dull, rarely feeble-minded	13.00
Border line, sometimes dull, often feeble-minded	6.00
Feeble-minded	1.00

Taking facts like these at their face value, some writers have concluded that any political institution (like a democratic or representative form of government) which places much responsibility upon a general electorate for wise decisions is doomed to failure. But such conclusions are too hasty. People in groups, as in a political state or a corporation, do, of course, have to be directed with definite reference to the degree of discrimination they can and will exercise. The wise leader is always mindful of the intelligence level to which he must appeal to get the response he wants. But to be truly wise he must also be mindful of what might be called the "desire level" and of the educational level of his group. And these two levels and sets of forces are clearly affected by other influences than intelligence. What the people in a group want in terms of self-realization and cultural outlets is undoubtedly modified by intelligence. Indeed, for that very reason, leaders in any walk of life—in industry no less than in politics—can no longer soundly assume that they alone can express or bring to pass the means of expressing the aspirations of others. They lead only as they have that sensitiveness and degree of foresight which feels the aspirations which are at work in the breasts of their followers, are articulate about those aspirations, are sympathetic with them, and are ready to work with "the people" for their fulfillment.

In short, the fact of degrees of intelligence among those led is merely one important conditioning element in the task of every true leader, the task of being the bellwether of his flock rather than its autocratic master. This fact is certainly not of sufficient significance to call into question the validity of democratic purposes and methods in society, however much it may be made an argument for modifying some specific plan for voicing public choices. Such plans, of course, are at best experimental today and are good only as they prove to be means to the end of helping to assure conditions that will minister to life, liberty, and the pursuit of happiness. The assurance in industry, as in politics, that there would always exist direction by people of intelligence (as defined above) would be a worthless assurance were that intelligence not coupled with other intellectual qualities and certain broad purposes of goodwill and fraternity which promised a democratic use of power.

Special Aptitudes.—In addition to this general faculty for dealing sagaciously with experience, there exist also special abilities or aptitudes enabling one to deal with special kinds of activity in a uniquely effective way. What all these aptitudes are is not yet clearly established, but it is known that some people have special facility in dealing with colors or with music, with numbers, with drawing, with tools. No doubt, as time goes on, aptitudes will be more clearly defined, and more and better tests of their existence will be devised so that people can be helped to identify and utilize their best abilities. Meanwhile, it is important to note that these aptitudes are motivators to conduct. They impel, especially after their existence is realized, to behavior which will give them expression. They offer, moreover, stimulus to the reasoning process. People are prone to think about the fulfillment and the expert use of their special abilities in a way which is distinctly fruitful.

Conclusion.—The picture of how we learn that is here presented intentionally emphasizes the motor and active phases of the process. There is need in all industrial training work,—and especially in the more general training for upgrading, for executive effort, for conference efficiency,—for methods that produce mental changes of attitude and working approach by directed experience within somewhat controlled situations. This is not at all to deny the power or necessity of reaching reasoned conclusions or of reflection about the outcome of experience. In fact, both parts of the learning process are essential. There should be motor performance and there should be reflective activity. And each should play into the hands of the other. It is the latter phase of the process which the next chapter elaborates.

CHAPTER VII

HOW TO ENCOURAGE REASONING

Learning, it has been pointed out, takes place through motor activity induced by various motives and through reasoning. The reasoning ability seems to be uniquely human, seems to be the one which enables mankind to learn more rapidly, more comprehensively, more effectively than those animals which employ only the trial-and-error method. Understanding of the reasoning process, of the conditions under which it is evoked, of the ways of stimulating it into wide use becomes, therefore, of the utmost importance.

Reasoning is the process of mental exploration undertaken in order to find or infer the significant and practically useful relation between things already known and some new fact or experience whose existence or use constitutes a problem. It is a search for meaning in a novel experience by tying it up in a way that proves workable with meanings already derived from past experience.

In this study, the words "thought" and "thinking" will be used as synonymous with "reasoning." The spontaneous and continuing flow of ideas in consciousness is sometimes referred to as thinking; but here thinking means the definite act of reflection, and some other phrase will be used where the random drift of ideas is meant.

An illustration of the working of the reasoning process may now help to get clearly in mind its essential character. Here is a company president who is anxious to provide in some systematic and humane way for his ageing employees. This is his recognized problem. He probably at once asks himself what experience other companies have had with industrial pensions. He has his secretary or his personnel manager prepare a bibliography

83

on the subject, and he reads the literature—the recorded experience of success and failure of different plans under different conditions.   He talks extensively with employers who have such plans.   He also consults an actuarial specialist who may eventually prepare for him a tentative draft of a plan based on the president's suggestions and his own technical knowledge.   This plan is the newly discovered basis of action which the president hopes will be the answer to his problem.   There is a presumption in favor of its being suitable, because he has tried to take account of all the experience possible.   He therefore submits this plan to other employers and executives for suggestions and then to his employees for consideration.   After emendations, people tell him to go ahead and try it, which he does.   And if the plan is soundly conceived and actuarially correct as to reserves required, etc., he finds, through the experience of the years, that he has reasoned through his problem correctly.

What, then, have been the steps in this process?   They are:

1. *Recognition* of a problem.
2. *Accumulation* of all possible data which throw light on the nature of the problem and, perhaps, therefore, on its solution.
3. *Classification* of all the data into significant groupings—groupings which, if intelligently made, supply clues as to the probable nature of the solution.
4. *Formulation* of a tentative conclusion, a solution, or "working basis" or "hypothesis" (as it is called in scientific inquiries) which is to be tried out in action to see if it works.
5. *Testing* of the tentative solution in action, and if it works,
6. *Adoption* of the solution as a working method considered to be effective as long as all the supporting conditions of the case remain the same.

If everyone when thinking about problems would get this sequence of processes firmly in mind and make the conscious following of it a practice, there is no question but that the reasoning process would go forward much more smoothly, rapidly, and correctly.   For convenience, remember the six italicized words and deliberately work through these six stages in solving a problem and the results are almost certain to be highly gratifying.   *Conscious use of these steps in the reasoning process is one of the most clarifying aids to sound thinking.*

A similar but also suggestive description of the successive stages in the thinking process in its problem-solving aspect is supplied by Graham Wallas in the four words "preparation," "incubation," "illumination," "verification."[1] The words themselves suggest the process to be encouraged to get new ideas formulated and tested.

Remember, also, that it has been said that *the essence of the educational method is the essence of reflection.* This means something enormously practical and important. It means that the way to carry on the educational process with oneself or with others is to present the educational matter—the material or skill to be learned—as a problem to be mastered and then to follow through the successive steps until mastery is achieved. The significance of this dictum is that it puts the emphasis upon the necessity for self-activity as the condition of education and of reflection. The president who studied pensions knew about them after his study. But he was really educated about them only after he had had actual experience with operating the plan which he had himself put through. And everyone, in respect to countless day-to-day problems of choice, reflects upon them and acts rationally only as he himself goes through the above processes, rather than, as so often happens, taking the ready-made conclusions of others as his own.

The Occasions for Reasoning.—The occasions for reasoning, the various kinds of problems which puzzle individuals, may helpfully be characterized in various ways, since knowledge of the ways of arousing reflection is suggestive as to how the process can be stimulated in others.

Dewey, for example, starting from the point of view of habits and the conflict among habits occasioned by the promptings of impulses and emotions at odds with established habits, says that "the occasion of deliberation is an excess of preferences,"[2] which gives rise to a conscious search for the right preference. Rationality or a reasoned way of acting is thus considered not to be "the attainment of a working harmony among diverse desires." It is a quality of effective relationship discovered and worked out among one's desires. "Activity does not cease to give way to reflection, activity is turned from execution into dramatic rehearsal." One chooses and transfers activity from deliberation to overt conduct when a unified and, therefore, more strongly felt preference finally emerges out of competing preferences. The search is not for an end of action but for a *way to act*. Thus, there may be reasonable and unreasonable choice—fully reasoned reflection in which all possible factors are really taken account of, and partially reasoned reflection in which action occurs too soon in the sense that some impulsive motive gets the upper hand before all factors have been fully weighed.

There may also be an excess of reflection. People are known to become occasionally too interested in thinking about alternatives to dare to decide and to act. They may get so occupied with remote and abstract matters that they are impatient with the limiting conditions of the immediate present. Those who talk and think much of "ideals" and who are fond of utopian programs are peculiarly in this danger. They find the world which they can easily build up in their minds so congenial, so easy to mould, that they hate the hard work required to find out how they can take the next steps which might lead them under the actual complex conditions of today, a little way in the direction in which they want to go.

People who professionally have to think a great deal in one special field are all too often unthinking, impulsive, and inept in other fields, as, for instance, in practical dealings with other people. Their reasoning is partial and fragmentary. To be adequate to life's needs, it must be laboriously applied to *all* kinds of situations continually. Deliberation is irrational to the extent that one end becomes so fixed or a passion or interest becomes so absorbing that only those consequences are kept in mind which forward its fulfillment. Deliberation is rational to the degree to which the choice among old impulses and habits and the proposed new aims is flexibly controlled by an honest weighing of *all* the determining elements in the situation.

To executives who have enjoyed an exclusively technical engineering training, this point is especially important. Their frequent failure to apply scientific thinking to personnel problems creates a serious defect in their managerial conduct. For them solicitude to see that they think honestly, which in this case means with full psychological knowledge, about the human aspects of their problems, is one of the great needs.

People think, someone has said, in order, first, to get satisfactory channels for the expression of their innate capacities and acquired desires; second, to find new ways of expression when normal channels are obstructed; and, third, to bring a harmony out of conflicting desires and alternate ways of expressing their capacities.

Woodworth identifies at least six kinds of situation which provoke thought—problem solving, self-justification, explanation, application, doubt, verification. A word on each of these should prove further illustrative as to the stimuli helpful to reasoning. The example given above of the search for a pension plan is the problem-solving kind of reasoning.

Self-justification, frequently called "rationalization," is the search for reasons either before or after an act in order to meet criticisms of the outcome by ourselves or by others. Frequently, action has been unpremeditated, been uncritically impulsive, is ineptly out of line with old habits, or is prompted by motives one does not care to admit. The wisdom of the outcome, in the particular event, is, perhaps, in doubt. Hence, people try to find a reason for doing it or for having done it.

A good deal of reasoning is in response to the more or less disinterested desire to know why—to know the explanation. People like to see a fact as an illustration of some general truth or principle with which they are already familiar. Much scientific research is thus prompted.

One also reasons from a general principle to specific concrete cases. One wants to see if it applies in this case, if its application can be extended to cover a new example. Thus, the principle itself becomes more completely understood.

One reasons because one doubts a principle or statement and wants to see if he cannot find instances which deny or contradict it.

One reasons, finally, because one has a theory or a principle which one seeks to verify. The assembling of cases where the theory works, the trying out of examples where it has to be employed, are reasoning for purposes of verifying.

Two broad ways of going at the reasoning process are thus seen to exist. Special names have been given to them. They are *inductive reasoning* and *deductive reasoning.*

Inductive reasoning is the utilizing of a variety of individual instances in order to arrive at the formulation of a conclusion, solution, or hypothesis which fits and explains all the facts. It is proceeding from the particular to the inference of a general conclusion.

Deductive reasoning starts with an established conclusion as true and tries to deduce certain facts from it. It is proceeding from the general to the particular case, in the effort to bring the case under the clarifying heading of the general. Mathematics is the most conspicuous case of the use of deductive, and the typical methods of the natural sciences are a familiar case of the use of inductive reasoning. In general, the inductive method is called into use most frequently. Yet it must at all times be realized that one's inductions are themselves often based on deductions, on already formulated general principles, and are, therefore, only as true as those principles. Suppose, for instance, that a scientist is studying inductively the activity of radium. He has probably assumed the existence of what is called the "law of the conservation of energy"—a general principle which says that energy is never lost but is only transformed into some other manifestation. Yet he finds that energy seemingly does disappear in radioactivity. His conclusion has to be either that energy is transformed in some way that he has not previously known or that the principle does not apply to this particular case and to that extent is not a law for universal application in the physical world.

Other Problems Requiring Reasoning.—Still another way of conceiving of the types of problem which prompt the individual to reflection is to characterize kinds of conflicts which are typical. One finds that people deliberate about the relative value of:

    1. Immediate and remote ends.

    2. Individual and social ends.

3. Lower or "animal" and higher or "spiritual" ends.

4. Future alternatives, as in the case of careers.

5. Old and new habits and beliefs.[3]

And another writer points out that if the individual is reflecting upon past experience and trying to evaluate it, he is likely to ask:

Was it pleasurable or unpleasant?

Did it leave me elated or depressed?

Did I get what I wanted and does that still seem desirable?[4]

Testing the Correctness of Reasoning.—Questions such as these lead one to ask how it is that the reasoner knows that his reasoning is correct. There are two points to consider here. As the three above questions imply, the reasoner will come through an experience impressed with the soundness of his conclusions if in and after action they have brought him back to a state of satisfactory adjustment and harmony with his surroundings. Then he "feels good." The fundamental satisfactions yielded by the solution discovered are felt to be undeniable. The solution worked in a basic and reasonably permanent way and was, therefore, correct.

The other question is as to the soundness of the inference from a logical standpoint. People do undoubtedly carry on activities which give satisfaction for reasons which, as consciously formulated, are illogical. But a persistent use of bad logic in thinking would be found to be disastrous over a period of time to successful adjustments and to happiness.

The process of logic is the process of checking up reasoning to see that the conclusion reached is the only one which follows as a result of the acceptance of the premises (facts) and that the premises do, in fact, bear a correctly causal relation to the conclusion drawn.

Aids to Reasoning.—A good reasoner is partly born and partly made. And there are a number of important surrounding and supporting conditions which can be created to help foster the deliberative process.

The first aid is to get the individual to be aware of and concerned about a problem. People differ much both in their native propensity to seek out difficulties or realize that they are

in them and in the habits they build of sensitiveness or indifference to those maladjustments which do not fall under their
immediate noses. Some people are content in a total setting
in which others would be stimulated to thought as to how they
could remove themselves. There are those of a bovine or
phlegmatic temperament who ignore or escape from problem
situations with a minimum of thought expenditure. It seems
to be true that the fertile problem solver, the individual who
confronts and tackles problems rather than sidesteps them, is
the one who has a goodly endowment of what is called "nervous
energy." People who have plenty of nervous energy, who have
a surplus of energy above the minimum demands of eating,
sleeping, and routine daily labor, are the ones who can be looked
to as likely thinkers. But even with them it is necessary in
many situations to have the fact of a problem brought to their
attention.

The situation of the employees in an unprofitable business
concern often presents an interesting example of people being
party to a problem without being aware of it. Of course, under
such circumstances, they are not, in their ignorance, in a position
to help solve the problems which bring the adverse condition to
pass. If a manager in such a case wanted employees' help in
cutting costs, eliminating wastes, and the like, his recognition
of the problem would have to be extended to them.

Take the case of a firm asked to submit a bid for a job on
which other competitors are bidding and are known to be figuring
closely. The clever manager will take this problem to his men
and ask their help in solving it. This means that he must give
them at least *enough facts to work on so that they are in a position
to do some thinking of their own* and reach a conclusion. And
the more facts the better, for this indicates the manager's
confidence in them and invites a favorable response from them.
Case after case could be given to show the importance of this
big truth—namely, that *only as the management will take the
trouble to make the elements of its problems real to the rank and
file can help be expected from them in attempting to solve these
problems.*

The basic prior condition of the use of reflection is consciousness of a problem. Let everyone who wants to encourage thinking remember this as his first cue. Remember, also, that problems cannot be productively worked upon without knowledge of the facts. This is the underlying reason why all intelligent efforts at publicity among employees on corporate affairs and problems is good business. They make the employees conscious sharers in that cooperative thinking process which is the essential factor in running any business.

One's physiological condition can also help to facilitate the use of the mind. If one is free of fatigue, is not overtaxing his digestion, is warm so that blood flows readily to the head, is not distracted by fear or anxiety or depressed by dread, pain, or by narcotics, one is predisposed physically to thought. But one must not be too comfortable. Those, for example, who try to study and think in a deep chair after a hearty meal and a day of vigorous physical activity should not be surprised that they go to sleep. Better an upright chair, an erect posture, and a light meal.

People do, of course, think when they are worried and fearful. But the pronounced tendency is to center the thinking on the source of the worry and the means of escape. People who would do effective thinking in one direction cannot be too preoccupied with other concerns, too stirred up in their emotional state.

Also, distraction should not be too great. It may be that the regular rhythm of some accompanying sound does not draw attention away from the thought problem. But certainly unless one has trained oneself to unusual powers of concentration, the more quiet and free from distraction the surroundings are, the better.

In the same way, one must have leisure in order to think clearly. This point should not be misunderstood. People do not "just think" if they are doing nothing; they tend to daydream and let their minds wander aimlessly. But if and when they have something which they want to think about, they can do it satisfactorily only when attention is not required for other matters. Thinking on a problem takes time, and it is important in all educational work, of self and of others, that, *once the problem is set,* free time be provided in which reflection can take place.

Thinking takes time, also, in the important sense that as one gets "warmed up" mentally by getting into his subject, the whole process tends to flow forward more freely. Restraints drop away; the material at hand is clearly seen, and the ways of working at it are often disclosed as if a veil were suddenly drawn away. But this productive and satisfying experience comes only if one is able to stay at one's mental labors consecutively and uninterruptedly enough to get a sort of "second wind" and free field. The condition of spontaneous reasoning out of the subject, which comes as one stays with it, is seemingly one of the requirements of the most creative reflective work.

The state of one's own mental equipment is of further importance. In part, this is inborn. Intelligence in the sense of ability to discern relations between old and new, a ready detective sense to discover cause-and-effect connections, a native inquisitiveness, a faculty for keeping to the point during deliberation—these qualities are all invaluable and are all seemingly a matter largely if not wholly of original endowment. On the other hand, the use of proper thinking habits can be acquired. By this is meant the conscious use of the steps in the reasoning process as outlined above. The good thinker uses the scientific method in reasoning; and the scientific method may be cultivated. To collect facts, classify them, to form and test conclusions, to hold only to what one has evidence for and can prove—these are steps which all can learn.

Again, one has partially in his control the extent of his prior knowledge about the subject under consideration. Access to ideas and facts and mastery of them are of vital importance. This access may require the use of a whole apparatus of study— books, journals, files, laboratories, and what not. In some way, one must get in mind the relevant data. How it all bears on the special problem, how an orderly and suggestive arrangement comes out of a great mass of material, may not at first appear. There is interesting evidence in the testimony of many thinkers that their method of work is to steep themselves in all the fact material that they can get hold of and then get away from the problem for a while. The common phrase that one is going "to sleep over the question" reflects sound psychological experience. There is something about leaving the problem alone and subsequently coming back to it freshly, which seems to give the thinker possession of a new clarity, a new power to bring a useful synthesis and a correct conclusion out of a mass of data. To "see where the facts lead" is a necessary, helpful process, but it requires living with all the facts thoroughly enough so that there is enough grist for the mental mill to grind. From this point of view, also, the thinking act cannot be too hurried. The teacher no less than the learner has to realize that time is of the essence of his problem and has to have faith that in mental as in physical matters there is "first the grain, then the ear, then the full corn in the ear."

People also tend to misconceive how it is that creative thinking comes about. Individuals do not generate new ideas in a vacuum and without relation to existing ideas and conclusions about a subject. New ideas are practically always built up as one significant new combination of a lot of facts or ideas already established. Inventions have hardly ever, for example, been conceived full grown in the mind of one man. They are the development of known ideas, built up step by step, often accidentally, with suggestions from one source and another, until, finally, a workable creation results. The practical conclusion to be drawn from this fact is that in constructive thinking one should always try to know how others have tried to solve a given problem before going on with the development of new suggestions.

A further aid to clarification in thinking lies for many in *writing down* their ideas. The organization of one's thought required for clear verbal expression is almost inevitably a means of showing up discrepancies in one's logic and confusions in one's conclusions. It is in this sense that "truth grows more quickly out of error than out of confusion of mind." If one will make some coherent formulation of his thought, he and others are far more likely to discover his errors than if he merely says "I know what I mean but I can't express it."

Another tremendous aid comes from the assistance of those with whom one associates; too much stress can hardly be laid on this condition. If those whose approval one values praise and encourage clear thinking, that is a great inducement to reflection. If they are able to discuss a problem, to criticize tentative conclusions, to aid in testing hypotheses, that is all of immense aid. Thinking is essentially social in its larger aspects. And the reenforcement, the criticism, and the clarification which association with others who are thinking yields, are at once an incentive and a positive influence upon the soundness of one's results.

Finally, there are certain considerations in this discussion of the aids to thinking which have to do with the character of the thinker. Thinking of a sustained sort, the solution of any problems really worthwhile, are *hard work*. Make no mistake about that. Thinking accurately and constructively is the hardest thing that people do. It is an ability the intensive and controlled use of which comes late in the development of the human equipment, and it needs the most deliberate and affectionate solicitude of each individual to foster and develop his reflective powers. Such powers are the crown and glory of humankind, and in the possibility of surrounding individuals with favoring conditions, with encouragement and the sense of satisfaction and delight in successfully exercising their reflecting abilities, lies literally the hope of civilization.

If all this is true, persistence in thinking, tolerance as to the results of thinking, patience with the process of thinking, courage in the application of conclusions reached—these are all character requirements for him who would develop his own thinking ability. It is often at one or another of these critical points that many individuals fall by the wayside in the fulfillment of their reasoning heritage. People get tired of trying to think straight in the light of so much surrounding muddleheadedness and of so much material success which has come by chance. Or they are afraid to endure the consequences of conclusions at odds with the outlook and customs of their fellows; or they draw conclusions from their own independent thought but keep them rankling in one unopened chamber of their minds, keep them isolated and unrelated to actual affairs, meanwhile becoming cynical because of the contrast between their own cherished truths and the folly or stupidity of others who do not share them. Or, possibly, they stop thinking because they become convinced that thinking does not influence life but rather runs parallel to it. This last view is the most insidious of all in its paralyzing effects. Whatever the ultimate philosophical answer to this question may be, it certainly is demonstrably true in respect to concrete managerial problems that thinking *seems* to help to solve them! And if people could be reminded that they do, in fact, *act as if* their thinking had constructive effect, they might continue to think more unreservedly.

Fundamentally, a passion for truth and a faith in the practical efficacy of truthfulness and "sweet reasonableness" will constitute the most effective, long-time reenforcement to the one who seeks to use his deliberative ability consistently and continuously upon all the puzzling problems of life.

Imagination.—Imagination is a flowering of the reasoning process, a building up out of existent factual material of new combinations which seem likely to work together practically and then by experience are found to do so. Imagination works more freely than reasoning in that the results sought are not quite so specific nor so obviously implicit in the facts. It is a seeking for a relationship which can be rationally established, rather than for one which is there already. Invention is the use of imagination for the solution of a special kind of problem. And one can be inventive in the field of corporate structure or human relationships just as well as in the field of mechanical contrivance.

Why do people exercise imagination? The answer is that they like to and that occasionally they have to. Daydreaming is unregulated and unproductive imagining. It gets nowhere; does not put together familiar facts in a fresh way that can be made use of. For those who indulge in it too much, it becomes a vice—an escape from realities into a world of revery and fantasy where practical and pressing issues are habitually ignored and deferred.

People have to use imagination where the need for real creation arises, where past experience gives only a slight hint or guide, where, clearly, a novel line must be taken. A man wants, for example, to build up his business with the sale of an unexploited product, such as safety razors were when first put on the market. This is a problem requiring the exercise of a great deal of imagination, a great deal of ability to build up pictures of what he would like to see done and of how he should go about it. The prior imaginative construction of at least the broad outlines of his plan is *the essential prior condition of any worthwhile action on his part.* Once he gets in mind what seems to him a reasonable picture of the whole program involved, the rest is relatively easy. But this picture, in order to be imaginatively productive, *must be clear, appear desirable, and include within it a view of the means whereby he will take the first steps.*

It is this truth which has led one recent apostle of mental control (Coué) to say that imagination is the factor more important than the "will" in trying to secure effective action. Get the right picture, see clearly what you want, and reenforce the desire by constant verbal reiteration of it, and the desired action should result; this is the formula that was advocated. The one other important element in the process—knowing the steps toward getting what you want—was the only omission from an otherwise helpful prescription.

Like reasoning, and in much the same ways, imagination can be cultivated. In the case of the man promoting a new venture, if he can sit down at his desk and satisfy the following conditions, there is a good presumption in favor of a fertile imagination's displaying itself. First, he must not be too old. Generally speaking, new ideas are the fruits of those from twenty to fifty years of age. He should have good physical condition, be fresh and undistracted. He must know his subject. That means he must have practical knowledge in the field of finance, production, personnel, and sales. He must know what he wants—a condition already fulfilled, in this case, since the launching of the unexploited product is his project. He must be hopeful, have confidence in the merit of his offering—a confidence backed by sober judgment. Finally, he must be willing to take the chance, be eager to embark on the plan, and be ready to assume the obvious risks.

These conditions are not beyond the control of many people who might try to exercise their imaginations. But the conscious bringing of them all together is where we tend to fail; yet it is the royal road to a more effective use of mind.

To prove this, let anyone take one of his own problems and see what good results he can obtain by thinking of it imaginatively. There is, for instance, the question of the best possible use of one's income. Almost everyone could profit by an imaginative consideration of this subject, by a thoughtful creation of pictures of new or eventual uses of income and of the steps required to make such use a fact. The truth is that most people do not know the essentials of this important subject and do not know that they do not know them. Realization of how much there is to it and of how many factors should be analyzed and considered is one of the conditions of letting the imagination play upon the theme.[5]

Judgment.—The quality of judgment should be defined in relation to reasoning and imagination, because it is an essential concomitant of them at their best. One must exercise judgment in the use of reason and of imagination in the important sense that there comes a time when one must decide that both must give way to action.

"Judgment" may be defined as "that quality in mental behavior which assures that one gives proper weight to the various facts, that one shows shrewdness in forming a conclusion which is plausible because consistent with the facts, that one sees a given problem in reasonable proportion to other problems to be faced, that one has confidence in one's processes and solutions in direct relation to benefits shown." If intelligence is the kind of sagacity made use of in sizing up situations, judgment is the kind of good sense shown in sizing up the results of the reflective process and of its application. Good judgment is thus usually a derivative of experience. An estimation of both probable and actual consequences is best gained out of a background of activity;

and as such it is a possession relatively rare in youth. But anyone who will cultivate the habit of critically weighing, evaluating, and analyzing the experiences of himself and others is in a fair way to develop good judgment. And it is a priceless asset in executives.

Conclusion.—The practical possibilities of individual improvement in the use of reasoning are among the most promising aids which psychology brings to mankind. Awareness and conscious use of the necessary steps in sound reasoning are required, and character qualities which prompt to applying reasoning in actual affairs against all the obstructive odds should be insisted upon and cultivated. The aspect of behavior which can be uniquely human is the applying of careful thought to all problems of living; and everything which can be done to foster, support and win action out of reflection is the least help that teachers and executives can give. The use of reasoning, the encouraging of imaginative thinking, the exercise of judgment,—these are hard enough at best. They call for all the reenforcement of favoring conditions, approval and honest willingness to experiment with reflective conduct which organizations and groups can furnish to individuals.

CHAPTER VIII

THE MEANING OF WILL AND PERSONALITY

The Will.—In popular thinking, there is often supposed to be a definite entity which can be "cultivated," spoken of as "the will." In strict psychological parlance, there is no such thing. But there is a certain group of facts which people usually are thinking of when the word is mentioned; and a clear understanding of these is important. One is supposed to "exert his will" in order to overcome some internal conflict or some external obstruction. What the phrase "an act of will" usually connotes is either the arriving at a decision, the making of a choice, the embarking firmly on a course of action, or the effective mobilizing to remove an obstacle. But all of these activities have already been described and the process of the experience explained in explaining reasoning and the reaching of decisions.

One looks in vain for any distinct entity in these activities or in the human equipment which is a "will." One finds, in fact, a variety of means whereby integrated and unified behavior is brought out of confusion and strife. And from a practical standpoint it is gratifying to see that when these processes are analyzed by steps, there are found to be specific helps which can be offered to facilitate action.

No fact about behavior stands out more clearly than that the individual is confronted with conflicting claims on his attention and energies. One's impulsive and habit life supplies *not guides but grooves* for possible lines of conduct; and those grooves collide in a most confusing way. Somehow, action has to be achieved in the face of contradictory demands. Some motive or some possible combination of motives has eventually to get the upper hand and get through into action. Vacillation is unpleasant; one wants action or peace but not constant indecision. This reaching of a decision is one of the facts that is often thought of as an act of will. In reality, the decision is reached because, in one way or another, one motive gets favorable attention and influence. This may come about through reasoning, impulse, social pressure, or arbitrary acceptance of the motive nearest in attention.

Embarking resolutely on a course of action requires a combination of stimuli, and no one of these can rightfully be isolated and called "the will." Yet all working together produce the result usually attributed to a "will." The following conditions seem essential for securing action in oneself or in others:

1. Have a definite purpose or goal.
2. Be sure that a purpose is really desired and is wholeheartedly and enthusiastically adopted so that the activity develops its own inherent interest.
3. Have the purpose reasonably attainable.
4. Have mileposts by which progress can be measured, and, if possible, get someone to compete in the effort.
5. Accept responsibility, as helping to get the full fruits of action.
6. Enlist as many subsidiary motives as possible.

If these six commandments with all the implications they contain could be pasted in the hat of every executive, he would not have to worry about having a weak will. He would find that if, when undertaking any venture large or small, he laid it out in these steps and provided the necessary surrounding conditions, he would, almost without knowing it, be on the highroad to successful accomplishment.

Another aspect of the problem of deciding requires mention because it reflects a situation which is experienced by almost everyone. It is the experience of knowing what one "should" do and doing something else. One sees the better and follows the worse. "When I would do good," as it has been said, "evil is present with me." It is not here necessary to consider what may be meant in a given case by better or worse, good or evil. The fact is that motives occasionally get the rein against one's better judgment. How, practically, motives so adjudged are to be overridden by others which have the approval of one's judgment is a big problem. Analysis of cases reveals the fact that what usually happens when the "better" motive wins out is that other motives are brought to its aid, are rallied around it, so to speak. One does what one thinks one should, for example, because of fear of ridicule or criticism; because of not wanting to have the regrets and the loss of self-respect which might ensue if one took the opposite course; because of the picture one has of an ideal of one's self; because of loyalty to a person whom one does not want to hurt; or to a group whose favor one seeks; or because the welfare of another is involved. If one can get into the forefront of consideration one or another of these supporting factors, if the attention-getting and attention-holding power of these factors can be given force, then the hold of the worse motive is loosened. What is required is not an exercise of will or a determination not to succumb. Again and again these fail.

What are required are *the positive, interest-arousing claims of those stimuli which will take attention away and center it elsewhere.* Get one's self into a total situation in relation to all the surroundings where there is reasonable expectation that "better" factors will claim attention and divert activity. That is the real counsel of wisdom. The force of "oughts" is notoriously precarious and weak. *The influence of the right kind of surroundings to project and sustain different and more productive motives plus the power of a picture in the imagination of the kind of person one wants to be—* these are the things to rely on. The prescription for the realizing of all sorts of aspirations in the face of motives that might deflect them is not emotional fervor about one's aspirations nearly so much as it is *impassioned thought as to how to get and keep oneself in an environmental setting where the pressure of all circumstances helps to contribute to forwarding the aspirations.* One is helped, it has been wisely observed, "when the hard labor of observation, memory, and foresight weds the vision of imagination to the organized efficiencies of habit." The biblical injunction to be not overcome with evil, but to *overcome evil with good*, means just this and is the soundest kind of psychology.

A final qualifying consideration should be noted. Decisions, choices, and entrances into new lines of endeavor influence not only the immediate results of the specific event. Each decision makes repetition of that particular kind of event more likely and probable. Each new line of conduct taken predisposes one to follow a similar line the next time a choice arises. Every act of choice is a building into the self of a tendency, however slight, to go that way again. Always, in a literal sense, the self is either being built up and strengthened along lines it wants to follow or it is being weakened and transformed into some other kind of self. What kind of person one wants to become, what kind of world one wants to see in the making—these are vitally and irrevocably affected by each selection from alternate choices. This is not a preachment nor a platitude. It is a description of a relentless fact about the nature of mental change and growth. And we disregard it at our peril.

Rejected Motives.—The picture that is now presented of the effective following through of one line of motives, as the real meaning of the so-called "process of willing," implies that something becomes of the motives which are not followed but are rejected. An understanding of the place of rejected motives is important in getting a total view of all the influences in behavior. For modern psychology has shown that unless they are handled intelligently they may bring trouble in their wake.

Woodworth points out that several alternatives are possible. The rejected motives may lapse; be deferred; be disguised; be substituted for or sublimated; or they may give rise to the appearance of "defense mechanism." If they are unimportant to the individual, the rejected desires are soon forgotten. If more important, they may remain dormant and await an appropriate occasion for satisfaction.

Sometimes, the motive is disguised or set forth to one's self in a different form by rationalization, and then followed. A manager may, for example, want to discharge an old employee (in the absence of a pension system to care for such workers), but he hates to turn onto the street a man who has been employed so many years; and he puts off the disagreeable hour. Finally, he bethinks himself that the slackened working pace and lessened output of the man are a bad example to the younger workers; he thinks of the man as a demoralizing influence, a handicap to efficiency; and in such a frame of mind he gets up his courage to tell the man that he must leave. "Sublimation" is the name for the process of getting energy that seemingly desires to vent itself in one channel directed into another. Further discussion of it and of the so-called defense mechanisms is deferred to the next chapter.

The Need for Choice.—The fact remains that a vast range of activities is possible and no one can undertake more than a fraction of the things he sees that he wants to do. Physical incapacity. mental incapacity, limitations of environment, conflicts between one wish and another, the opposition of others, mere lack of time—all compel a selection out of possible lines of behavior, "Renunciation is the order of the day." And it is part of one's knowledge of reality to realize this and undertake the job of pulling coherence and a sense of unified direction out of the confusion. This means selection, coordination, and a sensible handling of the motives to be subordinated.

One fact to keep in mind is that, in practice, one is not concerned merely with separate and isolated impulses and motives and their expression. *"It is the individual that must be satisfied, rather than any specific one of his tendencies"* (Woodworth). The task is one of coordinating energies and motives, of bringing a temporary harmony and sense of self-fulfillment out of the clash of desires. Indeed, this underlying and constant effort to make activity yield a sense of self-realization is one of the experiences that people often think of as manifestations of "will." In reality, the tendency to self-assertiveness is so dominant that it is usually to be counted on to help the individual to integrate motives in such a way that a sense of accomplishment results.

The conclusion is, therefore, that in whichever sense one thinks of the will and the process of willing, one is really thinking of a rather elaborate chain of internal events which can be separated into several parts, each of which is a somewhat controllable unit. People with effective wills are really those with strong desires and clear purposes and a shrewd sense of the conditions required to realize them including the selection or creation of the right supporting environment. "The world turns aside to let pass the man who knows whither he is going" is a fair commentary on the conditions implicit in a healthy "will."

The Expansion of the Self.—The phrase "the expansion of the self" is used to characterize the process which everyone experiences of seeing the range of his reactions widen and gain in meaning and of seeing the estimation of the things he values extend over a broader area. One writer has given the picture of four "levels" of conduct. He calls them

1. The instinctive modified by pleasure-pain experiences in instinctive activities.

2. The instinctive modified by rewards and punishments.

3. The level where conduct is controlled by anticipations of praise or blame.

4. The level where conduct is regulated by an ideal of conduct which is deemed "right."[1]

Of course, this is a highly artificial and arbitrary classification, and no such clear line of demarcation is usually observable in actual events. It is too simple and too static. But it does call attention to the fact that different kinds of influence and motives do operate in the individual life. And growth for the individual means progressively giving effect to motives which seem to yield conduct which is more satisfying because seen in its wider relations and social influences, because more permanent in its effects, because in line with satisfying the major purposes one holds in view. The end of activity, it should be realized, is not merely more activity but more thoroughly satisfying activity. "Not perfection as a final good, but the never-ending process of perfecting, maturing, refining is the aim in living."[2] And recognition of the significance in all educational work of getting the individual to understand and respond on a wider and wider front of interests and to interests of a finer quality is basic to an understanding of the nature of growth and of the expansion of the self.

For expansion is not an unnatural or forced process. It is, to be sure, a somewhat conscious process, because it depends upon the uses to which experience is put. It depends on what encour-

agement is offered to the individual, which is calculated to
stimulate and build up a wise expression of native tendencies.
Compounded of those original desires his expansion most certainly is. And viewed basically there comes eventually, if
intelligence is used, to be no real conflict between this self-
expansion and the most effective use of one's powers "for others."

A highly artificial opposition of "selfish" and "service"
motives has been built up in the mind of many by religious and
moral instruction; and that there are facts in human nature and
experience to which such a contrast gives substance it would be
idle to deny. But everything which modern psychology thus
far shows indicates that *when people are intelligently, critically,
and sincerely trying to "make the most of themselves," they are at
the same time being* ipso facto *the most useful and serviceable
citizens.* This is not identical with saying that self-interest and
social interest coincide at all times. The point is, rather, that
the effort of *self-fulfillment when guided by reason and affection
yields fruits which almost inevitably are worthy and desirable,
which to a large degree reconcile and harmonize the impulses of
self-expression and the claims of social utility.* How important
a part both *critical intelligence* and *emotional warmth* play in
this process cannot be overstated.

One finds, of course, the utmost divergence in individual estimates of what self-realization is. Yet there is good reason to
think that psychology can help to answer questions as to what
qualities, characteristics, and directions are qualitatively to be
preferred, as well as why and how these can be encouraged.
Adequate consideration of this problem would involve examining
experimentally and historically the esthetic, social, and religious
sensibilities and experiences of people. If it is pointed out that
at some time and somewhere practically every conceivable
esthetic, moral, and religious standard and practice have found
social favor, that only shows at what an early stage the world
is at in its process of behavior evaluations.

The contention here merely is that in a given set of cultural
and social circumstances it should be possible in time to evaluate
conduct from a psychological point of view. And the necessity

for this kind of judging process and standard of judgment is realized the more if the notion of an expanding self is admitted and seen in its significance.   How necessary such a standard is, is recognized if one remembers that native impulses as such offer no such standard of value, that social approval does not constitute a standard, and that self-approval can be a valid criterion only if the self has been wisely and generously educated.

Two other factors qualifying behavior and growth should be defined at this point.   For they both have to do with the underlying effectiveness of the individual personality as a whole. These are temperament and mood.

Temperament is the name for that dominant characteristic in the tone of the individual's reactions to life, which is seemingly determined by his peculiar native chemistry, by his special combination of muscular, digestive, nervous, and glandular interactions.   A person who has a phlegmatic temperament is chronically sluggish, undemonstrative, and slow in all his responses.   He cannot help it; it is the tone his activity takes because of the conditioning effect of his peculiar combination of secretions.   A person who is sanguine is chronically so because, in some undiscovered way, his secretions give him a tone of buoyancy, power, and hopefulness.

This whole subject is as yet hardly explored; it is possible to do little more than make explicit the fact that people do have great differences in the underlying character of their organic responses to all situations.   Whether with further knowledge about glands and their control there will come knowledge of ways of modifying temperament, there is as yet no means of knowing.   At present, all that can be done is to deal with people in the light of the facts as to the temperamental bias they display.   Even a precise classification as to what kinds of temperament there may be is not now obtainable.   Many people do seem, however, to show a strong tendency toward one or another temperamental type. And the practical thing to do is to bear in mind the kind of temperament one is dealing with at any given moment.

Mood.—Mood is the word applied to a temporary quality which responses take, due to physical and mental conditions which are more transitory in their influence than is temperament. One is in a cheerful mood, a gloomy mood, a hopeful mood, a sulky mood, etc., when all the effective conditions contribute at the time to a total outlook which is of that particular kind. People differ in the duration and in the intensity of their moods and in the extent to which they are affected by any modifying influences.

Here, again, the only prescription can be to "know your man." It is futile to try to deal with certain people in certain of their moods and seemingly equally futile, in many cases, to try to help people get over their moods. One thing that can be done is to work with a person when he is known to be in a favorable mood and, if possible, only then. Many executives, for example, are notorious among their subordinates as being "in a bad mood" during the early part of each morning. Where this is the case, subordinates should studiously avoid taking up any important matter until the mood is known to be more favorable. The psychology and physiology of moods is, at present, so little understood that hardly more than this can be stated helpfully.

Personality.—The word "personality" is used in a number of senses. Usually, it indicates either a *total* of personal attitudes or a *conscious organization* of those attitudes in a fairly definite direction. It is in the latter sense that the word will here be used. Personality is the name for *that total working together of forces in an individual for the achievement of his unique objectives.* It is thus always in the making, always becoming. People are necessarily concerned throughout life to pull themselves together in an effective integration of activities. The strength and significance of personalities is seemingly disclosed by the success they achieve in building up on one main line of trend and accomplishment.

The implications of this notion of personality deserve mention. First, individuals achieve personality as the result of the constant reciprocal interplay of outer environmental and inner impulsive and habit forces. Second, this achievement requires that individuals have purposes and that those purposes shall change and grow with experience—as they inevitably do but, also, can be made to do more effectively. Third, personality is achieved and it ripens only under conditions of conflict.

The practical implications about the first two of these truths are developed in other chapters in this book. It is sufficient here to state in this connection the principle that educational efforts of every sort must capitalize upon the truth *that growth is always a matter of working from two ends at once, from the end of the environment and from the end of the individual's desires and purposes.* The individual in a corporation, for example, wants joy in work and security of livelihood, both of which are legitimate desires. But they remain only desires and perhaps baulked desires, unless someone provides the objective arrangements in the way of training, transfer, promotion, regularized work, unemployment compensation, etc., which tend to create conditions under which these desires will be realized. In other words, the attainment of joy in work and a sense of security at work are the result of creating a variety of working methods at and surrounding the job, far more than they are a matter of the mere desire of either employer or employee. A real guide for the executive is the principle that *if he wants to get people into new actions or new attitudes, he must work as much, if not more, on the surrounding conditions which have made their present responses what they are* as he does on the desires themselves or on the specific purposes now held in view.

Conflicts of desire and aim are a constant factor in the life and growth of personality. The struggle to bring some coherent organization of activity out of contrary desires may result, when not successful, in a number of kinds of reactions known as "defense mechanisms" (see p. 112). If these so-called "mechanisms" work in a manner too pronounced, uncorrected by contact with reality, real and serious disorders of the personality result. One of the responsibilities of the modern executive should be to recognize when he sees them the evidences in behavior of such disorders. And the earlier the stage at which they can be identified the more likely it is that something can be done to correct them. If, on the other hand, the conflicts perennially encountered are faced and resolved in line with the major purposes of the individual, the development of personality becomes a fact.

It is in this sense of a conscious and progressively effective process of using experience to contribute to personal power that the creation of personality becomes a real life objective. It is in this sense that the aim of living is the growth of personality. And a discriminating and realistic sense of the elements to be conserved, of the characteristics that do, in fact, make personality qualitatively important, is one of the great possessions of life. It is a sense which, when possessed, makes living a fine art.

The achieving of personality can thus be made an objective of large importance—one which can supply a basis for judging every kind of hour-by-hour activity. The executive responsible for the labors of hundreds of persons finds real meaning in his directive labors only as this broader attitude and aim are grasped. Employers and managers are not merely responsible for materials, machines, and dollars. They are, in the last analysis, jointly responsible with the individuals associated with them in work, for the personalities of those individuals. If employers and managers have purposes which do not envisage the growth of personality in workers as a part of those purposes, just so long will they fail to be the best possible executives. For the performance of labor dissociated in aim and effort from the development of personality is not only a hollow activity when long continued; it tends to become a degrading experience. Life cannot be permanently divided into those activities which contribute to growth and those which through stupidity or cupidity are not so organized that they do.

Fundamentally, life, to have meaning, has to be lived so that all its major occupations and activities contribute vitally and consciously to growth, to self-expression, and to accomplishment.

Knowledge of psychology supplies positive evidence that in the working life where so many waking hours are spent, the major desires of life must be served. Responsibility for making this a fact in modern business life rests, in part, upon those who direct it. The kind of creative thought which will recognize and establish conditions which make possible the fulfilling of this purpose is a mark of the newer executive leadership. Throughout the balance of this book, both general policies and specific methods are suggested which may, perhaps, be of concrete value in this task of making industrial life minister to the growth of personality while at the same time securing the immediate ends of productivity.

Psychology has some definitely helpful things to say as to how industry can be conducted so that personality is enhanced rather than denied, so that the work of life can be, as it should be and often was before the Industrial Revolution, one of the most important and valued channels of self-fulfillment.

Self-knowledge and Self-improvement.—Techniques for self-analysis which will help the individual to hold the mirror up to nature are still in the highly experimental and tentative stage. Numerous approaches to the problem are possible. One of these which is simple, popular, and practical is offered in the breakdown of traits suggested by Dr. W. W. Charters. It is quoted here not so much because of any psychological profundity as because of its common-sense check-up of qualities which business values and gives value for. As Dr. Charters says, the following traits are those without which we cannot compete with other men, "though you have ability, brains, skill, and information:"[3]

1. *Ambition.*—Have you the will to improve yourself? This means *real* will; not merely a vague, intermittent desire.

2. *Industriousness.*—Have you the ability to drive yourself *steadily?*

3. *Persistence and Patience.*—Look back over the various plans you have made during the past year; enumerate all you can remember and see how many of them you have actually put through.

4. *Dependability.*—Can you be relied upon to carry out plans assigned to you by other people?

5. *Forcefulness.*—Do you give people the impression that you are capable and self-controlled? Are you self-reliant?

6. *Effectiveness of Speech.*—Can you express your ideas clearly and *convincingly?* Do you speak with a "piping" voice, or have you studied how to place your voice so that you are not unpleasant to listen to?

7. *Self-confidence.*—What are the things you have done of which you have a right to be proud?

8. *Friendliness.*—Are you too critical in your judgment of other people?

9. *Adaptability.*—Do you find it easy to listen to what other people are saying? If you are hardly able to wait for a chance to air *your* opinion, you need to cultivate this trait.

10. *Tact.*—Can you work in harmony with other people? How often do you find yourself praising people for what they have done?

11. *Cheerfulness.*—Do you depress other people or are you a cheerful companion?

12. *Good Judgment.*—Examine yourself particularly as regards *initiative* and *resourcefulness.* How many suggestions have you made to your employer in the past six months? How many of these has he approved?

13. *Sensitiveness to Criticism.*—How do you take the criticisms, direct or implied, from employer, friends, and associates? If you brood over them, if the sting of criticism keeps you from seeing that it may be *useful* nevertheless, you may be *oversensitive.*

14. *Ability to Size Up People.*—Do you see only good in some people and only weaknesses in others? Are you observing enough to be able, after talking with a new acquaintance for 15 minutes, to specify how he impressed you as regards neatness of dress, effectiveness of speech, friendliness, tact, cheerfulness?

15. *Memory.*—Are you good at remembering names, faces, and personal incidents about the people you meet?

16. *Neatness.*—Are you painstaking in regard to your personal appearance?

17. *Health Habits.*—Ask yourself whether your *habits* are those that make for or against good health, and how they tell on your working ability and mental attitude day by day.

18. *Discrimination.*—Can you discriminate between more important and less important matters? Do you clog your daily routine with unnecessary work on comparatively unimportant details?

19. *Economy.*—Do you save time and effort by doing things in the right and easiest way without waste motion?

20. *Capacity to Delegate Work.*—This quality is especially important for those who are, or hope to become, executives. Executives often fall short in this trait because they lack *persistence* of a certain kind or because of *vanity* or *selfishness.*

CHAPTER IX

WHAT ARE THE DEFENSE MECHANISMS?

The obvious fact that no one can do all that he wants to, follow all his desires, and satisfy every prompting gives rise to individual difficulties of adjustment to life which extend all the way from momentary irritation to deep, profound, and disrupting rifts in the personality. It has been the valuable contribution of a group of psychiatrists that they have identified a number of typical abnormal ways in which individuals react to conflict situations that do not promptly come to a solution.

The phrase "defense mechanisms" has been used as a class name for these several unusual ways of adjusting oneself to conflicts in which desires cannot readily be fulfilled. The name means that the reactions have in common the characteristic of trying unsuccessfully to produce an adjustment which defends and restores to working effectiveness the whole personality. The word "mechanism" should not be understood too literally. It is, rather, a general pattern, tendency, or process of defense which is implied.

The sources of conflict on which certain psychiatrists have laid particular stress are (1) those in which an individual's *sex* desires are baulked, (2) where one has a feeling of *inferiority* which he is trying to overcome, and (3) where one has some profound *fear* or *anxiety* from which he is trying to escape.

In meeting all these conflicts, the idea of substitute release or *compensation* plays a basic rôle. If some fundamental desire is not able to get expression, if some deep feeling of inferiority prevails, or some great fear, the tendency is for the individual to compensate for this by finding some behavior outlet that will release the energy and seemingly restore the individual to serenity. Whether or not the compensatory behavior really does

112

provide a satisfactory channel depends upon which of two experiences takes place—upon the degree to which *sublimation* rather than *suppression* occurs. The word "repression" is used here as synonymous with "suppression."

Sublimation is the process of discovering for a desire a substitute outlet which proves in behavior to have really equivalent value from the point of view of expressing and unifying personality. Suppression or repression is the obstructing of a desire in a fashion so conclusive that it cannot get expression at once in a natural way, thus leading to building up more or less unconsciously a nucleus of ideas and activities which seem to the individual to be providing compensatory relief and a channel for the desire's expression. This nucleus of compensatory ideas and activities is spoken of as a "complex." Defined in another way, a complex is a fixation of attention, stimulated by some particular desire or fear, that is directed toward a way of release which is not normal and which can never restore the individual to a truly satisfactory adjustment between desire and reality.

There are many sorts of complexes which have frequently been grouped into those having to do with sex, with the enhancement of the "ego" or self, with fear, feelings of inferiority, and hatred. And there are, also, more particular complexes dependent on accidental circumstances.

A worker may, for example, as the result of an accident on a certain machine, develop an aversion for that machine which becomes practically a complex. Or a worker may, as a result of a quarrel with a foreman, develop a complex against the foreman. What is meant in such cases is that the individual adopts a way of behavior in relation to the source of his difficulty which is too intense, too inflexible, too unrealistic, too unadjustable to be an effective practical way of meeting it. The object on which the emotion is fastened becomes automatically the stimulus which arouses a whole pattern of unadjusted and ill-advised behavior.

Undoubtedly, a great deal of behavior can now be explained and understood from this point of view of compensation as it never was before. An interesting and illuminating study was made a few years ago of the strikes and riots among an itinerant group of farm laborers in the west in which the author pointed out how workers were trying to compensate for their abnormal condition of being "womanless, jobless, and voteless." There can be little doubt that both as respects individuals in specific cases of aggressive conduct and as respects groups acting together in riots and violence, they are often trying quite naturally to compensate as best they can for fears, feelings of inferiority, and thwarted wishes, relief from which they see no other way of securing.[1]

The idea of compensation helps, also, to explain an interesting variety of inferiority feelings. The newly appointed foreman who tries to impress everyone with his power, the short-statured executive who blusters and bullies, the self-made manager who has no use for college graduates—these are all familiar figures. And in all such cases, what is happening is that people are trying to cover up a sense of inferiority by the kind of behavior which they think will impress the world.

The process of *rationalization* has already been mentioned. One wonders why and how the victim of a complex can really believe that he has made a satisfactory adjustment to reality. The answer lies in the tendency to seek reasons only on the side that one wants to believe. Rationalizing is seeking plausible reasons to justify and support what one has done, is doing, or wants to do. Everyone indulges in it to some degree. But it becomes a serious mental abnormality where it helps some deep-seated maladjustment of personality to continue by allowing the self to continue to believe that all is well.

In an interesting study conducted by J. D. Houser to discover the attitude of employers in relation to their personnel problems, much is made of the fact that rationalization frequently enters into managers' thinking to the detriment of their actual personnel activities. He states the two following instances of rationalization as being somewhat typical of the kind of "water-tight" thinking that was characteristic of many executives with whom he talked:

The extremes of rationalization are well presented in two illustrations based on several interviews. One concerned the owner and executive of a moderate-sized manufacturing organization. Aided by very favorable general conditions, he was making his enterprise a profitable one, although his wage scales were as low as he could keep them and yet maintain a supply of labor. He was active in a religious body. At a meeting largely attended by members of this church, he heard a certain plan of "industrial democracy" discussed. Feeling the intense appeal of the plan to the idealism of these people, he sought further details regarding its operation. He even authorized preliminary steps toward introducing it into his own industry. When he learned, however, that he would be obliged to reveal something of the financial details of his enterprise, he quickly withdrew this authorization, refusing to consider any further application of the plan.

Another illustration of obvious rationalization was found in an executive's explanation for his feeling that any form of profit-sharing was dangerous. Under such a plan, he thought, employees could legally examine the books of the company at any time. They might find, for example, that 80 per cent was deducted each year for depreciation of machinery and equipment. Being ignorant of such matters, they might think this too large a percentage (since it reduced their share in the profits) and might insist that the figure be cut to 2 per cent. The man of straw which this executive carefully constructed out of his objection to profit-sharing was hardly convincing.[2]

The process of *transference* is an interesting defense mechanism of which everyone has seen instances. A woman employee had a most unreasonable and unexplainable sense of grievance against her foreman. It was of such long standing and so bitter that the personnel manager finally decided to take the matter up with her and see what was wrong. After a good deal of questioning, he finally discovered that a former foreman who had resigned years before had promised her a promotion and then had left before he made good his promise. Of course, the new foreman knew nothing of the promise. Yet she transferred to him all her sense of disappointment and ill feeling which she had previously centered on the other foreman. This instance well illustrates how insidious and unfortunate can be the influence in behavior of such a "mechanism," which allows a person to get so far removed from the realities of her own relationships.[3]

Projection is the name given to the experience of imputing and attributing to someone else feelings and ideas which one really

entertains himself.   One writer tells of a worker who kept going
to his superintendent to complain of his foreman.   He insisted
that the foreman was not loyal to the company or conscientious
in the performance of his duties.   Eventually, the truth came
out that this worker had very much wanted to secure the foreman's job when it was given to the other man.   And when he
did not get it, he thereupon got discouraged, put little heart
into his work, lost interest in the company, and compensated
for his frustrated desire by projecting his state of mind upon
the foreman and then complaining to the superintendent that
the foreman had become disloyal.[4]

Obsessions are ideas and impulsions to act which stubbornly
recur and secure expression in spite of every effort to banish
them.   Sometimes they are caused by an obstruction to desire
which experience has brought.   But in other cases, they are the
result of lack of balance and stability in the individual, which
gives rise to undue centering of attention on one set of urges.
In a mild form, obsessions are very general; but in such cases,
they are not sufficiently intense or prolonged to have any serious
consequences in conduct.

Whiting Williams tells of a certain union official whose zeal
in behalf of the union's cause was peculiarly intense and zealous
and whose bitterness toward employers was so intense that his
attitude was really obsessive.   Prolonged inquiry as to the
reason for the bitterness of his attitude brought out the fact
that 20 years before, when this official had been a coal miner
employed in a company-owned town, there had been a serious
strike.   The company dispossessed the strikers from the company
houses and it happened that this worker's wife was about to give
birth to a child at the very time the attempt at dispossession
was being made.   The emotional disturbance naturally caused
by such an unfortunate combination of events was great.   A
bitterness was aroused which the years had never modified.
The kind of shock and feeling of hatred which an experience of
this sort precipitated became definitely obsessive in character.

Delusions are beliefs without foundation in fact, usually
regarding one's status or welfare.   There are delusions of

persecution and delusions of grandeur.[5]   In their severer forms, they are symptoms of insanity.   But the milder manifestations, especially delusions of persecution, are to be met with among people who otherwise seem quite normal.   Their identification is important because individuals who are telling their own delusions to their working associates who do not realize their falsity, may become a seriously disrupting influence.   Workers, for example, develop persecution manias regarding foremen who are supposed to "have it in for" them.   Foremen sometimes develop such delusions about their superiors.   Also, every executive has had experience with the worker who "talks big." This exists in every degree of severity; but where workers tell of wages much higher than those they really get or tell untruly of promises of advancement made to them, a difficult situation may be created.

Delusive and obsessive ideas and emotions may become so disruptive in group activity that their recognition at an early stage is highly important.   This makes it all the more valuable for executives to become familiar with the facts about the manner in which such abnormal behavior displays itself.   For in their first-hand dealings with their men, executives and especially foremen are in a position to discover the evidences of delusions and obsessions.

People may also develop some outstanding characteristic manner of response which marks them as belonging to a type. While the idea of human types as rigid groupings of individuals possessing special traits is not valid, there is a certain practical justification for indicating some frequently seen types of people. Some of the familiar types which are off the normal are:

a. Unambitious and unresponsive persons.   Often, they are somewhat sullen and sulky as well.

b. Too ambitious persons who find every position they secure not worthy of their powers.

c. Persons with the *wanderlust*.

d. The excessively reckless.

e. The "man-crazy" or "girl-crazy."

f. The excessively timid or overfearful.

Any of these characteristics may grow to abnormal and pathological proportions and require corrective efforts similar to those necessary for the removal of complexes and obsessions.

Other Ways of Release.—A number of other ways of escaping the difficulties of conflict deserve mention as helping us better to understand human behavior. Unquestionably, the use of alcohol or drugs is at bottom prompted by the urge to escape from the strain of conflicting desires and aims into a position of achieved desire, power, and freedom from anxieties. Tam, in Robert Burns' poem, "o'er all the ills of life victorious," was in the mood that alcohol, while its effect lasts, is calculated to induce and which he had not been able to get out of his work-a-day life.

The chronic daydreamer secures his release by building up an inner world of fancy where he makes every dream come true.

The cynic is likewise avoiding the responsibility of conflict and choice by asserting that nothing is worthwhile.

The Process of Reeducation.—Various techniques of analysis and self-restoration are employed by those who work professionally to cure cases of mental difficulty. These are of less immediate interest to the layman than is a knowledge of the general principles of attack underlying all such efforts at rehabilitation.[6]

It is first important to recognize that the point at which an individual's complex requires corrective effort is not always easy to determine. No one is mentally in perfect balance at all times. It would be a dull world if we were! But from the industrial point of view, concern needs to be exercised about the behavior of one's self or associates, if one's working efficiency or theirs is impaired from such causes as those described above, or if it is clear that one is unhappy and ill adjusted mentally in ways that distract him and, therefore, often disturb others about him.

Underlying all the methods of reeducation—by which is meant efforts to get the individual back into a normal relation to his total setting—is the idea of a *fresh and honest confrontation of reality*. The attempt must be to get the sufferer to realize honestly the dilemma he is in, to see that he is trying to reconcile two sets of ideas and actions which are incompatible, to admit that a choice must be made which will definitely put one set in the ascendancy.

Early in this process, the effort is made to have the individual help first to lay bare and then to understand the causes from which the complex or fear or inferiority feeling originally started. He must be shown that the original complex arose because of a failure to realize some desire or inability in some other way to cope with reality. He must then come to see that the desire itself when properly understood can probably secure some adequate satisfaction and outlet in ways that do not disrupt the personality or introduce a standing discrepancy between what he wants to do and what he can do.

This process of reeducation cannot usually be quickly accomplished. It may take a considerable time to discover the origins of the complex. It is sure to take time for the individual to adjust his mind to the idea that some reconciliation can be effected between what he has come to desire and what he can reasonably expect to get in actual fulfillment. And, finally, it takes time for the individual to try out a new way of action and see if, in daily life, it brings satisfaction to him and proves as well to be socially admissable.

The increasing recognition of the importance of mental factors in personal adjustments to life has naturally given rise to the opening of a great variety of consulting offices. Services are offered both to individuals and to companies on everything from "vocational counsel" to elaborate psychoanalysis. Whether one seeks personal or corporate assistance, it is, therefore, highly important that one deal only with thoroughly accredited psychologists, doctors, or psychiatrists. The chance for imposition in this field is so peculiarly great that too much care cannot be taken to get trained and experienced practitioners. Departments of psychology in universities, mental hygiene associations, the Psychological Corporation in New York City, are among the sources to which one can turn to learn of the professional standing of consultants in the different schools of mental hygiene.

Conclusion.—Even the most general knowledge of some of the kinds of abnormal mental reactions and behavior which may be encountered in people will forewarn the executive that the treatment usually accorded to normal people will produce no results with the abnormal. Special consideration and handling are necessary. But the corrective process is a highly specialized and technical one, which should be conducted only by those specially trained for such reeducational work. Nevertheless, even such a brief statement as to the nature and general outline of the reeducational process as that given above should be useful. The basic ideas have, in fact, a very wide application. The whole conception of "confronting reality," in all that this phrase implies, is an exceedingly valuable one. Realization of the influence of unfortunate and forgotten experiences is most helpful. The importance of the time factor in helping readjustments must also be realized. The necessity for reconciling desires with the claims of a complex social environment must be appreciated.

Occasionally, one encounters an executive who has a real flair for personal work among his associates. They trust him; they seek his advice; they lean on him for support; they make him a father confessor. It is, of course, a pity that there are not more of these sympathetic, helpful individuals in the world. But it is undoubtedly true that such persons can carry on their efforts at personal service with greatly increased effectiveness if they have consciously in mind the principles of reeducation which modern psychotherapy has discovered. And every individual who will take thought of these principles in his own personal mental career can also better understand and control his own desires.

CHAPTER X

THE IMPORTANCE OF MANAGEMENT'S PURPOSES

Conscious purposes have a rôle in human behavior in industry which it is of great importance to understand. Since for some this assertion may require explanation, the point that they *do*, in fact, influence conduct, will first be discussed. Practically, too, one wants to know how purposes may be changed. Purposes also come into conflict in ways which it is essential to realize; and with this understanding it is then possible to consider how they can, in a measure, at least, be brought into working harmony and, as the current phrase is, "be integrated." It is these phases of the subject which the next two chapters will treat.

Definition.—A purpose in the sense here used is an aim or objective held definitely in view for reasonably immediate and specific accomplishment. It is the name for an effort directed to the achievement of something unrealized. "A genuine purpose sets up the goal as an end to be striven for."[1] A purpose is distinguished from a desire which has already been defined as a fundamental and usually inborn impulsion in a given direction. Desires are either native or have become deep seated through the influence of habit. Purposes are always acquired; they are the specific ways in which individuals or groups seek by specific activities to realize their desires. Unquestionably, there are motives which influence behavior without explicit awareness on the part of the individual. But such motives are not purposes as here defined, although the importance of unconscious motives should not be minimized. That conscious motives do influence conduct has to be established only because of the contention of some that conduct is predetermined in a way which leaves conscious direction no part to play.

In the illustration, used in a previous chapter, of an employer confronted with the problem of making some systematic provision for aged employees, one sees a combination of motives giving rise to a definite purpose to do something about this problem. And in so far as the employer is moved to look into other pension plans and think through some arrangements for application to his own conditions, his purpose does, in fact, exert a real influence on practical activities.

Purposes, like other conditioning factors in behavior, result from the driving force of desires, confronted by the stimulus of specific objects and the problems of any given situation. Their existence is to be explained only in relation to both factors—desires and surrounding conditions. In a word, they arise out of efforts to realize desires, and they always have a relation to the entire situation at a given time and are intelligible only in connection with it. Understanding of people's purposes always requires an understanding of the environment, which must be thought of broadly enough to include the purposes of other individuals or groups related to the individual or group affected, no less than to the related physical environment.

To ask how an individual's purposes come to be what they are is, in effect, to inquire what his total experience has been, that is, what his education, habits, cultural setting, and social environment have been. All of these contribute to forming purposes, as does, also, the glamor of a new idea caught from some strong personality or from reading or from imagining some new combinations of characteristics or from some "ideal." But in every case, whether one is considering why his own purposes are what they are or considering how those of others can be influenced in definite directions to become something else, the *necessity of participating in experience—both mental and motor—as the prime agent in acquiring purposes has to be realized.*

The Purposes of Groups.—All that can be said about the influence of purposes in an individual's life is true of the effect of purposes upon the conduct of conscious groups. A group purpose is the desire of its members to secure for themselves by acting together those conditions which will enable them to satisfy certain individual purposes which they consciously share. Trade associations or labor unions, for example, have group purposes in the sense that each is forwarding policies and measures that will assure for its members certain things which each member desires.

The quality of a group's purposes, however, is likely to be different in a number of ways from those of individuals. A group tends to keep its purposes simpler and more "single track" than an individual and tends to hold them more intensely. Group purposes usually change more slowly than those of individuals, because of the necessity of changing the minds of a considerable number of persons. These differences, however seemingly slight, entail big differences when it comes to devising and using methods to influence purposes. Obviously, each group necessarily strives for ends which grow out of its own setting and experience. And the statement of purposes will naturally be couched in terms of a group's special interests and functional responsibilities and in relation to the point of attainment from which they start. Proper understanding of this truth is highly important to an appreciation of the work of any groups, such as a trade association, a craft union, a foreman's council, or an employees' shop committee. What each wants is inevitably related not to some ideal demands but *to the particular achievement, status, and outlook of its members at that particular time.*

The Process of Changing Purposes.—It is vital to an understanding of all executive work to know just how it is that a change of purposes can be brought about, in individuals and in groups. The nature of the problem and the direction of its solution are best seen by giving one or two examples.

The experience of a considerable number of corporations with safety committees of employees supplies a good illustration. A few years ago, many plants undertook to reduce their accidents by appointing a safety committee of their employees as a point of contact through which educational and preventive work could be done on the safety question. The purpose of the managers was to reduce accidents. But in the course of time, they found that they were discussing not only accidents and their contributory causes with employees but also many other common problems. It was natural that the area of discussion should widen. The conference idea was thus gradually extended to include questions of general grievances and shop problems. From this it was a natural step to the creation of an employee-representation plan to which members were elected by departments rather than appointed. By the time that this point was reached, the purposes of the manager had obviously come a long way from the aim of accident prevention. The process of going through the experience and the logical impact of events upon the minds of managers brought out a willingness to adopt and work with an employee-representation plan, which was at the outset an idea wholly foreign to their thinking.

Another example is that of a well-known plant in which the management believed that the inclusion of a certain few key employees in a stock-ownership plan would be beneficial to company morale. This company had, also, a shop committee which eventually urged the extension of the stock-ownership arrangement so that all employees might participate. After careful examination of all the facts, the request was granted. Thus, as the result of several years of going through a certain kind of experience, the purposes of the management as to the advisability of employee stock ownership were considerably changed and broadened.

A further illustration is that of the experience of a manager in a Middle Western factory who found in one of his departments a serious condition of limitation of output. He finally went into the department, gathered the men about him, and said, in effect, that if they would give up the practice of restricting output, the management on its side would guarantee that there would be no rate cutting, no laying off of workers, and that it would do everything possible to improve manufacturing conditions so that high production could be obtained. He asked the group if they would try out this policy for a month and then reconsider the situation with him. They agreed to this, and at the end of the month the experience of everyone with increased earnings had been so satisfactory that there was no desire to return to the former restriction policy. *The worker's experience of higher earnings and security of position had demonstrated to them that what they wanted was better obtained under the new conditions than under the old.*

More effective than any preaching, moralizing, or coaxing, the way of instruction in all these cases, was the method of self-disclosing activity and experience commonly shared. The impact of the total situation brought about a change of purposes which was shown to yield more satisfactory results to all concerned than the purposes previously followed.

The new experience was thus a large factor in helping to create the new purpose. Purposes were changed not by an intellectual plus an emotional appeal merely but also by the process of actually working through the situation and creating a shared experience. As one writer has put it:

> on a basis of what has already been experienced, things are desired; on the basis of what has been desired and experienced, new things become desired; this extension and growth of desire takes place through the influence of similarity and analogy.[2]

There is, to be sure, the added important factor of having someone or some group suggest or supply the idea as to what the new purpose should be. But this creative aspect of the broadening of purposes is itself a result of experience almost as much as it is a result of any reasoned thinking.

In short, purposes do change and evolve. Because people have minds which reflect upon experience and evaluate it, and even more because external conditions modify, redirect, and restrict experience, people's purposes *must change.* There is an innate craving in human beings for economy in the means adopted to realize ends as well as in the choice of the ends to be realized, all of which predisposes to the changing of purposes. The carrying through of purposes changes situations and surroundings, and these, in turn, help to suggest and unfold new purposes. Thus, there comes to be the possibility of the purposes of individuals and groups being molded and integrated. And thus it is that the nature of this process of changing and integration is suggested.

The wise executive may now draw the obvious and highly practical conclusion that people's purposes will be influenced most effectively where the individuals involved are forced by all the circumstances of a situation to readjust themselves to it. And the process of readjustment, if critically gone through, will be the process of changing purposes. All the surrounding conditions must, therefore, be made to support and foster the new purposes and contribute to their realization.

Show people that the realizing of present purposes is either impossible or not likely to yield them what they really want; start them into a series of activities where the new experience will of itself lead them to draw fresh conclusions about what they want and about the ways of getting it; and then foster by suggestion and further experience the obvious inferences which they are likely to draw from their activity as to the new purposes which they will find attractive. This is the line to be taken by anyone anxious to influence the purposes of those about him.

Are All Purposes Equally Attractive?—But a warning should be issued. Purposes can be permanently altered only when people are clearly convinced that their own underlying desires are thereby being truly served. The *kind* of purposes which an executive holds, has a definite bearing on the likelihood of his success in bringing employees to subscribe to them. The general principle here is that those purposes *will find most ready acceptance which can most readily be seen by people to square with their underlying desires.*

In the example given above of the manager who was trying to get the members of one of his departments to drop a policy of limitation of output, his success was clearly due to the fact that he made the abandoning of a former purpose desirable and, hence, inevitable because of the unquestioned attractiveness of the new terms he offered.

The guarantees which a number of companies are making today in order to foster productivity supply further evidence in point. The Chicago men's clothing industry, for example, functions on its labor side through a strong union which is deeply concerned to cooperate with employers in getting large production

at low costs. This purpose by itself is not calculated to appeal
to the workers. In order to make it acceptable to them, it has
been found necessary to secure from the employers guarantees
against rate cutting and of continuous employment or of unemployment compensation. With these provisions assured, the
interest of the workers in getting out more work has been stimulated. It becomes obvious to them that their purposes and
desires are truly served by a policy of greater productivity when
it is thus administered. Nor is it sufficient that there be mere
affirmation by the executive that he believes that, in a given case,
purposes of manager and worker are or can be identical.

It is essential that this sense of identity be assured *by some
concrete plans and arrangements which are permanent evidence
to the worker that his own desires will be fulfilled when they thus
embrace the purposes of the employer.* In Chicago, the men's
clothing workers' union operates as a guarantor to prevent rate
cutting and insists upon an elaborate plan for unemployment
compensation conducted under the joint auspices of the organized
employers and the union. The possibility of getting employees
to adopt purposes of high production is clinched by *tangible
evidences* of ways and means in which their protection is continuously assured and their interests safeguarded and advanced
more effectively than with their former purposes.

The Changing of Executive Purposes.—No less important than
consideration of the way in which workers' purposes change
is a discussion of the way in which purposes of owners and managers grow and change. Indeed, within the executive circle
there frequently exists a problem of reeducation respecting purposes which should usually be attacked *before* other matters of
personnel policy receive intensive consideration.

What forces can contribute to the process of broadening
managerial purposes? Several at once suggest themselves.
First, a manger may run into a real difficulty and be forced to cast
about for some new method of securing his ends. And often,
in the course of following newly discovered methods, he may find
exprience gradually revealing to himself a new and larger purpose.
All sorts of applications of this simple truth are at hand. A man-

ager, for example, decides that unit costs in a department are excessive due to the absence of an incentive method of payment. He decides to change from week work to piece work. The workers in the department object so vigorously that they walk out on strike. Perhaps some executive colleague or friend in another company suggests that if he had taken up the matter with the department in advance and explained that no real reduction in wages was contemplated, but rather the opposite, no strike would have taken place. This leads the manager to question whether he should not have some organized method of conference with his employees, which may, in turn, lead to the consideration of a plan of employee representation. Thus, a purpose of lowering unit costs becomes, when the problem is seriously confronted, a broader purpose of improving conference methods.

Indeed, it is, in general, true that the most vital force that gets an executive into a sufficiently open frame of mind to formulate and work at new purposes is a *serious problem whose solution he has not thus far discovered.*

A second way in which a change of purpose may be brought about is pressure from the stockholders or from executives higher up locally or in the holding company of which the individual plant is a unit.

A third possible way is the pressure of public opinion. This may either be in general or it may be brought about more or less compulsorily because public opinion has been able to secure restrictive legislation which requires the manager to alter his working methods.

Again, purposes are changed more and more today by the influence of what someone has well called the "prestige motive." If an executive finds, for example, that he is playing golf or hobnobbing with associates who take pride in progressive labor policies in their own concerns, his desire for prestige with his associates may lead him to consider measures of a similar sort. Once a sound personnel policy becomes "good form," a powerful lever is at hand for use with backward executives.

Finally, purposes may change because people are bored with their present methods and present motives. And boredom has started them in the direction of an inquiring frame of mind which makes them receptive to suggestions as to new methods. Again and again it has proved true that the actual experience of trying out these new policies has brought with it a drastic change of purpose.

The Fact of Conflict in Purposes.—It is important to realize the nature and extent of the conflicts experienced in the working out of the purposes of the different groups in industry. In general, the strife of these interrelated groups arises out of both economic and psychological divergences. A picture of just how these affect the attitudes and behavior of people should help materially to point a way toward adjustment and integration. For the fact is that, despite these group disparities, the basic desires of the individuals composing the several groups tend to remain similar and constant. The craving for approval, security, creative outlets, domestic well-being, satisfying leisure— these persist much the same in kind, if not in degree, throughout human life in a given time and place. And because this is so, it is possible that, in spite of fundamental intergroup conflicts, there may be created a considerable degree of harmony in the pursuit of specific purposes. If inventive ingenuity is great enough, experience has shown that conflicting groups can achieve a level of cooperative effort which minimizes even if it does not actually remove conflict.

The Groups in Industry.—What, then, are these groups, sometimes in opposition, that typically compose the industrial community?

In popular thinking, the group alignment usually thought of is that of "capital and labor." This is a wholly unrealistic, oversimplified and stereotyped conception. Analysis reveals that there are typically the following functional groups: (1) the investing group; (2) the managerial group; (3) the manual-worker group, sometimes sharply divided into office workers, skilled and unskilled workers; (4) the customer group; and (5) the general public group.

The same individuals often participate at different times in sharing the purposes and loyalties of different groups. But the fact of a defined content for each group's purposes remains, and it is subject to alteration only as the environment or the functions of the group are modified or if, for any other reason, new purposes are evolved.

The purposes which are typically manifest in the behavior of these groups may be safely generalized about, if it is always remembered that there are numerous exceptions. Indeed, it is these exceptions which constitute the hope of the present situation, because they point the way and offer suggestions as to how the purposes of groups have, in specific cases, already been altered and reconciled.

1. Typically, the purpose of the investor is to secure a return on his investment as large as is consistent with the security of his principal. The fact seems to be, however, that this purpose is, in practice, somewhat tempered by the fact that the size of the typical dividend return in industry today is diminishing as the fundamental risks involved diminish. Recently, it has become clear that the return to the investor is becoming relatively standardized except in new and experimental industries.

2. It is usually supposed that the purposes of managers is to assure that a yield as high as possible is earned on the investment while, at the same time, the plant is operated in an efficient manner. Where managers are also holders of stock, their purposes become to that extent identical with those of investors. Yet if their stockholdings are small, they may feel that their interest lies first in a high salary or in an enhanced reputation for efficient management. Indeed, the increasing emphasis upon professional status in managerial work has greatly modified the purely money-maker purpose suggested above. The purposes of managers are thus likely to be far less simple than is usually realized. They are usually moved by several purposes. First, they, like everybody else, work, in the first instance, because they must. Economic activity is today normally characteristic of people in temperate climates because they must anticipate their need for food, shelter, clothing. We are all under the necessity of extracting a living from a reluctant nature. And as the demand for sheer activity, as such, is an outstanding characteristic

of human beings, it is natural that much of this satisfaction in being active carries over into the economic sphere. In a word, people are active in industry not only because they have to be, but also because they get considerable satisfaction out of the activity.

Examination of particular situations reveals a further interesting variety of motives. Profits are, of course, a pragmatic test of the business solvency and commercial utility of an enterprise. Profits are today the accredited device for measuring economic utility; and in the absence of any other universally accepted measure, they have to be reckoned with. But one can find more and more corporations where profits are thought of as one necessary condition of operation rather than the only test of managerial success. This is true in that large segment of industry covered by public-utility corporations, where dividend rates are, in effect, limited by government. And profit motivation is, of course, absent, also, in all the various economic activities which are governmentally owned and operated.

There are, also, plenty of managers who are obsessed and controlled by the desire for mere size in business, anxious to build up a volume of business which shall be greater than any other. There are others in whom the pugnacious disposition to oust competitors and win out in a fight for markets is a controlling consideration. There are still others with whom a desire for a serviceable output and a sense of creative accomplishment in supplying useful goods finds outlet through business. Many managers are proud of their trade mark, anxious to be known as dispensers of a quality product at a reasonable price.

There are an increasing number of cases, too, where managers also take pride, even at the expense of exorbitant profits, in the goodwill of the employees of the organization and take pride in fostering, by the adoption of special measures, a genuine feeling of the employees' essential partnership in the enterprise.

Unquestionably, some or all of these as well as numerous other purposes mingle in bewildering complexity in the motivation of managers.

But the business man has been told so often by the economists that he is "in business to make money" that he has himself tended to take this statement as a complete account of the truth about his purposes.

Yet because of this wide range of possible motives, there exists in any given situation the possibility of effecting a change in the relative emphasis among these purposes.

3. It is as impossible to simplify the numerous motives at work in the industrial activities of working-class people as it proves to be in the case of managers. Nevertheless, the general statement can be made that manual workers desire to secure a share from the income of the enterprise as large as is possibly consistent with a reasonable expenditure of energy and a reasonable satisfaction secured from the carrying on of the working process itself. The power of economic motives is necessarily great because of the narrow margin on which so many manual workers live. On the other hand, plenty of evidence will appear that where subsistence is assured other motives tend to become increasingly operative. Here, again, the fact of a plurality of motives makes it possible to bring about changes in the relative influence which each exerts.

4. Customers desire to secure an adequate supply of needed goods of sufficiently good quality and at prices as low as is consistent with that quality and with ready accessibility to the desired commodities.

5. The general public in its relations to industry functions largely through regulative bodies and government bureaus. But, on the one hand, these agencies tend to want to be left alone to the pursuance of their routine. And, on the other, the voters, except sporadically, show no great anxiety to regulate or interfere at all closely.

The Fact of Group Conflicts.—Brief and summary as is this exposition of group purposes, it points out the current divergences. On its economic side, the conflict grows out of contention among these functional groups over the division of a limited volume of national and corporate income. This comes to focus in such issues as those of price, wages, return on the investment, and the extent to which surpluses shall be reinvested in a business. In other words, it involves purposes regarding which no absolute standards are derivable; and the absence of standards makes it impossible to remove completely and permanently the element of conflict.

On its psychological side, the conflict grows out of the fact that the characteristic environment and the work of each group inevitably breed attitudes in relation to the other groups which are charged with distrust if not with downright antagonism. There is, I submit, a subtle and almost inevitable resentment between, for example, those who work with their hands and those who work with their heads; between those who manage and those who are managed; between those who secure income from investment and those who secure it from direct labor.

This admission of the fact of conflict will be disparaged by many who honestly feel either that fundamentally no conflict exists or that any acknowledgment of its existence inevitably leads to undue emphasis upon it. Both views seem to me to be unrealistic and the result of an inadequate viewing of the facts. Those who wish to deny the existence of divergences of aim do so because of a mistaken conception of their nature and creative significance. Those who feel that the idea is inevitably over-emphasized when discussed at all seem to be reaching their conclusion on a basis of a too close view of those industries and corporations where the conflict idea has admittedly been all too prominent and pervasive, due largely to a repressive policy on management's side. I would certainly agree heartily with those who hold that constant dwelling day by day upon the aspect of divergence of interests among the groups is bad and wasteful. But a proper analysis would point out that, from time to time, those elements in the relationship which involve differences of purpose—such as wages, standards of output, and hours—rightfully imply the necessity of negotiation. Differences have to be reconciled; a working basis has to be agreed upon. To ignore this is to leave unprovided any agency which might be the means of a peaceful and amicable adjustment of differences.

The way of intelligent control is to provide some agency for settling recurrently the controversial questions, while *emphasizing at all times that production can go forward to everyone's best advantage only in a day-by-day atmosphere of harmony, understanding, and cooperation.* Put in another way, the occasional and possibly stormy periods of adjusting the terms of the labor contract point clearly to the need of some kind of representative machinery for arriving at a new working formula. *But once the labor contract has been agreed to (preferably, for a stipulated period of time), every group's best interest is served by fostering a non-conflict attitude.*

One of the most important tasks for the executive is to create instruments and channels of a truly representative character through which this periodic reconciling of interests and merging of purposes may take place and to help deliberately to build up a permanent tone and sentiment throughout the organization characterized by mutual helpfulness. If the bickering, bargaining, controversial atmosphere is continually rife, it is due, in many cases, to causes well within management's control.

On the other hand, the view that there is a complete identity of interests and purposes among the industrial groups seems to grow out of a mistaken idea of conflict rather than out of candid analysis of the motives actually at work. It is, in short, feared by some that conflict necessarily implies physical violence or an unethical exercise of power.

The newer view of conflicting aims underlying the present discussion is that *conflicts are inevitable in intergroup relations, that imaginative reflection upon ways and means can, first, narrow the area of conflict and, second, create a new formulation of purposes.* This newly invented, newly conceived, newly phrased formula or solution can then quite naturally gain adherence from the affected groups and thus bring about an integration of purposes wherein the conflict factor is greatly lessened in force and influence. Just what this means in practice can be concretely suggested by illustrations, but it must be understood that the examples of integration here given are not suggested as models or panaceas, but merely as supplying instances of efforts to carry forward this process of formulating and agreeing upon new purposes.

That the idea of conflict does not necessarily have immoral implications is also well pointed out by Lindeman when he says:

Conflicts are not in and of themselves bad, or immoral, or unethical. They simply are. Life is conflict. The whole concept of life as adjustment implies that there is a resisting force or object to which the organism must adjust itself. The adjusting process may produce either good or bad results, but this does not imply that the conflict itself is inherently either good or bad.

The scientific viewpoint asks us to investigate this adjusting process minutely. What is it that happens when an organism adjusts itself to its environment? Is it the organism acting upon the environment or the environment acting upon the organism? Obviously, it is both. The organism is changed, but the environment is also changed. The process is one of interaction and not simply action and reaction.

The scientific viewpoint indicates that no significant adjustments are made until conflict appears. This does not mean that life is all conflict. Nor does it mean that life is all cooperation. Life is adjustment, and conflict and cooperation are parts of the adjusting process. Conflict and cooperation are not antithetical qualities or quantities placed over against each other; they are merely two ways of viewing the life process.

Adjustment always takes place in parts and not in wholes. That is, the organism does not adjust itself completely to the total environment but rather adjusts a portion of itself or a part of its function to a portion or a function of the environment. The total environment is involved in each adjustment and must eventually become a part of the total adjustment, but the total adjustment is a building up of minor adjustments.[3]

The Alternatives to Conflict.—This more profound view of the rôle of conflict situations is also supported by a consideration of the alternatives. Miss Follett has wisely pointed out that there are three:

1. The conflict element can be ignored—which is a failure to confront reality and thus leads nowhere.

2. The conflict element can be denied—which results in a failure to supply machinery for negotiation and adjustment and leads equally to trouble.

3. It can be assumed that a balancing of interests, a compromise, can be effected which will remove the conflict.

The last of these is the only one requiring further analysis. Why is a compromise not a permanent resolving of a real conflict of aims—especially since it is the means so frequently resorted to?[4] A compromise is an arbitrary yielding of certain points in one's efforts to fulfill one's purposes, coupled, usually, with a yielding of points by the other party or group involved. Each group agrees to remove from the discussion certain facts which are nevertheless elements in its case—aspects of its desire. Each group trades cleverly from a tacitly admitted extreme demand down to a point as near to it as it dares to hold out for. Hence, neither group goes away satisfied in point of what it really wants. All of which implies an effort not to arrive at a solution based on all facts in the problem including the conflicting purposes, but one based on bargaining skill and on leaving the purposes still largely in conflict.

Furthermore, bargaining skill, in its turn, really implies for its relatively effective use that the bargainers are in an approximately equal bargaining position. This assumption is so definitely contrary to fact in the economic arena today that it of itself should vitiate the fundamental validity of the compromise idea. If groups are to reach a *modus operandi* by compromise, it should be possible to assume that they have fairly equal power. Otherwise, the scales are always weighted in some one way. Unless and until each group in industry is organized, is articulate, is able equally with all the other groups to sell what it has to offer only when it finds the terms equitable, equality of negotiative status does not exist. And, in fact, it does not. Consumers are organized not at all. Managers in relation to owners are in a dependent position. Manual workers in relation to owners and managers are poorly organized, inarticulate, and in possession of something to sell—their labor power—which is highly perishable and in need of an immediate market. Under such conditions, compromise, however popular it may be as the lazy man's way out, is not a fundamental remedy for psychological and economic disparities.

This leaves for consideration the fourth possible method—that of utilizing conflicts in constructive ways to bring out by creative thinking a new basis for getting together. This new basis should be one which not only does not ignore what each group really wants, but also helps each to see its purposes in relation to the limitations of circumstance and to adapt, adjust, and further them accordingly—a process quite different from the rough and ready, static, uncreative process of compromise. It is this fourth method to which the name "integration" has been given.

What is Integration?—Integration is the process of discovering out of the divergences of group purposes those new methods and procedures which are found to compose group differences by yielding a new purpose—one which the several groups find satisfying because in harmony with what they really want.

The process of integration requires

1. Recognition of real differences and of real identities of interest and purposes, both in whole and in part.
2. Encouragement of cooperation wherever an identity can be discovered.
3. Frank acknowledgment of the remaining differences.
4. Efforts to resolve the differences by creating a new basis of activity more inclusive of the various purposes.[5]

The further strengthening of existing common purposes is a desirable objective and one needed in almost every organization. And it takes a clear head to recognize these purposes as distinguished from those as to which there are basic differences. Examples of the former would be the provision and maintenance of sanitary, light, airy, and cheerful work places; the provision of a good job instruction system; the maintenance of contributory group insurance or a mutual benefit organization. What is required in relation to these commonly valuable aims is only to have it made plain to all concerned that they *are* common and are worth striving for.

The bigger problem concerns the purposes not so readily agreed to be mutual. It is the method of dealing with these which is discussed in the next chapter.

CHAPTER XI

THE INTEGRATION OF CONFLICTS OF PURPOSE

The Methods That Forward Integration.—The real problem of resolving conflicting purposes arises in regard to issues where an identity of interests is not readily apparent.

Take, for example, the question of the possibility of interesting employees in high productivity at low unit cost. Here the only attempt which has any likelihood of success is one in which all the contributing conditions make the employees come to realize that they have more to gain than to lose by working more effectively.

They have more to gain than to lose if they earn more, if they are not overfatigued, if they do not more quickly work themselves out of a job, if they can share in the greater gain accruing in profits, if their sense of accomplishment is enhanced. Any plan which will give them specific assurances on these points has a good chance of acceptance by them.

In actual industrial practice, this integration of purposes is today being obtained by a combination of methods. (1) Some type of incentive payment method is adopted either with or without a differential piece rate under which the employees' rate of pay increases both relatively and absolutely as the productivity increases and as unit costs decrease. (2) Some assurance of regular work or regular income is given so that employees will not by working hard work themselves out of employment. (3) An assurance is given that there will be no rate cutting unless the character of the job is radically altered.

Given these several procedures for protecting the employees, it has been found possible in many companies to bring employees into agreement with the management's purpose of increased productivity. If, however, the employees should ever come, with their new experience, to the point of making a careful analysis of the entire fiscal situation in the company which employs them, they may find in specific cases, that despite all these provisions there is still a rate of profit being made for the stockholders which seems unduly high. If and when employees feel that by the outlay of their energy in behalf of productivity, even if it is relatively well repaid, they are making unduly large profits for managers and investors, it may still be hard to retain their whole-hearted cooperation—that is, hard to get them to adopt the purposes of these other groups.

Indeed, it is because of a sense that such a questioning feeling may possibly arise among employees that certain companies have already been led to experiment with some method of stock sale to employees or with profit sharing. Both of these devices aim, by use of somewhat different legal means, to effect an identical psychological result, namely, to make it worthwhile for employees to interest themselves in the creation of profits, because of the fact that they will share in them.

Another possible new purpose growing out of employees' experience with an extension of knowledge and power in purely shop affairs would be a desire to share in decisions about the major policies of the company. This may come about through a realization that such decisions must, also, inevitably affect their group destinies more or less directly. This purpose has already appeared in a few companies. And if the logic or pressure of such an employee purpose leads a company to allow the election of one or two employee members to the board of directors, this may constitute another experimental step in the direction of integrating and harmonizing purposes.

Once a corporation has, for example, a shop committee with some power, an incentive payment plan which is felt to be fair, guaranteed employment or unemployment compensation, a sharing of profits by employees through a substantial minority stock ownership, a sharing of ultimate directive control by employees, the result is that the employees are in a position where they quite naturally share in an entirely novel and unrestrained way, in forwarding the same purposes as the investors and managers to a degree never previously possible.

How true this analysis is will be seen when one examines the results obtained in improved working attitude, efficiency, and sense of industrial partnership in the few companies whose procedures are experimentally including most or all of the features just suggested. It is risky to name individual companies, because policies may change with the intervening of banking interests, with the death of individual owners, or because of economic reversals due to shifts in demand or other reasons. But there are perhaps a couple of dozen companies which seem to me to be set in a reasonably permanent way toward a combination of working procedures that are resulting in a true integration of the purposes of managers and manual workers. The extent to which the absentee investor can be included in this harmonizing of purposes is more doubtful, unless it is agreed that a cumulative preferred stock with a fairly liberal yield can be said to take adequate care of his interests. If and when industry can and desires to do more financing through bond issues the rate paid for the money which must be borrowed will, of course, be less, and the investors' opportunities will be reduced by so much.

The working procedures, then, in these progressive companies are today including the following provisions: a well organized and well rounded personnel department for the intelligent handling of all routine matters of employee concern; provision for accident, sickness, disability, old age, unemployment and death; employee representation or collective bargaining with full negotiative power; some well arranged plan of incentive payment; some carefully conceived plan of stock-ownership or profit-sharing; some formal chance for expression of opinion by workers in the board of directors. I do not say that all of these advanced companies have yet adopted every one of these features; but they have certainly included all but one—usually the last. And half a dozen of them do make a point of having employee-directors.

What has happened in all these cases is not that the employees have adopted the typical purposes of present-day managers and investors. For in these companies the managing and investing groups have, at the same time, *had to modify their purposes* in order to bring about a fuller integration of their purposes with those of employees. They have had to modify the typical objectives of such groups to the extent of letting the employees in on a share of the profits, of paying them during periods of idleness, of giving them information heretofore considered confidential, and so forth.

The result is a *new* purpose or set of purposes satisfactory to all concerned. And they prove satisfactory because in the process of experience each group has found the old purposes inadequate to give it what it wants and has found that a modification in purposes is not so bad as it may have seemed in advance. *Indeed, in the light of experience, the modified purpose is found to be desirable and satisfying in a new and more profound way.* And as far as the employees and managers are concerned, one of the chief elements in the experience of finding this new satisfaction is *the realization that the purposes of the other groups have also modified in a broadened direction.*

Whether or not, under the conditions such as those named above, the customers and the general public can be in harmony with the shared purposes of the three directly interested groups constitutes, at present, a further and real question. And the creating of conditions under which they can and will share purposes with these three groups is going to require a great deal of inventive thinking. Much depends on the direction which the new common purposes of investors, managers, and workers take. If they virtually conspire in a given case to raise dividends, salaries, and wages and take it out of the public in high prices or shoddy goods, the possibility of a further integration of purposes with customers is delayed and reduced. But if the combined desires of the three primary agents in production look toward rendering public service consciously and willingly on reasonable terms, they will find consumers and everyone else able and willing to share in the forwarding of their purposes.

It is significant to see that a prominent contemporary business leader whose powers of reflection and vision are widely recognized comes to much the same conclusion as the above when he says:

Perhaps some day we may be able to organize the human beings engaged in a particular undertaking so that they truly will be the employer hiring capital as a commodity in the market at the lowest price. It will be necessary for them to provide an adequate guaranty fund in order to buy their capital at all. If that is realized, the human beings will then be entitled to all the profits over the cost of capital. I hope the day may come when these great business organizations will truly belong to the men who are giving their lives and their efforts to them, I care not in what capacity. They then will use capital truly as a tool and they will be all interested in working it to the highest economic advantage. Then an idle machine will mean to every man in the plant who sees it an unproductive charge against himself. Then every piece of material not in motion will mean to the man who sees it an unproductive charge against himself. Then we shall have zest in labor, provided the leadership is competent and the division fair. Then we shall dispose, once and for all, of the charge that in industry organizations are autocratic and not democratic. Then we shall have all the opportunities for a cultural wage which the business can provide. Then, in a word, men will be as free in cooperative undertakings and subject only to the same limitations and chances as men in individual businesses. Then we shall have no hired men.[1]

Is Conflict Thus Eliminated?—I do not say, however, that these efforts at shared purpose remove and eliminate the likelihood of any future conflicts of aim. They do lessen the sense and the fact of conflict; they do raise the level of cooperation to a higher, fuller, and freer plane. But in a given case, whether a company pays 7 or 8 per cent on its preferred stock, pays $25,000 or $50,000 to its president, pays $1 or $1.10 an hour to its skilled workers, works 40 or 44 hours a week, builds up a surplus equal to its capital fund or equal to half of it—these and other questions of policy and practice are *not susceptible to absolute and final decision on a scientific basis.* Facts can and should illuminate discussion of such points. But they remain points of essential disparity of interest. And further integration will require further inventiveness. In a word, we do not want necessarily to wipe out conflict—because we cannot. We want, rather, to utilize it for ends that different groups see as contributory to their best purposes. We want to keep on attempting to integrate as new conflicts emerge and thus obtain a progressively intelligent and rational control of the wayward and intractable facts of growing and complex experience.

Limitations upon Integration.—A further important qualifying consideration has to be made as to the possibilities of integration. Where the relative amount of power among the groups involved varies greatly, the difficulties are increased. A strongly entrenched economic group gives up power reluctantly, especially if it feels that thereby it loses economic advantage. Our self-assertive trait drives us to seek power and to hold on to it once it is secured. The possibility of integration appears, admittedly, only when, in a specific case, the more powerful group believes that there are other purposes to be served as important as the possession of power. All sorts of qualifying factors may enter to modify the urge to power such as a feeling that it is better to have less power and more peace of mind, that power over others is an unworthy and unsatisfying experience as compared with building creative power of a cooperative sort, that power is today threatened anyway and that, hence, it is better to make a good gesture of conceding some of it. In any case, a group's resolute and unyielding will to autocratic power is a foe of integration and should be understood as such.

Such a candid observer as Bertrand Russell says on this point, perhaps with undue pessimism:

I am compelled to read that science will be used to promote the power of dominant groups rather than to make man happy. The men who administer the science of the future will have a power beyond the dreams of the Jesuits, but there is no reason to suppose that they will have more sense than the men who control education today. Technical scientific knowledge does not make men sensible in their aims, and administrators in the future will be presumably no less stupid and no less prejudiced than they are at present. Furthermore, science enables the holders of power to realize their purposes more fully than they could otherwise do. If their purposes are good, this is a gain; if they are evil, it is a loss. In the present age, it seems that the purposes of the power-holders are in the main evil . . . Therefore at present science does harm by increasing the power of rulers. Science is no substitute for virtue.[2]

Finally, there is the difficulty that it takes real brains to invent and adopt new ideas for use by a given organization. Stupidity and inertia must thus bear their share of the blame for the slowness of the working of the integrative process in modern industry. It is not easy at one and the same time to conserve the best in present incentives, to assure clear-cut controls, regular working habits, and a well-defined sense of responsibility while also making provisions which foster security, ambition, and creative power. To embody in concrete provision of constitutions, by-laws, standard practices, profit-sharing contracts, etc., the conditions which will support and evoke new unity of purpose is a hard mental task. But there is ground for real hope to be found in the present variety of experimental efforts, all of which offer more concrete guidance to executives as to possible next steps than they have ever before had to study and draw upon.

The Principle of Integration in Industry.—The view which this whole analysis seems to me to support may be summarily stated as a principle regarding the method of achieving a sense of corporate unity in any organization.

Corporate unity of purpose and action can be brought out of conflicts only when, in a consistent and reasonably permanent way and in terms of practical working procedures and not merely in verbalisms, the organization is demonstrating clearly to all its members that it considers them as partners in a group enterprise and not as hired agents for the piling up of excessive profits for absentee owners or for fulfilling purposes to which they naturally do not find it possible to be a party.

Objection may, however, be raised at this point that my discussion here is not scientific and psychological but personal and opinionated. I want to meet this certain objection by asking the reader to look into his own experience and employ a little introspective psychology to check my point. Let anyone ask himself how long he is willing to follow purposes (1) which he did not have a hand in making, (2) which he is more or less enforced to accept if he wants to get the wherewithal of life, (3) in the results from the realizing of which he has no stake, (4) the real meaning of which he does not understand, and (5) the process of fulfilling which he finds a bore.

It is in much this situation that typical manual and clerical workers in the general run of companies find themselves today, if only they and we had the psychological acumen to see their negative and unliberating motivation. No; it is not unscientific to call attention to the psychological shortcomings in the kind of purposes that many corporations today espouse. It is the essence of the problem. Indeed, leadership in its best sense appears in industry only when the objectives to which it summons devotion are those which experience shows that people can embrace as an integral part of their search for self-fulfillment.

Warning should again be offered, however, that the way of integration *is not reducible to a formula*. The methods which will secure it are not necessarily the same for all organizations, nor are they, perhaps, the same today and tomorrow. The examples offered as the types of procedure now being found salutary in a number of companies are to be taken as *suggestions only*. They are merely illustrative of the principle to which each corporate group must give expression in its own way in the light of its history and the inventive genius of its leaders. It is sufficient if the point has been established that the sharing and harmonizing of purposes—this indispensable condition of true corporate effectiveness—requires the creative and persistent use of plans, methods, and institutional arrangements in a setting where the fulfilling and growth of everyone's purposes is a rational result of the whole group's evolving experience.

Two important corollaries of this truth should be explicitly stated by way of summary. First, *group purposes cannot be changed solely by exhortation or by appeals to the intellect*. Purposes change in the process of active experience. How the change gets its start has already been shown. It is by the impact of those actual events into which the individual or group is more or less inevitably thrust. For if one unsettling suggestion regarding present purposes gains a hearing or if one failure to achieve present purposes occurs, new experience begins at once, either tending to confirm or to deny the validity of some already tentatively considered new purpose. Experience has already tended to suggest a purpose which is more tenable and likely of fulfillment.

Second, *individuals or groups do not accept the purposes of others ready made.* One writer has wisely pointed out that for specific purposes to be fully apprehended *one must have a share in creating and accepting them* as well as in devising ways and means to realize them. This should be axiomat c, since purposes which are taken over and given only intellectual assent have not come through the vivid and vital channel of motor and emotional experience and thus have not the living quality necessary to make them influential in conduct. The process of sharing in the formulation of a purpose and in inventing the means of realizing it provides a strong psychological presumption in favor of having it continue to influence action.

This fact gives support to the case for the use of the so-called "democratic method" of conducting organizations, as suggested below:

The best guarantee of collective efficiency and power is liberation and use of the diversity of individual capacities in initiative, planning, foresight, vigor, and endurance. Personality must be educated, and personality cannot be educated by confining its operations to technical and specialized things or to the less important relationships of life. Full education comes only when there is a responsible share on the part of each person, in proportion to capacity, in shaping the aims and policies of the social groups to which he belongs. This fact fixes the significance of democracy. It cannot be conceived as a sectarian or racial thing, nor as a consecration of some form of government which has already attained constitutional sanction. It is but a name for the fact that human nature is developed only when its elements take part in directing things which are common, things for the sake of which men and women form groups—families, industrial companies, governments, churches, scientific associations, and so on.[3]

In conclusion, if this discussion of the importance of purposes and of ways of changing them still seems lacking in practical application, it should at least be of value in calling attention to two basic and homely truths: first, to the impossibility of getting far with industrial peace while *the purposes of groups are at odds,* are limited, selfish, narrowly construed, ingrown; and, second, to the necessity for courageous experiment and new insight in the direction of methods and structural arrangements which will be the outward condition and channel for allowing people in organizations to manifest goodwill and generous and constructive purposes without being exploited in the process.

CHAPTER XII

THE TECHNIQUE OF CREATIVE LEADERSHIP

This chapter aims to see what leadership is from a psychological point of view, to consider to what extent it can be trained for, how the training should be carried forward, and how leadership can be effectively exercised.

This topic yields today entirely new and fresh, practical conclusions in the light of modern psychological knowledge. What is now known of human motivation has radically altered both the concept of leadership and ideas as to the kind of technique most useful to the leader. The importance of the problem is realized as never before because of the necessity of enlisting from large groups of individuals a harmonious, willing, and integrated working spirit. This kind of working spirit, experience has taught, is not a spontaneous growth. It has been found to develop in direct relation to the proper exercise of real leadership in the organization. In an important sense, progress toward industrial amity, productivity, and good governance depends on a display of the new leadership which this discussion outlines. Executive work, considered not merely as such but as the opportunity for displaying leadership, has become today one of the biggest challenges to creative effort which life holds.

This new leadership is to be contrasted with ideas of leading which were primarily military or religious in origin. Domineering power, the demand of absolute obedience, overbearing exercise of authority—these were attributes of the old leadership. Results were obtained by subjugating others to the carrying out of one's own purposes.

Whatever may have been the success of this kind of leadership in other fields and in other days, it is certain that it does not today produce in industry a satisfactory attitude in working

148

associates. The situation in the past has been all too much like that in an army of mercenaries—paid soldiers working for hire—and all too little like that in a volunteer army of citizens fighting for a fatherland or the members of a college football team playing for their alma mater. Hence, the timeliness of examining from the standpoint of the leader how he can best acquire and exert influence.

Leadership Defined.—*Leadership is the name for that combination of qualities by the possession of which one is able to get something done by others chiefly because through his influence they become willing to do it.* It is ability to secure *willing* action in behalf of an established purpose. Leading means that others follow. The fact of following indicates that action is secured in a desired direction. Ability to lead is ability to get people to act—mentally or physically—toward an objective.

The elements, first, of a definite objective and, second, of influencing people *so that their own desires harmonize with those of the leader* are both essential. It is this which is *creative leadership*, as distinct from ways of getting people to act which do not take their desires into account. The new and distinguishing element is the creation and direction of positive desire in the led. Something over and above mere consent is implied. It means actually taking over as one's very own the purpose of the leader. Or, more fundamentally, it implies the evoking by the leader and the led together of new reaches of purpose, the realizing of which is discovered by all to bring about a more effective fulfillment of the desires of all. The creating and evoking of purposes no less than the popularizing of purposes are a mark of the best leadership. For, as already shown, purposes do not stand still. Changes in them are dictated by the experience of encountering new problems.

Of course, leadership in industry is a familiar fact. It is the creative, self-generating aspects of it that need emphasizing. There has always been that type of leadership which is exercised under conditions of compulsion due to economic pressure upon the led. The limitation upon this type is that as economic pressure lessens and as the desire for the sense of freedom grows in the community, the power of the leader diminishes. Again, there is a good deal of leadership which achieves only a sort of resigned following, a passive consent. This is an advance over enforced, grudging consent; it is a leadership of the half-hearted. But it does not go the whole way and become what is really desirable in its power to liberate and create unified effort—a leadership of the whole-hearted and active minded.

Kinds of Leadership.—It is probably valuable to distinguish certain differences in leadership problems. Yet the general principles, to which this chapter is largely confined, apply quite generally. The president of a corporation employing 100,000 people working in different plants has certain problems unlike those of the superintendent of one plant. And he, in turn, has a task not identical with that of his foremen, who have from thirty to sixty men in a department. Leadership may be exerted directly, face to face; indirectly, through other lesser leaders; or intellectually, through the medium of the written word or the oral statement of policies.

Also, my definition suggests that every executive down to the straw boss or gang foreman is a leader. It suggests, also, that some who are not the acknowledged directing heads may be most important leaders; and that a great many people are occasionally leaders in the sense of trying to get other people to want what they want and see things their way.

Surely every executive *is* a leader and the job is to make every one of them a creative leader—a builder of a group animated by satisfying, common purposes.

Surely, too, every organization is familiar with the able but unacknowledged leader who must work through the titular heads. He has a special and difficult rôle to play, requiring unusual powers of tact and patience. His problems merit special study.

And it is true that everyone in an organization is at times and to a degree a leader. It is one of the values of this emphasis on the creative aspects of leadership that the characteristics and status of the leader are seen to be those of normal people and not of geniuses. The aim should be to try to extend as widely as possible that combination of normal human qualities which make average people effective as leaders.

A further fact, which observation confirms, is that progress in improved personal relations in industry is crucially dependent upon the right kind of leadership.   In every organization where notable work along these lines is being done, it is due to the devotion, vision, intelligence, and persistence of one or two outstanding individuals in positions of high responsibility.   The world depends upon individual persons to supply the stimulus and the ideas which push it along, and no greater work can be done by personnel executives than to encourage, support, and supply constructive ideas to other executives who have generous desires but little technical knowledge as to how to translate them into progressive and humane methods.

Why Discuss Leadership?—The notion that leaders are born and not made dies hard.   The reason why leadership can be talked about today with some assurance that it will yield new and productive results is because *a new conception of human nature* is one of the first fruits of the study of modern psychology. As the earlier chapters have shown, human nature is no longer to be conceived as an empty goat skin into which desires, feelings, and ideas are poured instead of wine, or as a putty image which is impressed only from the outside or, again, as a lovely angel fallen from its high and perfect estate.   Human nature is now conceived as dynamic, self-generating, self-energized, outreaching, expanding, emerging, evolving, striving, growing.   It is at once a product of its own inner, living forces and of the pressure of outer forces of all sorts to which adjustment must be made. Because the total situation perpetually conditions conduct, the control of the situation at any one point means a change in the resulting activity.   What people want and the way in which they want to get it change with experience.   And this fact supplies an important reason why leadership can be effective if only the leader knows *how to get the environment to help him to bring pressure in the right way to yield the right response.*

In short, because people's purposes are fluid, amenable, and emergent, the leader has his chance to work with natrual forces and psychological influences, to help direct the line that conduct will take.   How he may do this should be explicitly pointed out.

Indeed, the examples given in the previous chapter of how managers worked to change the purposes of employees are equally in point here. The manager who is trying to change purposes is, by that token, trying to lead in a fundamental way.

A still further example may, however, clarify the relation of the leader to this process of influencing what people consider desirable. I watched recently the operation of an employee representation plan in a New England textile plant. The traditions there were the usual textile traditions of autocratic management and the autonomy of the individual, old-school foremen. The second generation of manager-owners decided to try to install an advisory shop committee which should be a channel of communication and of adjustment of all difficulties. I was present at a foremen's meeting held two years after the plan had been initiated. The personnel manager was in the chair, and he was bringing to a head a discussion of the foremen's estimate of the plan's success. I had known of the great opposition encountered among the foremen when the plan was first proposed, and it was extraordinarily interesting to see them voluntarily testify to their own new sense of the value of the committee in helping them to get on better with their men. No amount of lecturing at these foremen could have done what was done by a wise management's gently but firmly inducing them to give the new idea a trial and thus through experience change their attitude of obstruction to one of endorsement and use.

The reason why leadership should be discussed afresh is, thus, that more is known about the *how* of it than ever before. And this applies not alone to the tremendously important problem of influencing the desires and purposes of others but to the specific activities of teaching, giving orders, disciplining, arousing enthusiasm, and other tasks.

The Leader's Purposes.—The character and the quality of the things the leader is trying to do with those he leads make a great difference in the likelihood of his success. Creative leadership has proved much more possible in companies which are giving *tangible evidences* of their goodwill toward those led than in those where military and autocratic methods are still relied on. For the more liberal companies show a realistic knowledge of how to bring about unity of purpose among human beings. And since this is what the true leader is fundamentally after, it is essential that he have the support of surrounding conditions which buttress his efforts rather than counteract them.

There is but one answer which any reasonably intelligent employee of the typical old-fashioned company would make to the question "Why should I respond whole-heartedly to the leadership of an executive whose one idea is to make as much as possible for a lot of outside investors?" He would and does answer "I should not respond *and I will not.*"

The slogan for the successful leader is, Get right with your purposes! This means that you must have judgment and insight enough to realize what sorts of purposes will gain favor with the groups you lead, will win favorable response because their acceptance in action gets the groups along in the direction in which they already know they want to go, or in which you can show them that they want to go.

The Characteristics of Leaders.—The chief value of listing the desirable characteristics of a leader is to distinguish the traits which conscious training can strengthen. Merely to say that the leader should have a sense of humor or a deep voice or a decisive manner helps little unless a statement as to the *how* of acquiring these attributes can be offered at the same time.

There is probably a good deal of difference in the qualities required for different types of leadership. A leader of the face-to-face type will, perhaps, require certain characteristics that are unnecessary in the intellectual leader who supplies ideas for a new movement. The qualifications differ, also, with the levels of intelligence and culture of the group to be led. Differences are likewise to be noted, depending upon the character of the group, on the race, the generation, and the place in which the leadership is exercised. For our immediate purposes, we are concerned primarily with the qualifications for face-to-face leadership of people in corporate organizations.

Certainly among the necessary characteristics of the leader the possession of *physical* and *nervous energy* is of first importance.

There is a subtle sense in which strength goes out from him, in which power is imparted by the contagion of his own physical energy and nervous drive. This quality as much as any other seems to be a factor always present in successful leaders.

Whether or not it can be cultivated is a question. But surely what energy one has can be conserved and directed. Fatigue, indigestion, a chronic sense of being "run down"—all these unnecessary limitations upon one's native endowment of vitality can and should be guarded against.

Related to this magnetic quality of vitality is that combination of physical and psychical qualities spoken of as *enthusiasm*.

To be enthusiastic means first of all to have caught sight of a value, a purpose, a vision, an ideal, that kindles all that is deepest and richest in the human heart. Then, and only then, have we opened the door to the incoming of rich and upbuilding enthusiasms.[1]

Here, again, is a factor seemingly universal among leaders. Of course, every enthusiast is not a leader, but every leader has a generous endowment of enthusiasm. This quality is, in part, a by-product of a good physical condition; in part, a matter of temperament; and, in part, a result of a conviction of the significance and interest of the enterprise in hand.

Adequate command—even though not a perfect command— of the *technical knowledge* or skill as to the project in question is also important. All first-hand studies of the qualities of successful face-to-face leaders indicate that they "know their stuff." They call out the admiration of colleagues and assistants by their ready technical skill. This does not necessarily mean, however, that the best technician makes the best leader; in fact, this has again and again been disproved in practice.

Intelligence is essential in the psychologist's special sense of that word to mean alertness and cleverness in "seeing the point," in making the necessary inferences out of past experiences in their relation to present situations. Although no tests now distinguish successful leaders from others who are able to rank high in mental tests, this may not always be true. Meanwhile, an executive who does rank high in general intelligence has a certain presumption in his favor that he will make a good leader. As already shown, education in this quality appears to be difficult if not impossible.

Imagination is required—namely, that ability to work with the data of past experience in newly conceived and illuminating combinations. A lively curiosity and sense of excitement about new ideas usually contribute to the finest flowering of imagination. How this characteristic can be cultivated has already been discussed.

Knowledge of human nature, whether or not it be what is called intuitive or however it be acquired, is important. This ability to understand the probable reactions of people and to judge of individual differences is an indispensable quality. Executives differ in the amount of this quality that they bring to their work. But that it can be improved and cultivated by thought and study has been shown again and again. And it is the purpose of all such books as this to help point out the specific ways by which this helpful knowledge can be greatly extended.

In addition, we find that there is required that something which is meant by the phrase "having faith in people." One essential aspect of the conception of creative leadership is a belief in the creative and self-generating powers of individuals in groups if they are given a chance to act together. The fact that people respond to confidence imposed in them is a familiar truth which the leader must apprehend.

Other characteristics which can be identified are courage, persistence, initiative, tact, patience, self-confidence, a sense of humor, and purposiveness. This last is of great importance. The leader is distinguished as one who believes in his purposes hard enough to work unremittingly for them. But to be continually reflective about the wisdom of the purposes in hand is to be a philosopher rather than a leader.

Over and under and through all these characteristics, I cannot but feel that the particular thing that distinguishes leaders is the special quality of *their attitude toward those whom they lead.* They are interested in people; they are sympathetic with people; they like people. I suggest that to be successful they must have *positive affection for people,* especially for those whom they are leading. I believe that I am not unscientific when I say that the creative leader is a warm-hearted individual—warm-hearted while still remaining cool headed.

If one asks how this desirable combination of qualities can be cultivated, the answer is not easy; but it is not hopeless. One sees people change enough in respect to the effective display of leadership qualities to make it possible to believe that some improvement can be brought about by special intention and effort. Perhaps the most important thing is *to want to improve.* All that was said before about the loving attitude and its contagious character applies here. And people love by *letting themselves go,* by forgetting themselves, by reaching out in sympathy and affection to the interesting, varied, attractive—yes, and pathetic—individuals with whom they associate.

Where, now, comes in the attribute so often spoken of—"personality?" The word is here used in its popular sense rather than in the psychological one defined and explained in Chap. VIII. In this popular sense, what is usually meant is a quality of personal charm, winsomeness, a certain magnetic attractiveness. The psychological elements of this have proved difficult to analyze; and as yet there is little that can be said about its nature or possible cultivation that has scientific value.

Dr. Charters, in an interesting study of "The Discovery of Executive Talent,"[2] suggests a somewhat different statement of basic, leadership qualities which may usefully be considered in this connection. He finds necessary:

a. Forcefulness enough to put across ideas which we believe to be right and persistence enough to stay with an idea until it is used.

b. Dependability in performing well those tasks for which we are responsible.

c. Criticalness which enables us to see those things that are not right.

d. Constructiveness in suggesting practical methods for improving the things we criticize.

e. Kindliness of spirit as a background of all our contacts with people.

Can These Qualities Be Assured by Training?—Even this brief and necessarily tentative outline of leadership characteristics can suggest a constructive approach to the problem of training in leadership qualifications. The answer is that some qualities seem capable of development by training and some do not. And the practical problem of the head executive or of the training department is to work specifically on those elements where training has shown itself able to yield definite results. The magnetic personalities usually spoken of as born leaders are and always will be strictly limited in number. There will never be enough to go around. That is why the practical problem lies elsewhere.

Every corporation requires a certain quota of executives; and every corporation head who knows his job realizes that these executives are most effective if they are also consciously leaders. The practical aim is, therefore, to make executives just as good leaders as possible. The opportunity here is by no means discouraging, since experience in industry and elsewhere has shown that careful attention to individual personality development can secure marked improvement in the character and quality of executive action. On the physical side alone, for example, the change that can be brought about in an executive's attitude if he happens to be dyspeptic is marked, if by careful attention to the matter his digestion can be improved and his liver made to function normally. The difference between a crotchety executive and an inspiring leader is, undoubtedly, in certain cases, the difference between a man who is in poor health and a man who is robust.

What we must come to recognize is that there is the need for many leaders in many places, rather than for heroes as leaders. The need has been aptly phrased as one for pluralistic leadership.

Special Phases of the Leader's Work.—It will be useful to discuss a number of special phases of the leader's work in order to show more specifically how the meaning of the idea of creative leadership discloses itself in action.

The good leader in action is likely to exhibit characteristic qualities of (1) a planner; (2) a technician; (3) a commander; (4) a coordinator; (5) a trainer; (6) an energizer; (7) a critic. Ideally, he might combine all these phases. But that all are equally required of the leader in every situation is doubtful. These represent, perhaps, the maximum of the good leader's qualifications.

The Leader as Planner.—The point has sometimes been made that under the conditions of systemization which good management entails, there is no room for leadership because everything is cut and dried, and direction and supervision become impersonal and automatic. The profounder view is that the kind of systematization which good management involves is not a static fact but is dynamic, and involves careful and constant coping with numerous changes in the whole setting of the organization's activity. New changes in the broad economic scene, such as changes in demand, business depressions, in technology, in the labor market, all require an adjustment within each company which removes systematization from the realm of the absolute and final.

It is vital to a proper understanding of the idea of systematized management to realize that planning for effective group cooperation is not an undertaking which can ever be stopped at any moment with the assurance that it will continue of its own momentum. Planning to secure cooperation is essentially an evolving and continuing task. While it is true that the conduct of the routine details should be more automatically assured under scientific management, the perpetuation of that spirit in which all the details work together in a continuing harmony requires constant planning of a high and special order. This is a phase of planning in which the true leader will show himself conspicuous.

Also, businesses, like individuals, reveal a certain rhythm in their life. They tend to be either growing and developing or the opposite. They cannot stand still because of the number of outside forces at work to affect their success. The true leader is conscious of and sensitive to this rhythm in the life of his organization and is deliberately trying to tone it up.

In this connection, a word of warning is necessary. There is a serious danger that the energetic leader may get too far ahead of his staff and his rank and file. A consultant friend of mine tells of a corporation in which this was true to such an extent that he advised the head of the company to take a trip to Europe for a year in order to allow his plans to work out into actuality before he brought in further new ideas to confuse and distract his associates.

The Leader as a Technician.—The leader has special problems as a technician. One of these concerns his relation to those more expert than himself in branches of the organization for which he is the coordinating agent. The old formulæ regarding this relationship seem no longer to apply with complete accuracy. The relation of the cost accountant to the foreman, the relation of the chemical engineer to the superintendent of chemical works, the relation of the personnel vice-president to the manufacturing vice-president, the relation of the purchasing agent to the financial head in a company where purchasing is the key problem— none of these relations can be stated any longer in terms of clear-cut divisions of authority. In these cases, each executive definitely assumes some large responsibility. The relationship of the head executive to all staff advisors is not necessarily best stated in terms of relative degrees of responsibility. It must be thought out today rather in terms of the kind of relationship which will best bring the technical judgment of the expert into proper relation to the effectiveness of the working of the organization as a whole. The head executive has the responsibility of seeking out new combinations of practical ideas, a new creative synthesis, which will be better than a mere compromise of the views of staff assistants who may come to him to settle their differences. The effectiveness of the true leader is measured not by his ability to reconcile the opinions of his staff experts but by his ability to invent out of their divergent points of view a unified, corporate policy that will carry the whole organization forward wisely.

In other words, the best technician, as stated before, will not necessarily be the best leader. Indeed, an executive will tend to be a good leader only in so far as he shows himself able to subordinate his own special technical knowledge to a grasp of the problems of the corporation as a whole. The danger has proved real that an engineer promoted to a position of leadership or a sales manager promoted to such a position or a banker brought in as the head executive may lead not as the creator of a functional unity but as an overgrown and one-sided technician with a special interest. The real leader must be a harmonizer of the claims of the various technicians under his direction.

The Leader as a Commander.—In emphasizing, as I intentionally do, the function of the leader as a creator of spontaneous initiative among the led, I do not want to be thought to ignore that aspect of the leader's work in which he acts as the commander, or order giver. While it is true that the emphasis on order giving can be increasingly subordinated, while it is true that each function can increasingly be made to carry with it its own responsibilities which the functionary fulfills without having to be ordered so to do, it nevertheless is true—and, it seems to me, always will be true in larger groups—that immediate and clear-cut decisions will, at times, have to be made by leaders. And these decisions will have the effects of commands.

In so far as commands must be given, it is important for the leader to recognize some of the inherent dangers. Order giving has a technique of its own which can, in a measure, at least, be reduced to formulæ. Some of these injunctions would be:

1. To avoid negative in favor of positive commands, which are explicit and arouse interest.

2. To give as few commands as possible.

3. To let those commanded understand the degree to which they are to use their own initiative in carrying out orders.

4. To be sure that the commands are understood; this involves the important work of setting forth clearly, in language that those commanded understand, what is to be done—it is not sufficient that the command be clear to the one who gives it.

5. To give *in private* any reprimand which has to be given for failure to carry out an order.

6. To give commands without the use of sarcasm or of ridicule.

7. To use the right tone of voice in giving commands. The tone of voice in which commands are given is exceedingly important—to be firm without being overbearing; to be pleasant and cheerful without seeming to take the matter too lightly; to be

personal without being unduly familiar; to be confident without being overbearing—all this requires the employment of a tone of voice and total bearing which deserve special thought. Improvement in this direction can be definitely cultivated. It is largely a matter of taking thought and of forming better habits. The executive can improve himself in respect to these important items. Deficiencies are due more often to heedlessness than to a wilful desire to make those commanded seem uncomfortable or humiliated. That the habit of a courteous, cheerful, considerate tone of voice and bearing in setting forth commands can be inculcated has been shown not only by the work done in the army and navy but also by the training work done with foremen as well.[3]

The Leader as Coordinator.—Some students of business administration have stressed particularly the function of the leader as coordinator. Bringing into working harmony the activities of numbers of people in groups working upon various functions is rightly felt to be one of the unique attributes of good leadership. And in this connection, two special problems emerge. First, the mechanisms of coordination must be supplied; and, second, the desire to act in the direction of coordination must be aroused.

Mechanisms by which coordination must be brought about are admittedly experimental as yet. But the principle which a psychological approach to this problem suggests as sound is one which can be stated in general terms. This principle is that *coordination effectively takes place only where every group specially interested in carrying on a function or activity is represented in making the decisions which affect the success of that activity.* The invention and installation of structural arrangements—conferences, committees, etc.—which will give this principle actuality in any given organization is one of the special challenges to leadership today.[4]

The desire for achieving coordination from among numerous diverse functionaries is not one that can be taken for granted. The leader is the person who sees his organization as a whole and helps all of his specialists to subordinate their personal whims to their larger desire for a smooth working together of the whole organization of which they are members. Everyone familiar with the amount of personal jealousy, interdepartmental feuds, and personal frictions in large organizations will realize that the leader has problems here of personal adjustment which are not simple and which require much thought and time to iron out.

The Leader as Teacher.—On every hand today, managers are giving at least lip service to the thought that the best executive is the best teacher and that a major function of the executive's work is teaching. All this is doubly true of the creative leader. He can get nowhere unless he is mindful in the most concrete way of what the teacher does and how he does it and is applying this knowledge in his own hour-by-hour contacts.

The leader will make the best trainer if two or three broad facts are in the background of his mind. He should realize that formal schooling and intellectual discipline stopped between the ages of ten and fourteen for many of those associated with him, that a grammar school education is as much education as was obtained by probably 85 per cent of his group. Also, he should realize and not be bowled over by the facts about the distribution of intelligence or mental alertness in the community. Apparently, the figures supplied out of the army experience about the distribution of mental alertness reflect, in a rough sort of way, the condition in the community as a whole. Some exceedingly somber conclusions have been drawn by certain writers from these facts. Writers like Lothrop Stoddard, Goddard, MacDougall, and others have, perhaps, prematurely become apprehensive about the possibilities of further education and even of self-government for people whose intelligence quotients fall so largely in the lower ranks. They tend to ignore the fact that mental-alertness tests attempt to test only mental alertness and that other qualities are quite as essential in life and in industry. The value of factual knowledge, of persistence, of purposiveness, of the cultural setting in which one's experience occurs, should not be lost sight of. And the discerning leader will realize that the possession of different degrees of so-called "intelligence" on the part of his group argues little about the possibility of having them become increasingly effective, loyal, and happy. His problem is, rather, to fit responsibilities to individual capacities while looking always for the brighter members and doing everything possible by drill, information, example, and enthusiasm to stir people to exceed their own previous performances. Differences of intelligence do not supply an argument against efforts to exercise leadership—they argue only for leaders who reckon with these facts and, as Lord Morley said, realize that he who would successfully lead mankind must not expect too much of it!

Another fact which the leader as trainer encounters is the fear and suspicion of further education among most adults whose education has stopped at an early age. It is felt by many to be a sign of weakness and a confession of incompetence to carry on with an adult educational program. The leader has this feeling to work against. He must realize that any contemplated educational program must be along the newer lines discussed in later chapters.

The leader must know how learning takes place. And without anticipating the discussion of training methods in Chap. XVI, it is useful, in this connection, to emphasize the truth that *the experience to which the leader exposes those whom he leads will be, perhaps, his most effective educational instrument.* For without discounting the values of learning by reasoning, we may as well be realistic in admitting the prevalence of learning by doing as the principal human method.

We learn more and we learn more rapidly when we are forced by circumstances to readjust ourselves to new conditions than we do from any other one cause. The surrounding conditions must support and help to foster the new objective and thus contribute to its realizing if a new habit is to be built. And the wise leader is the one who uses the whole environment to be sure that it does reenforce the new aim. Perhaps an example will make my meaning clearer on this important point.

Take the case of a plant which wanted to take the power of discharge out of the foremen's hands. The personnel manager "sold" the idea to everyone but the foremen, of whom a substantial minority had grave misgivings, but the policy was put into effect over their objections. After a year's experience with the personnel department handling this function and taking all the personnel adjustment problems out of the hands of the already overworked foremen, their opinion was again sought as to the success of the policy and the advisability of returning to the former method. All the foremen were found to be converted; and the change had come not through persuasion or even, it seems to me, through overmuch autocratic assertion of power. It had come through creating a total experience which, in its natural setting, showed the new way to be more advantageous for the foremen. The surrounding conditions were allowed to reshape their ideas as to how to get the departmental morale they wanted, and they found that they liked the new way better. Good · leadership had put the foremen through a successful learning process.

It is repetitious to say that learning takes place because of recognition of a problem to be solved or because of an urgently felt desire which is not satisfied. But these *are* the two great prime movers to new learning, and until they are called into use nothing happens. If industrial leaders would recognize and apply this principle about learning, it would surely yield a thousand-fold. Set people in a problem situation; guide the process by which *they* find the way out; stir people by the prompting of a new and strong desire; then help to show how *they* can satisfy it—it is this which constitutes good leadership strategy.

The relation of the leader as teacher to the learning process is thus crucial. He can help to supply facts included among which are the experiences of others; he can help to interpret facts; he can help to create and place people in problem situations where new and educational experiences will take place. He can inspire them to thought and to activity by his own interest in and enthusiasm for the project; but the learning itself must be done by each one afresh.

The Leader as Energizer.—The face-to-face leader certainly supplies by the contagious and energetic quality of his personality something which most people find indispensable if the leader is to hold them for long. Two facts stand out here: that almost everyone responds, at least occasionally, to the enthusiasm of some leader; and that most people require a good deal of personalizing of the objectives for which they will strive. This characteristic of human nature has undoubtedly been exploited in industry. "Popular" managers can often secure allegiance for ends which the led should not, in their own best interests, strive for. This has led many to be cynical about any personalizing of corporate aims, any deliberate centering of employee interest and loyalty in the personality of an attractive executive. But I submit that the real problem is not so much to be alarmed at any of the mild forms of hero worship which may occur as it is to be highly critical of the hero's aims. *Given the right kind of purposes* in the leader, and there is every good psychological reason for letting people get the energizing influence of a little personal devotion to him.

The leader will energize, also, not alone by being a radiating influence but by supplying the surrounding conditions which inspire to achievement. This may mean many things, from attractive buildings to well-organized production-control methods, incentive payment methods, unemployment compensation, honor rolls, and a thousand other measures. One particular feature which inspires when the leader uses it discreetly is *explicit appreciation of good work.* It is hardly an exaggeration to say that this one item alone can do more to help improve the working tone of most organizations than many more imposing and expensive procedures. For the whole tradition of industry is for executives to accept and expect hard work and to say something only if mistakes are made or inadequacy discovered.

Indeed, this condition is fostered today when the "exception principle," so called, rules so largely in management. When organizations are set up so that problems only come to an important executive when they constitute exceptions to standard practice or deviations from normal, the result is that the points which get the executive's attention are chiefly the deficiencies and failures. He may become involved in criticism to such an extent that it is easy for him to lose sight of the fact that he usually meets his subordinates on the unfavorable side. The one way to correct this is for him to be deliberately mindful of the value of encouragement and praise.

Obviously, people take praise differently, and to some it is a heady potion to be taken most sparingly. *But by and large, people yearn for, crave, and thrive on some occasional, affirmative mention by their executive superior of the good work that they are doing.* Appreciation energizes and stimulates in a way that executives rarely realize.

Let me introduce into the record an instance out of the experience of a former student, which substantiates this point.

The printing department, consisting of about twenty skilled workmen, in a paper box factory, had been known for over a year as a hotbed of sullen dissatisfaction bordering on revolt. The wage scale in the department was high—the turnover in labor always low. The foreman, known as a good production man, was lax in matters of discipline and sympathetic to an extreme with his men in their personal affairs. He seemed to be popular but was of the "old school" of foremen—jealous of his authority, telling his men just what they had to know and nothing more. The attitude of the department was hostile to the other departments. The printers turned out expert work and were very quick to pass the buck on any errors. The appearance of any of the printers on an athletic team or in one of the employees' associations was a sure sign of disturbances to come.

The foreman was dismissed and his place filled by a man of some vision, a strict disciplinarian, but just, and quick to give credit where credit was due. He was enthusiastic about the skill of the printers; enthusiastic about the high standing of the company. Within 2 months the presence of this new foreman had changed the department beyond recognition. A spirit of interest and cooperation began to be noticeable. The new foreman was bringing out the best in his men. Being a born leader, he knew good material when he saw it, and he made the most of it. The former foreman had destroyed the morale of really capable men by his own discontent and his distrust of every one, either above or below his rank.

The second instance relates to a coal mine and presents in explicit detail the incident briefly mentioned at the outset of the book.

A mechanical coal loader manned by the operator and three assistants was placed in our mine something over a year ago. This small crew displaced twenty hand loaders. The original cost of the loader is $13,000 and it is operated under heavy daily expense; much of the success of the machine depends upon the operating crew.

A man was chosen and carefully trained by the demonstrator to operate the new machine and his helpers were selected with discrimination. The machine gave an average daily output of 90 tons of coal and stayed at that average for several months. According to records of other mines that had the electrical machines installed, this average seemed very satisfactory. However, as our roof is particularly good and other conditions favorable for the operation of the mechanical loader, the superintendent thought that our record should be better and began to hunt about for leakage.

He noticed that there was dissension among the men. They did not pull together smoothly. The operator of the machine, while a college graduate and a willing worker, did not possess ability to gain cooperation among his men. When things went wrong he antagonized his men and generally ended by smashing things up a little more than they were when he started. The men grew to dislike the operator and dissipated their energy in arguments.

This lack of cooperation extended beyond the loading crew to the men who kept the machine supplied with empty cars and took the loaded cars away. There were frequent breakdowns, and considerable time was lost while the master mechanic's time went in on the repairs and adjustments. Expenses were on the increase.

Meanwhile, another loader was installed. A second man, always in harmony with the men around him, was chosen to operate machine number two.

The two machines worked side by side and number two worked up to the record of number one and for a few weeks held the same average. The operator of the second machine was studying his men as well as his machine. Each time there was something wrong he got down where the trouble was and helped the mechanic run it down and learn what caused it. His men got about and watched. Soon the operator and his men were able to eliminate or run down their own trouble and thus save the expense of the mechanic's time and also speed up the time given over to repair. To this operator and his crew the machine became a personal thing. They took pride in its achievements and took pride in keeping it in the best condition possible. "She's runnin' pretty" was an affectionate way the men had of showing their admiration. They were all pulling together—and pulling for their machine.

As time went on, there was less and less trouble. The machine worked more smoothly and continuously. "Runnin' pretty" expressed it. It began to show a gain over the record of number one each day. It struck an average of 100 tons. The superintendent took men from number one who seemed to be the cause of friction and transferred them to number two hoping to increase the efficiency of the first loader. By spurts the first machine ran its average up for a few days and then dropped back.

The company was satisfied with the record of number two but not the operator and not the superintendent. They were certain that it could do better. They studied the crew, eliminating a little friction here, a little antagonism there. They studied the thing until every leakage of energy and enthusiasm was eliminated. By stimulating a little good-natured rivalry between the two crews they kept the interest keyed up.

The crew of machine number two held a big advantage. They had a leader who led them; one who never asked his men to do anything that he did not lend a hand to; one who knew his machine and took pride in its achievements; one who knew his men and took pride in their achievements; one who encouraged his men instead of antagonizing them. The energy, interest, and enthusiasm of the second machine had been mobilized and directed to one purpose—the maximum output of coal with the minimum expense in operation. The average daily output of machine number two reached 200 tons and stayed there.[5]

I have deliberately devoted some space to these accounts because I cannot be too emphatic in stating that there is far too little outspoken appreciation today in all kinds of organizations. More of it would supply a much needed lubricant and stimulant, assuming always that it is discreetly used.

Mention should be made of one further condition which may supply an energizing force where the tradition is or can be built up. There are instances of which the work of coal mining offers a good example, where the workers do better work when not closely directed and when allowed to work on their honor. A feeling for the dignity and pride in working on one's honor is, of course, far from universal and it will not arise spontaneously. It is a cultivated product, but where it exists its moral value is great. With the increasing tendency to have a supervisor over the work of smaller groups of men, it is important to remember that adequate supervision is only half the story; the other half is a deliberate appeal to individual and group honor and pride in work which enables people to want to do their best without the necessity of too close oversight.

The Leader as Critic.—The task of criticism is so necessary that the manner in which criticism is conveyed should receive attention. Here, too, as in the case of giving orders, the tone of voice is important. And since the end in view is to change the way in which the worker is acting or thinking, the emphasis in criticism should be constructive. A mere reprimand is likely to leave the worker disgruntled or wounded in his self-respect.

Other valuable points in this connection are that criticism:

1. Should be square.
2. Should be definite—the man should know exactly what is wrong.
3. Should always include definite instructions as to how to do those particular things right.
4. Should not be accompanied by any "bawling out."
5. Should usually be given in private.[6]

The Dangers in Leadership.—No program for the development of leadership can be successfully executed which does not realize that certain dangers are likely to be encountered, hurtful alike to the leader and the led. What has been called the "will to power" describes a real fact about human nature. We are all familiar with the situation where a leader has found that power comes readily to him and thereafter takes short cuts to maintain his prestige. He then tends to become much less sensitive to criticism and suggestion. He may delight in the personal adulation that comes when the personalizing and hero-worshiping influences get unduly to work.

He may so quicken his own mental process that he gets too far ahead of those he is leading. It is comparatively easy for a brilliant executive to conceive policies and plans much more rapidly than they can be carried out all the way down through an organization. *To allow those led enough time to do what is required of them and what is involved in their sharing in a new educational experience is one of the important requirements of good leadership.*

The leader may also lose his sense of the value of continuously developing a cooperative technique of group action and be impatient if his way is not followed in every particular. That his way is the right way should not be held to be a foregone conclusion but should be regarded by him as a matter for education with his group.

Another serious danger especially likely to develop in big organizations is that the leader will become surrounded by "yes-men"—those who tell him only what he wants to hear and assent enthusiastically to everything he proposes. He must be at great pains to avoid the deceptions to which this situation leads; he must keep close to the *"pungent sense of effective reality."* This means keeping close enough to his following to know the flow of sentiment and opinion at first hand. The man whose principal contact with subordinates comes when he presses a button and they are summoned "onto the carpet" is in serious danger of getting away from an awareness of the public opinion of his group.

One way to get and hold a corrective view to offset some of these dangers is for all executive leaders to remind themselves occasionally that, in an important sense, *they are the servants of those at the bench or the counter; they are most effective when they best facilitate the hour-by-hour activity in the shop.* This is not the whole truth but it is an important phase of it to realize that the rank and file of the producing organization are the firing line and the front-line trenches. Everything that goes on behind the lines and "overhead" is, in reality, being done to enable the front line to go forward. The staff and its leaders are, in this sense, the servants of the privates of industry; and to look at the matter this way, at times, conduces to a proper sense of humility and proportion in the leaders.

Another aspect of this same truth is that the leader may come to think that his own aims and objectives are worthwhile *in themselves* without reference to the opinions and desires of those led. Nothing in the long run is so fatal to successful creative leadership as the attitude which says that when one's own ends are set up, other people's wills must be bent or broken, in order to secure their adherence to the leader's ends. Creative leadership means nothing if the leader does not realize that the fulfillment of life by each individual in his own way is a legitimate end which has always to be adjusted to the ends of the organization. The leader, it must repeatedly be emphasized, is not a beguiler, a bully, a seducer, or a hypnotist in respect to the purposes of those whom he leads. Only as he is a teacher and inspirer and one freely envisaging broader and broader aims can his appeal remain effective.

Dangers in Being Led.—The people who are led may, in turn, become the victims of a policy which does not sufficiently employ an educational motive. They are peculiarly in danger if at any time the leader develops pathological tendencies, as leaders have all too frequently been known to do under the strain of responsibility. If the leader has a physical infirmity or handicap, he may try to compensate for this by unduly aggressive conduct. If he finds some definite limitation in his mental or emotional equipment, he may try to compensate for this in some harmful way. Numberless examples of both of these phenomena could be cited. Those led are also peculiarly in danger where the leader does not for any reason keep up with the times, keep up with the facts of the technology of the enterprise or facts regarding the current temper of the members of the enterprise.

Conclusion.—Emphasis throughout this discussion of leadership has been upon the aspect of evolving purposes—upon the psychological process by which both leaders and led come to have a meeting of minds and desires because the desires are integral to the growth and fulfillment of each. It is because human nature works best this way, by learning through shared experiences and by sharing experience that it believes will bring it a sense of self-fulfillment and by evolving out of experience an awareness of what it really wants, that what are called "democratic tendencies" are abroad and are on the increase. Industrial leadership has, therefore, more and more to work under conditions of progressive awareness of democratic forces by all concerned as well as an increasing sympathy with them. As they are reflected in industrial behavior, these forces mean that people are more and more demanding that their purposes and aims shall be self-chosen and the realizing of them be self-achieved.

This does not mean nor imply necessarily that such forces are going to lead to wilful, uninspired, and unguided shifts of popular desire and aim. It is here that the new rôle and basic significance of leadership in industry appears. These inevitable and psychologically sound, democratic impulsions uniquely require the wisest kind of leadership and guidance. "A people," said Mill, "may be unprepared for good institutions, but to build a desire for them is a necessary part of the preparations." This is a dictum for the leader. His rôle is not merely to carry on with purposes already established. It is, in its best conception, to kindle and evoke new and finer aims—finer not because they conform to sentimental or arbitrary standards but because of the permanence, quality, and vigor of the satisfactions people experience in realizing them.

Industrial institutions, then, if they are to move in a more democratic direction—and there are evidences at hand that this is likely to be the case—require as never before a type of management in which creative leadership is the dominant note. They require this at every executive level, because the demand throughout business organizations is for structural arrangements and for an animating spirit in and through which people can grow in a sense of self-fulfillment—a sense secured not in their leisure hours alone but also in the process of living their industrial life. This insistence that industrial experience must itself become truly creative for the led no less than for the leader is the unique essence of the new leadership concept.

CHAPTER XIII

THE CREATION OF MORALE

Economy in the use of human and mechanical energy in the accomplishment of a given end is what is usually spoken of as "efficiency." Up to a point, it is obtainable by taking thought as to process and by having an explicit and fair labor contract. But more than efficiency is necessary for maximum performance, for sustained effort, for enthusiastic achievement. There is that "last touch which cannot be commanded." There is that zeal of whole-hearted and single-minded activity which makes the difference between an organization that merely operates and one that cooperates. That quality, that attitude and spirit, are what we mean by morale.

Morale is that attitude which results from the mobilizing of energy, interest, and initiative in the enthusiastic and effective pursuit of a group's purposes.

"Morale," says another writer, "is at bottom a state of will or purpose, and the first factor in any mature human purpose is knowledge, that is, knowledge of the thing to be gained by the purpose—the good to be reached."[1] This definition calls added attention to the relation of morale to purposes and objectives; and one reason why the place of purposes in behavior was stressed so greatly in Chap. X was because of the importance of an understanding of the close interrelation of sound purposes with good morale. What are sound purposes in this connection has already been suggested and will not need to be elaborated below.

Morale is, also, more than a condition of interest. Each worker can be interested in his own job, and morale still be poor. It is only as he is interested *in his relation to the organization* that the morale factor begins to develop. An effective grouping of

173

human wills interested in the purposes of an organization is what morale entails. And where that mobilization of desire has taken place, a working power has been generated which is considerably in excess of the sum of the working power of an equal number of isolated or emotionally uninvolved individuals.

Generally speaking, this truth of the "plus values" in team play does not have to be proved, it is so widely recognized. It is rather the necessity of adopting the combination of policies and methods which induce it that requires to be stressed.

Morale further implies performance which is self-sustained, enthusiastic, and in a measure self-directed. Under good morale, activity generates naturally from within, because a true identity of self-purposes and organization purposes has been attained. There has come about a change from a relationship of contract to one of willing and voluntary cooperation.

The Administration of Morale.—Recognition that morale is of tremendous value over and above technical and mechanical perfection has been relatively slow in coming in industry. But today the search for the conditions which assure morale is going on more seriously than ever. And no executive leader worthy of the name is ignoring the task of morale building. Naturally, a condition which relates so integrally to the minds and attitudes of every member of the organization is affected by almost every executive act. But from the administrative point of view, there must be some executive specially charged to keep the morale factors to the fore in managerial thinking. And the personnel manager is now recognized as the logical morale officer of industrial and mercantile organizations. As such he is the one who studies the attendant conditions which will foster and perpetuate good morale, the one who plans and advances the institutional provisions which tend to assure it.

The Factors in Morale Building.—Fortunately, knowledge of the elements that contribute to morale does not have to be arrived at *a priori*. The experience of all sorts of organizations, including armies, athletic teams, churches, fraternal bodies, and the like, points the way to what must be done. A reasonably complete list of the items will naturally include many points which are more fully discussed in other connections. Hence, in discussing the factors named below, I shall mention only their special relation to the morale problem.

The factors in good morale are:

1. Good physical health.
2. Good mental health.
3. Effective leadership.
4. Explicit purposes known and believed in by the group
5. Knowledge of the impressive traditions of the group.
6. Adequate knowledge of technique by each member.
7. A sense of fair treatment in relationships with others in the group.
8. A reasonable sense of the permanency of one's tenure in the group.
9. A sense of being recognized as partners in and not as servants of the group.
10. Clear identification of each as a member.
11. Knowledge of the results of each individual's and the whole group's progress.
12. Conscious organization of approval of good results.
13. Some participation in the results of the efforts of the group.
14. Confidence in the success of the group's undertaking.
15. Conscious assumption of responsibility by every member of the group.
16. The support of favorable home and community conditions and attitudes.
17. The elimination of unfounded rumors.

Good Physical Health.—Napoleon's dictum about an army marching on its stomach applies with force in industry. People cannot sustain enthusiasm if they are hungry or ill or in a chronic state of semi-fatigue. The attack on the health problem throughout the larger industrial organizations can hardly be carried too far—the only serious problem being as to the extent to which its cost should be borne by the employer.

Good Mental Health.—The serious importance of eliminating the worry, fear, anxiety, suspicion, anger, and hatred which displaces the positive emotional drives is being increasingly recognized. Attention has also been well directed recently to the ill effects of bad "reveries" or sustained daydreams which are pessimistic, hostile, or unrealistic in character. The kinds of thoughts that characteristically flow in one's stream of consciousness influence attitudes and enthusiasms; and individuals whose reveries are unwholesome or whose prevailing moods are morose or negative can be a very bad influence among their fellows.

In part, this is a problem which can be tackled through company policies on wages, health insurance, unemployment pay, pensions, death benefits, and the like. And, in part, it is a problem of helping certain individuals along recognized psychotherapeutic lines.

Good Leadership.—Leadership of the creative sort already discussed is indispensable. The good leader can often by his own devotion and ability make up for the absence of other factors which really should be present.

Good Purposes.—Second to none in importance as a morale-building factor is the explicit adoption of purposes for the organization which are known to all its members and believed in by them. The experience of the World War on this point was most instructive and conclusive. It showed that, in the long run, the relation of knowledge to effort was exceedingly close. Armies and stay-at-homes "carried on" on the basis of information about "war aims" or purposes, which was prepared and disseminated with the greatest care. Probably never before in the world's history has there been such a huge educational effort to convince friend and foe alike that the purposes of each group were right and should be supported.

In industry in those companies where the purposes in control are liberal and colored with a social outlook, the ways and means of making all the rank and file understand what the company is trying to do are selected with utmost solicitude. And that executive group is wise indeed which realizes that there is a distinct limit to the kinds of purposes for which employee support can be successfully sought. In general, *the purposes that can get support, if and when they are understood by the great body of workers, are those which can be shown to a reasonable being to fit in with and contribute to the attaining of the things in life which he himself wants.* Given such purposes, and the foundation for morale is firmly laid. Given any other kind of purposes, and all the other efforts toward morale are, *over a long period of time,* of negligible value. The saying about not being able to fool all the people all of the time applies here.

And how to make good purposes not only intellectually understood but also emotionally gripping and compelling is one of industry's big problems.

Knowledge of Traditions.—In all the older institutions of a religious and social sort, the fact of an honorable history, a long tradition, a worthy name, numerous adherents, and social prestige gives to new members a sense of value in association which helps build and support morale. Just what the equivalent of all this is in industry it is still too early to be sure. But there are already companies in which the record of fine service, a notable product, the reputation for quality, are of a character to be impressive and attractive to the employees if the story is translated to them in popular form.

Knowledge of Technique.—Good morale implies the fact of good workmanship. Good workmanship implies the existence of an adequate training program. The kind of training method amplified elsewhere in this book is, thus, one of the best contributing factors to morale.

A Sense of Fair Treatment.—Enthusiastic support of a group aim cannot exist if a sense of injustice or hidden grievances prevails. In all the dealings between a corporation and its workers, whether in the terms of the labor contract or in the face-to-face dealings of leaders and men, the group must feel that even-handed justice prevails, that favoritism is absent, that merit wins, that minor maladjustments will be recognized and removed. The whole machinery of open, fifty-fifty, joint dealing through representative bodies has this as one of its vital objects. The great problem is to be sure that what executives conceive to be "fair play" seems equally fair to the rank and file. For this sense of justice is a highly relative and shifting factor which alters as various social forces play upon the minds of the group.

A Sense of Permanency of Tenure.—This item in the morale-building program should be double starred and underscored. Thankfully, more attention than ever is now being paid to regularizing employment and compensating workers during periods of involuntary idleness. But from a national point of view, only a beginning has been made. Experience in industry on this point, short though it is, is conclusive that morale cannot be maintained unless provision is made in some way for reasonable permanency of position and income.

A Sense of Partnership.—The difference in the quality of the relationship in any organization of a partner and a servant is a commonplace observation. In professional circles, where quite large partnerships prevail, the incentive to the younger members of the group lies definitely in the hope of ultimately being taken into the charmed circle of partners. It is interesting to observe that in those progressive corporations where morale is being deliberately sought and worked for, there is some formal procedure of being admitted into the real ranks. The Columbia Conserve Company and the Dennison Manufacturing Company, for example, both have what amounts to probationary periods, after which one qualifies for the special benefits of permanent membership in the group. Of course, the partnership relation goes in quality beyond the perfunctory and contractual attitude of master and servant. That is one of its psychological values. Energies are enlisted, sources of power are tapped, which one usually seeks in vain to secure from servants. The implications of this thought are as yet hardly appreciated or considered in many corporations; but until they are, the finer manifestations of morale cannot and do not appear.

A Sense of Common Identity.—In an army, one knows one's own by the uniform; in the lodge, there are secret identifying symbols and signs; in the church, one is recognized, in part, by familiarity with the ritual. What is there in a corporation with 5,000 employees that can provide some comparable sense of identity with one's partners and associates in the enterprise? The problem, while not of first-rank importance, does merit attention. In some ways, especially as the size of a corporate group increases, it is desirable that both in the shop and, perhaps, in the local community, the individual workers should be able to know who their associates are.

Knowledge of Progress and Results.—Both for individuals and for the group as a whole, knowledge of how they are coming out, in terms of quantity and quality of product and in terms of earnings of the department or the business, is a necessary factor. Milestones of progress are psychologically necessary to hearten all of us for continued application at the same task. Every other important type of organized human effort reckons with this fact, and industry must come to it much more than at present.

Organization of Approval.—One important value growing out of a knowledge of results is the ability to accord praise for good results. Since one of the strongest traits in human nature is this craving for the approval of our associates, too much emphasis can hardly be laid on this feature. Whether the approval comes in non-pecuniary honors, promotions, changes in title, or higher pay is almost of less importance than the fact that one's fellows thereby know that one has won a coveted recognition and is raised, for a moment at least, and in a real way, above the common throng.

Participation in Results.—In the church, one gains as a member the peace of soul which its ministrations are designed to give; in the army, one shares more or less directly in the "spoils of victory"; in the university, one gains in knowledge and friendship and has a sense of being of an elect few. It may, therefore, be seriously contended that in industry there must be some recognition of the psychological importance of having every member of the group share in some way acceptable to him in the results of the group's effort. Those results in industry today are, to a large extent, disclosed in corporate income. And here, again, the companies which are morale-conscious have been the first ones to work on the problem of profit sharing. The growth of experiments with this device seems conclusive evidence that executives are more or less consciously recognizing that a sharing of the results is a vital element in the maintenance of rank-and-file enthusiastic support of corporate objectives. This is not the same thing as saying that profit sharing of some sort is a good immediate incentive at the job. Experience does not seem to show this to be true. But it is true, from a long-run point of view, that corporate loyalty and zeal to be sustained over a period of years must contemplate some sharing of the successes of the corporation by all those who have helped to bring them about.   This is the point at which many efforts at morale building waver and weaken.

Confidence in Success.—Most human beings are so constructed that unless their effort is carried on in an atmosphere of hopefulness and confidence, it soon drops and attention almost involuntarily turns elsewhere.   Fortunately, in a young country like America, where economic opportunity has been great, a spirit of confidence in corporate workers has not until recently had to be a matter of concern.   But as economic conditions become more stratified and economic power more centralized, the factor of individual confidence and hopefulness both for himself and for his group is one to which attention must increasingly be given. An interesting example of contrast in the amount of individual hopefulness which can be expected is, at the present moment, supplied by the contrast between labor conditions on the Interborough Rapid Transit Company in New York City and the Philadelphia Rapid Transit Company in Philadelphia.   The officials of the former company confront a problem of great complexity in the balance-sheet outcome of their labors, which makes the development of a fine morale a tremendously uphill task, and the results appear to be exactly what one would expect. In Philadelphia, under surrounding conditions of well conceived personnel work and a progressively improved profit situation, the morale appears to be at a very high point.

Assumption of Responsibility.—Loyalty to a group's efforts does not thrive under conditions of complete absence of responsibility.   There must be active participation, and the participation of each should be in close relation to his ability to achieve and grow.   This implies that executives who seek morale should consciously strive to decentralize responsibility so that each member of the group will feel that he truly has some chance to show what he can do to contribute to the corporate effort.

Supplying Favorable Outside Support.—Good morale does not develop, of course, if, in the home or elsewhere in the outside community, there is a constant fire of criticism and hostile sentiment toward the group in question. Usually, one is bound to admit, such outside detraction from the reputation of a company does not come without some justification. But, occasionally, there is deliberate and unwarranted unfavorable propaganda of this sort on the part of competitors, rivals, labor agitators, or others. In any case, if a company knows that a whispering campaign is under way to which the workers are exposed, it is essential that steps be taken to see that unjustified comments are stopped or that justified criticism is promptly met by correction of the trouble.[2]

Eliminating Rumors.—Both from within and without the corporation's walls, false rumors may be spread which prey disastrously on good morale. Usually the line executive close to the rank and file is the one in a position to meet this problem best. He should be aware of the danger of letting such rumors get underway; he should have his ear to the ground; he should work closely with the personnel department and his higher executives to supply full information which will correct wrong impressions. Rumors are very likely to start from individuals who have a real or fancied grievance. A definite characteristic of certain types of mental disorder is the conjuring up of such rumors for purposes of compensatory self-assertion. Understanding of this tendency and early recognition of its expression are highly desirable aids of a preventive kind in the equipment of all executives.

These, then, are the factors which demand attention when good morale is sought. And if only the briefest mention has been made of them, that is because they touch upon many fields of effort more fully discussed elsewhere. In fact, it should now be clear that all the activities of the personnel executive who is the special morale custodian should be contributing directly to the objective of good morale.

Instruments and Agencies in Morale Building.—Similarly, a consideration of the ways and means of carrying out the educational program, which the cultivation of morale implies, would lead considerably afield. If, however, one realizes the close relation of adequate knowledge to good morale and knows, also, that such knowledge when conveyed must be touched with the warmth of emotion and conviction, the elements of the method will suggest themselves.

House organs or employee magazines can be a helpful agency. So, also, can booklets describing company policy, personnel provisions, and history. Other helpful items in increasing use include:

1. Booklets descriptive of processes, products, and uses of products.
2. Motion pictures of the same.
3. Occasional lectures by executives and selected outsiders.
4. Intelligent use of a company library.
5. Poster campaigns on special subjects.
6. Honor rolls.
7. Special incentives to take special educational courses.
8. Some use of music, as a company band, musical club, etc.
9. Intelligent and honest publicity in the local community.
10. Intelligent and honest use of company slogans, trade marks, and insignia.
11. Occasional and discriminating use of non-industrial types of group activity such as athletic teams, dramatics, theater parties, picnics, etc.

The Minor Executive and Morale.—No discussion of morale should ignore the important rôle played in its development by those executives who are closest to the individual workers in hour-by-hour contacts. Obviously, they must be convinced that good morale is of value; they must know its psychological sources and the objective ways and means which will call out and support the positive motives which morale implies; and they must have frequent and convincing evidence from their higher officers that morale is also seriously desired by them.

More specifically, they must realize that this is, in large part, an individual problem and that each worker supplies, to some extent, a special and unique challenge to his ingenuity. He will find, for example, that he can enlist the aid of his more intelligent and enthusiastic workers to influence the less intelligent. He can quickly run rumors to earth. He can see when company policies have not been "sold" to his men and when, in turn, his men's troubles have not received adequate attention from the company. He is in a position to give at the right moment that word of commendation which can be so heartening to the individual worker. And because all this is so, any executive training course which omits from its subjects the topic of Morale and How to Get It, is ignoring a vital constructive force.

CHAPTER XIV

THE TECHNIQUE OF GROUP ACTION

The best formula for social betterment would emphasize especially the improvement of the conditions of group activity with a view to making it more worthy of the efforts of the individual and more interesting and satisfying to him.

—R. S. WOODWORTH.[1]

The conscious use of small groups to forward the constructive thinking of the members of a corporation about its policies and methods is a possibility but newly recognized in the executive world. But that it has great potentialities it will be my purpose to suggest in the present chapter.

There is, in the first place, the always present problem which every executive and teacher faces of trying to get ideas translated into actions. Indeed, much of the so-called "educational work" of the world seems to go for nothing because the students never get to the point of using what they supposedly know. This is true within corporate groups in their training work exactly as it is everywhere else. There are so many good ideas abroad; why is there not more action embodying them?

Group conferences have shown that they lend themselves peculiarly to being the medium of individual clarification, formulation, and projection into concrete activities of events and ideas which may, until that point, be nebulous and unrelated to going realities. If in some way a group, by the impact of mind on mind and by insistence on a purpose of effective objectified results, can make ideas wieldy, practical, and available for use in an organization, that is no small feat; and it represents a big step forward in making education result in new and fruitful experiences.

Concretely, the problems that I am thinking about are of the following sort: Here is a management that is anxious to raise its wage levels but realizes that it cannot do it under market conditions except by new economies in the production process. How can it get this idea across to its employees? Not by preaching, not by posters, not by mass meetings. Cannot some use be made of small group conferences where this problem can be discussed and brought home to the hour-by-hour life of each man at the bench in terms of his working methods?

Or, again, there is the case of a company which has instituted some form of stock sales to employees or profit sharing or unemployment compensation, but which feels that the employees do not realize their personal part in the maintenance of such a plan, do not grasp the obligations that it puts upon them to uphold their end and do their part. My point is that the way they will most quickly absorb new ideas and attitudes is not by bookish, conventional educational methods but by carefully guided group deliberation and study of all the facts and of their relation to them, both actual and potential. It is this kind of mental problem as well as the equally significant one of securing employee contributions to the total creative thinking about corporate progress which I believe group activity has shown that it can help to solve.

What is a Group?—A group, in the sense here used, is a conscious coming together of individuals for the accomplishment of some specific results. A board of directors, an operating committee of executives, a staff group of departmental heads, a foremen's council, a shop committee—these are examples of groups frequently met in business. The group may be a regularly constituted body meeting at stated times; or it may be a special conference or committee brought together for a single specific task. The principles governing successful operation remain the same. If the group wants to economize time and energy in forwarding its agreed ends, it must take thought about its group mental processes and the development of its group total situation.

A group is, of course, an *organization of minds*. If that fact is held in view, its possibilities will be more likely to be realized. For the fact is that minds in activity together will respond and will reason and imagine in ways similar to individual minds but with enough additional elements in the process to make it a specially stimulating and enlightening one to all involved. It is these additional influences which it is most important to discover and use.

The Whole Greater than the Sum of Its Parts.—The hypothesis upon which group action is urged is that in group thinking *the new ideas evolved are more than the sum of the individual ideas* which might have been offered by the same persons sitting alone and preparing memoranda of proposals on the matter in hand. All experience shows that the stimulus, fertilization, criticism, and suggestion of group participation in the thinking process produces a new idea, a creative contribution, which will be distinctly superior in practical value to ideas evolved in any other way. Not only that, but the process of reaching the idea is such that, in a unique way, it becomes quickly and thoroughly a part of the working motives and active influences in the mental life of those who have been a party to reaching it. Thought and action are wedded more closely than they are when the thinking activity is isolated and subjective.

And there is the further value that group participation in creative thinking helps to keep executives and subordinates aware in a practical way of that truth which has already been discussed in this book, namely, that the total situation, setting, background, elements, and forces in any human problem are not fixed and static *but are always evolving.* That the total situation is an evolving one requiring that an understanding of it be kept constantly corrected by a knowledge of any new elements in it, is a generalization which is accepted readily enough. But it is one which will be remembered and acted upon in real life only if one provides structural mechanisms and plans designed to keep people informed of evolving factors. And the kind of probings and promptings on new aspects of a problem which group conference entails assures, in a unique way, that problems are handled not as solid, impervious entities but as fluid, changing issues requiring wide-awake and shifting attacks.

If, then, there are these substantial psychological values in group activity, there is here a productive force, a synthesizing medium for creative thought, which any organization ignores to its great loss.

Group Action as Experience Sharing.—A second hypothesis underlying the new interest in group deliberation is that, for most people in practical affairs, experience is the great teacher. Of course, this is a platitude. But the psychological reason why it is so, the extent to which it is true, and the relation of this truth to the uses of group action deserve special attention. In discussing learning, we saw the necessary part played by motor activity and the experience of going through problem-solving situations. The executive or teacher enables people, in a greater or lesser degree, *to share his experience.* The way of their learning about the matter in question is the way of sharing the activity in order that they may come naturally and voluntarily to share in the knowledge and understanding, first, of the elements of the problem and, then, of the possible solutions which can be applied.

To expect real agreement by any process short of this is out of the question. Real agreement on purposes throughout a corporate group means, it cannot be too much stressed, this intellectual and emotional involvement in the processess of solving its own problems and developing its own purposes. This process of enabling or requiring others to share executive experience, as a basis for eventually sharing conclusions and convictions, is education in the best sense, provided always the solutions and purposes are sound and true. For this is the process—and the surest process—which assures that actions are prompted *from within*, are the result of a genuine concern about the issue at stake, carry the intellectual and emotional endorsement of those involved; and are not merely inarticulate, reluctant, or uninformed acquiescence.

In what way, then, is experience shared in a helpful manner by group activity? The answer should be apparent, since over a period of time group action supplies a splendid medium in which the leader's knowledge naturally pools with that of those led to go forward to the discovery of new facts and a new orientation of the problem.

Take, for example, the case of a board of directors which has charged its president with the problem of finding out whether or not they should enter into export trade.   It will be relatively easy for him to reach a decision after study of the facts.   But to convince his directors that his decision should also be their decision is a much more difficult task.   Fundamentally, if done rightly, it is a task of getting them to share his experience with the facts of the problem so that they, too, will feel in a position to reach an informed decision on their own account.   And the group meetings, with their airing of all possible objections and difficulties, will be the best possible medium for the pooling of ideas and the formulation of a policy which takes account of all phases of the problem.

The alternative to this and the procedure so frequently encountered is that an executive makes up his mind about a new policy and then, when he is convinced that he is right, goes ahead and rides roughshod over all differences and objections.   Such an executive may, after his policy has been tested and proved sound, get his colleagues lined up with him.   But he will never have them lined up *cooperatively and helpfully in advance* by such domineering methods.   And since often this advance cooperation is the key condition of the really successful working of a new policy, he is taking the longer, harder, and slower road if he still sticks to his strong-arm, individualistic tactics.

Equally dangerous, from the fundamental educational point of view which the corporate leader should cherish, is the frequently met disposition of minor executives and members of the rank and file to say, "If that's what the big boss says, it must be right; and we'll stand by whatever he decides."   This is flattering to the leader; but it is the wrong attitude for him to encourage. For, once he makes a serious mistake on this basis, confidence in his judgment is almost sure to be gravely and permanently damaged.

In short, group conference proves to be an agency well adapted to the group's and the leader's education, because (*a*) it enables the group to share in advance the leader's ideas; (*b*) it enables the leader to get the benefit of the group's ideas; and (*c*) it enables new combinations of ideas to be evolved which constitute creative thinking in the best sense.

Group Action Affects Individuals.—In all proposed changes in corporate plans and methods, the executive comes back each time to the fact that *it is a succession of individuals whom he has to influence.* In the hurry of effort to get mass effects, in the reaction which is general today against methods that smack of "individual conversion" and "personal evangelism," it is too often overlooked by leaders that, after all, *it is individuals who must be reached and influenced.* More often than executives realize, their training job should be in the direction of personal contact and influence with other executives who stand in the way of change.

What, then, is the connection between this necessity for individual instruction and the use of group action? There seem to me to be several vital connections. First, the full force of a problem can be conveyed in conference. The difficulty is seen to exist not merely in the leader's mind but in the minds of others in the group. Second, the need for prompt action can be stressed by several in the group. And, third, the reenforcement of numbers can often be given to the wise proposals offered by one individual as a solution. Thus, obstinate and conservative members of the group can be worked on by the impact of the group's thought and emotion. That alone may not be enough to change their views; but it can be an important addition to other influences of a more personal sort which the leader brings to bear.

Group Objectives.—The purpose for which the group is being organized should determine its size and the whole manner of its operation. At least three clearly different possible objectives at once appear. A group may be organized (*a*) to create enthusiasm, (*b*) to impart information, (*c*) to foster deliberation and reach decisions.

A body that might grow to several thousands in number can effectively stir up enthusiasm. A body of several hundreds that hears one man lecture may thus receive information. But my concern in this chapter is only with groups having the third kind of purpose. Such deliberative groups must be small and compact in size. And if we focus attention on the conditions of securing their maximum effectiveness, we find available a large body of experiment and experience with effective methods of which use can be made to bring group thinking to much greater usefulness than is usual today.

These requisite conditions may be listed as follows:

1. Have the group the right size—small and compact.
2. Select its members to assure the voicing of every important divergent point of view on the question under discussion.
3. Surround the group with the right physical conditions.
4. Protect it from interruption.
5. Limit the length of its sessions to a fairly short period—usually an hour and a half is long enough unless the members are well disciplined in consecutive thinking.
6. Assure the right preparation for the meeting by issuing an advance agenda and memorandum of factual data.
7. Select the right chairman.
8. Have him understand the successive steps necessary in facilitating the process of bringing divergent views into harmony.
9. Have him recognize the types of intellectual and emotional complexes which he may confront among the individuals in conference.
10. Use the best possible method for registering decisions.
11. Adopt some system for recording decisions and transmitting them to other affected groups and persons.
12. Recognize the limits upon the nature of the work which a group as such can do.

It will now be useful to explain in more detail the procedures entailed in assuring these conditions.

The Group's Size and Character.—Up to a point, the group's size may be dictated by the necessity of representing important differences of opinion—either personal or functional in character. But this would not normally require a group of more than fifteen persons, which is as large as is usually desirable unless there is a remarkably skilful chairman who can keep as many as twenty people really involved in the discussion. A dozen people or less is ordinarily the most effective number.

Since the whole idea of group activity is to bring harmony and unity out of divergence and conflict, the recognition of conflict should not be looked at askance. One unique element in the use of groups for deliberation is this emphasis upon the value of different points of view and even of different purposes. Executive leaders must face realities here in acknowledging that widely different points of view *do* exist in an executive or representative functional group and that often conflicting purposes have grown up or are inherent in the outlook of some subordinate group (see Chap. X).

The selection of group members should, then, be made with reference to the matters to be discussed and the several distinct points of view about them which would typically arise.[2]

The Physical Surroundings.—Too much stress cannot be laid upon surrounding deliberative bodies with all the prestige and the conveniences that will conduce to real thinking. Without going into meticulous detail, it is worth while to suggest that the room should not be too large, should have good acoustics, good ventilation (this is very important), good natural and artificial lighting, chairs which are not too uncomfortable, a table—preferably round, large enough for each member to sit at. To have managers on one side of a table and employees on the other is not good psychology. The room should be located where it is quiet enough for people to be heard when discussing in a conversational tone of voice. And arrangements should be such that members are not called out or summoned to the telephone during the meeting. This is one of several good reasons why no session should be allowed to run more than an hour and a half. Another is that most people cannot sustain close attention and real thinking for a longer period.

The Agenda.—Preparations for the meeting should include advance notice to all as to what is to be discussed. On some matters, an advance memorandum of all the relevant facts should be distributed as well. Complete access to the facts, preliminary knowledge of the issues—these are vital points if time in conferences is to be economized and soundness of conclusions is to be assured.

The Chairman.—A good chairman is the beginning of a good conference. If he is the right sort, it will matter little to all whether he is appointed or elected, is of management or of rank and file, or holds his post for a longer or shorter period. For in his hands and in his handling of individuals lie all the issues of the group's conference success. He must, for example, know his objectives both in terms of methods of conference and in terms of the group's contribution to corporate purposes. For a conference group may have any one of three outcomes to its deliberations. There may be *subordination* of the views of the weaker to those of the stronger. There may be *compromise*, where some or all are knowingly prepared to concede some of their points temporarily. Or, there may be *integration*, where a new formula or idea or program has been worked out embodying the really desired elements in the thought of each member. The good chairman will normally have integration for his aim.

To attain this implies several definite efforts on his part. First, he should see that everyone understands the pending problem. This means a further analyzing of the problem into its separable elements, some of which will usually be found to be simple and readily disposed of. Thus, the time and ingenuity of the group should be spent on the really troublesome elements. Once these are made clear, a forceful statement of each divergent view is necessary. Every genuine difference of outlook should be explicitly voiced. The chairman should encourage this. He should help the timid to be articulate—to verbalize in ways that will be clear to all. He should discourage the bold from repetition. He should check digressions from the main argument—his tact and courage on this point should be exemplary.

He can help, too, by keeping everyone's mind clear when differences or clashes arise by helping them to distinguish between misunderstandings arising out of confusion about meanings and those which arise from conflicts of aims. The former frequently arise and can be quickly cleared up by care in definition. The latter must be made plain to all as conflicts, as the first step toward a new adjustment.

In a word, the atmosphere of a debate in which one makes "points" should give way to one of truth seeking in which everyone is helped to make himself clear to all and, that done, to think how the differing thoughts of all can be carried forward to a new idea to which all will give hearty support.

The chairman should then be able to sense when the discussion has run its course and be able to "pull the threads together" or get some one clear-headed member to do it for him.   If the talk has been made to lead toward a truly creative solution, an outlining of that solution by someone will be essential at this point but not before.   It will, indeed, require a sixth sense to combine all the qualities needed to make the chairman into this paragon of patience, tact, good pedagogy, and creative imagination!

He will succeed best, furthermore, when he is additionally equipped—equipped with conscious knowledge of the sources of the characteristic human reactions which he is almost sure to encounter.   He will, for instance, realize that people's hour-by-hour work preoccupations tend to influence their habits of thought and outlook.   And he must expect to find serious temperamental differences as among general executives with a broad view, staff executives with a special view, office workers, salesmen from the road, craftsmen, and machine feeders.

Again, he will often find that group surroundings tend with many to accentuate their typical characteristics.   The shy tend, usually, to become more shy; the bold, to become more bold in group action.   But just to emphasize the variety of human reactions, he will find, it should be pointed out, that in some people in the presence of groups there arises a desire to act in a way opposite to their normal individual responses, by way of compensation.

Another point for the chairman to watch is the tone of voice of the members of the group.   It is likely to reflect prevailing mental attitudes.   If people's voices become strident, loud, and disputatious, an element is creeping into the discussion which makes a consideration of the problem on its merits exceedingly difficult.   The chairman can by the right use of his own voice and by an occasional private word of warning help to keep the vocal tone of the discussion friendly, impersonal, and deliberative in character.

The Members' Mental Traits.—Experience shows that conference members tend to fall into certain types as regards their reactions to the discussion.   There are, as Dr. Alfred D.

Sheffield has pointed out, (1) those with a deep conviction, whose minds are virtually closed on the matter in hand. (2) There are those with a long experience which is limited to one narrow phase of the subject. They are those who "have been at this game for 30 years and I tell you it won't work any different." (3) There are those who take any discussion personally as a reflection on their own work, and who feel constrained to defend themselves as their contribution to the meeting. (4) There are those who personify troubles or settle them by a phrase—who see "the big boss" as the cause of every trouble, or "the capitalist system" as the basis of all ills. (5) There are those who oversimplify problems in other ways by seeing only a part of the cause or a part of the cure. (6) There are those with a strong authoritarian habit of mind who can be swung in any direction suggested by those whose authority and prestige they respect. And there are, no doubt, others personifying other stereotyped reactions. But the last, rarest, and best type, if integration is ever to come, comprises those with a really scientific habit of mind who are willing to "prove all things and hold fast to that which is good." It is these individuals who will be the "leaven in the lump" of any group, who should be encouraged and urged to help their fellow members to reach reasoned and sound conclusions.

The chairman who knows that reactions like the above are almost inevitable from some of his group can equip himself to lessen the inevitable frictions to which they will give rise. He can get those with invincible convictions to state their case fully. That done, they always feel better! He can often by a little preliminary touch of humor or banter—but not by sarcasm— lighten the tension of these perfervid presentations of deep conviction. He can point out to those with a long but partial experience some of the other phases of the problem. He can, if he is very adroit, make those suffering from defense reactions of fear, inferiority, vanity, or face-saving see that the group action seeks a larger end than merely the criticism of some member. Those who oversimplify, he can, over a period of time, help to see the tremendous complexity of most issues. And to those who toady to authority, he can make it clear—as can the organization's head executives at other times—that what is wanted is not bootlicking but independent and constructive ideas on the point at stake.

Reaching a Decision.—If a full and free discussion has been held and a solution has been outlined which seems to represent a real integration, the group then faces the question of deciding how it will vote or otherwise register its agreement. Any method of group voting after a caucus of smaller groups within the whole has been held, is psychologically unsound and bad pedagogy. Where this is now done in industry, it means that the employer group casts one vote and the employee group one, with the grave likelihood of a deadlock. Each member should at all times be encouraged to think and act as an individual. And if a consensus of individual agreements can be obtained without resort to a vote, that is surely the best way of all. What the Quakers call obtaining "the sense of the meeting" has much to be said for it as a rational way of reaching decisions. Under these conditions, those few who may still not be completely in favor of the new idea do not have to appear obstinate or conspicuous by voting "no"; yet, on the other hand, they tacitly allow themselves to see the new idea adopted and given a chance— in the course of which their own acceptance of it may gradually become more whole-hearted. If there is voting, unanimity is, of course, the ideal. But provision should always be made for allowing plans to be adopted if some substantial majority favors them.

Limits to Group Action.—It is probably true that the use of groups for creative deliberation has been retarded by the temptation to expect too much of them and to overextend their field of activity. If group action is considered by executives first and foremost as an *educational medium* and secondarily as a policy- or method-creating agency, the best results on both counts will be secured. For the tradition in industry for several generations and the mental habits which have resulted are, of course, at quite opposite poles from those here being urged. And the prevailing attitude of subservience and passivity in the rank and file cannot be expected to give way in a month or even a year to a completely self-respecting one where the most productive results will be achieved through group deliberation.   Before people can create together mentally, they must be able to communicate clearly, without reservations and inhibitions; and they must be able to grasp the intricacies of the problem before them. The educational work required for this preliminary state of affairs is the first task for many kinds of groups; and obviously it is a task which cannot be hurried.   Time, it should be emphasized, is of the essence of the successful development of group thinking into its finest flowering.

Interesting testimony on this point comes from William P. Hapgood, whose methods of utilizing group deliberation in the Columbia Conserve Company have been marked by great patience and foresight.   He says:[3]

During the process of securing the confidence of the workers in the sincerity of the owners we set up an educational plan by means of which more and more of the workers were taught the problems of management. This school, called the Council, consisted of meetings regularly twice a month, and sometimes as frequently as three times a week, in which problems of interest to the workers, and of interest to the business, were discussed, and decided upon.   It inevitably happened that in the beginning, and continuing for some years, most of the difficult problems were decided by a few employes, and those mainly in the more important offices.   I say this inevitably happened because the technical knowledge of the business in the beginning, and for some years later, rested largely among those in the more important positions.   Before those in other positions would enter fairly freely and with confidence into important decisions they had to become more or less technicians themselves.

Through our experience I can answer the question as to whether workers can be taught to manage their own industries positively to the effect that workers can be taught to manage their own business, if the technicians in the beginning who understand the problems are willing to impart their knowledge to the workers.   In my judgment the only way they can be given this knowledge is by actually entering into management and being permitted, in fact being urged, to make their own decisions.   I know they will respect the judgment of those more able than they until such a time as they feel confident of their own ability.

The other important limit on group action is upon the kind of action. A group's executive function must be radically limited. The detailed work must be assigned to individuals. And where reports back to the group are called for and where subcommittees are asked to do special things, the only way to get efficient results is, at the beginning, to set a time on a subsequent agendum for the matter in question to be followed up and reported on. Group deliberation can, of course, be executive in the sense of its bringing about the reaching of executive policies by agreement. But when such new policies are adopted, there comes the further problem, not to be ignored, of assuring the transmission and interpretation of that policy to all members of the larger organization. The machinery for assuring this is the *machinery of coordination.*

An important distinction is thus to be observed between the process of integration, which may and should take place as a result of effective group deliberation, and the process of coordination, which is the task of providing structural arrangements of a conference sort throughout the organization in order to facilitate the transmitting, interpreting, and carrying out of policies.[4]

Both of these processes are necessary in forwarding the corporate group's ends. And unless special attention is paid to the coordinative end of the problem, the values of integration may be seriously impaired. For nothing is easier than for a small group of informed individuals to agree on a new way of action, only to have the larger groups which they represent never come to understand and agree about the solution adopted. The small group conference has ultimately to share its experience of fact finding and creative thinking with the members of the several groups represented. Merely sharing decisions will not serve. That is why attention to the machinery of coordination becomes so important.

Conclusion.—The end of group activity as here considered is, then, the building up of the "functional unity" of an organization as the result of a process of creating group unity of thought and desire through integration. Integration means that agreement is reached on a new and creative level of idea or plan, where the best in the desires of all is embodied, and all know and feel that what they really want is being furthered and secured. Group action is essential to integration; but it must be carried on under the wisest possible guidance. Success in furthering group integration requires excellent leadership; it requires a wide diffusion of the necessary knowledge; it requires real fertility of thought on the part of as many members of the group as possible.

What have been called the "plus values" of group action are needed in all organizations that want to be more than an aggregation of hands and foot-pounds of energy. And any organization leader who will make a beginning along the lines here discussed can be confident that, in the course of time, the productive character of his group efforts will both surprise and gratify him.

CHAPTER XV

THE PSYCHOLOGY OF SELECTION

The use of psychology in the selection of employees is still in its infancy. Despite the extensive experimentation in the field, it is still easier to tell what not to do than what to do. And the upshot of successful experience to date with methods growing out of actual psychological study is still, one must admit, disappointingly small.

The present state of the art can be outlined in relation to:

1. The general conditions surrounding selection and placement.
2. The interviewer.
3. The interview.
4. The use of tests:
   a. Intelligence.
   b. Special abilities.
   c. Knowledge and trade skill.
   d. Special interests.
   e. Personality.
   f. Working capacity.
5. The placement.
6. The follow-up.

General Conditions.—What might almost be considered as the common-sense conditions surrounding the process of selection are so frequently honored in the breach rather than in the observance that it is important to mention these first. For money spent on elaborate test procedure will, to some extent, fail to pay dividends if the obvious prerequisite conditions are not observed.

For example, the physical surroundings of the interview should be cheerful. The applicant should not be kept waiting too long. He should be interviewed in private. He should be made to feel that the choice is a mutual one in which he is selecting the position as much as the employer is selecting him. The importance of the act of associating with a given company should be realized by the employing agent as well as it is by the applicant. His openness of mind and sensitiveness to the first impressions which he gets should be appreciated by the interviewer. And the man at the gate or in the reception room or whoever has the very first contact with the newcomer should be impressed with the necessity for courtesy and considerateness in all dealings with him. This applies equally to messengers or others who may be intermediaries between the employment office and the executive to whom the new employee is being sent.

Another important feature is to segregate as definitely as possible the rooms in which men and women are hired and in which factory workers, office workers, and executives, including salesmen, are interviewed. This last requirement may seem artificial from one point of view, but from the point of view of the usual seeker for employment in these several occupational groups it is one necessary way of supporting their natural sense of dignity and self-respect as to the kind of work they are to do and the kind of attention they have been led to expect.

The Interviewer.—It may not necessarily be required that the interviewer be a trained psychologist, since the services of such an expert can be used in a supplementary way. The important thing is that the interviewer have a sensitive and deft human touch, understanding, and sympathy. He should have a genuine fondness for people. Most interviewers can probably get the proper frame of mind about their work only if early in their career they have made it a business to go out and look for a job for a few days or weeks in order to get the feel of what it is like to be on the other side of the interviewer's desk. To have in mind the attitude and frame of mind of the anxious, nervous applicant is tremendously important.

This implies, of course, that the interviewer should not be too young. Nor should he be one usually without some close knowledge of the actual working demands of the departments for which he is hiring. Usually, also, it is better practice to have the interviewer of the same sex as the applicant, although experience seems to suggest that it works out better if a man has to interview women applicants than under the reverse conditions.

The racial background of the interviewer will often be another important factor, although this depends a good deal on how strong are his racial antipathies and prejudices. Certainly, where employees are predominantly from one foreign-born racial group, it is good sense to have an employment manager who can speak their language or at least to have ready access to a sympathetic and intelligent interpreter.

As to the different personal and working traits which different racial groups will bring to the job, there is little of a truly scientific nature that can be stated here. There is a great deal of popular attribution of thoroughness to Germans, stolidity to Poles, excitability to Italians, and similar generalities; but the interviewer who was governed by these notions would certainly go wrong. The fact is that we do not know in any accurate way how much the racial factors count in creating personal differences.

Increasingly, however, it will be valuable to use people with good psychological background as interviewers even when no elaborate use is made of tests. For quite apart from technical testing procedure, the interviewer will thus have some insight into the facts of differing aptitudes, intelligence levels, personal differences in temperament and character, nervous and mental peculiarities and abnormalities, and personality types such as pronounced extroverts or introverts. In other words, he will be aware of the complexity of personal characteristics and motives to be met in individuals and will have some notion of how to deal with them.

The Interview.—The interview will almost necessarily remain the keystone in the arch of the employing procedure. Admittedly, no completely standardized or stereotyped formula for its conduct can be made. Each new applicant faced presents some unique personality problem which has to be dealt with in a distinct and individual way. But a general line of approach is suggested by the best experience; and it can readily be adapted to the needs of an interviewer hiring an unskilled ditch digger and an experienced road salesman.

The first requirement is accurate knowledge of the job requirements. There must be the equivalent of a job specification providing the interviewer with a clear picture of what is demanded of the worker in point of education, special knowledge, special physical qualifications, age, sex, etc. However much it may seem to the interviewer that he knows all these facts as a matter of course, experience has shown that to have them organized and recorded always improves the quality of the interview. It gives the selecting procedure the clearest possible objective.

The second requirement is as full a knowledge as possible of the personal history of the applicant. We are indebted to Dr. V. V. Anderson[1] for the suggestion of four phases in this history: (1) developmental history (used only in clinical studies); (2) health history, including present health; (3) educational history; and (4) work history.

To get this entire picture requires time. The applicant must feel that what is taking place is not unwarranted prying but a sincere and intelligent attempt to find out his fitness for a job and a job's suitability for him. Hence, he must be put at ease and not made to feel the victim of an inquisition. It should also be freely recognized that he has a perfect right to resent questions which seem to him irrelevant; and this proper sense must be respected unless the interviewer can convince the applicant of the legitimacy of the question.

While securing the necessary personal history, it will usually be possible for the interviewer to begin to make observations about the third factor—the personality study. This Dr. Anderson has divided into studies of:

1. Intellectual activities, *e.g.:*

    A. Is the applicant's education commensurate with his opportunity for it?

    B. Is he alert?

    C. Has he seemed to learn from experience or is he naïve and gullible and does he repeat the same mistake over and over?

D. Is he attentive, and does he seem to fix and hold his attention well?

E. Does he give a consistent, intelligent, well-related story?

F. Does he seem distractible?

G. How suggestible is he?

H. Has he any special aptitudes, or special interests?

I. Is his memory good?

J. Does he show good common sense?

2. Motor characteristics, *e.g.:*

A. Does the applicant display tension or "push" in his activity?

B. Is he restless and overactive?

C. Does he seem inert?

D. Does he seem static?

E. Is he overtalkative, or undertalkative?

F. Would you judge his activity to be persistent and steady? Or capricious?

G. Does his life history indicate that he has or has not finished undertakings?

H. Does he seem sluggish or lazy? Does he slouch as he walks or sits?

I. Would you judge him easily fatigued?

J. Do you think that he could be speeded up easily? Or easily slowed down?

K. Do his movements seem well coordinated?

L. Are his posture and gait good?

M. Does he appear energetic?

N. Would you judge him to be tenacious and persistent in the face of obstacles and discomfort?

3. Temperament:

The leading question concerning any given individual may profitably be, What part do emotions play in his daily life? Some people have a characteristic mood that is very easily discerned. They are of a gloomy, sullen, sour temperament and disposition; or they are cheerful, optimistic and hopeful; suspicious, timid, embarrassed, oversensitive, self-deprecatory; or pompous, or cynical, or snobbish, or irate. These moods and emotional attitudes greatly influence one's relationship with others and are very important factors underlying work failure, or work success . . .

The interviewer is to bear in mind that the significant implications in this whole situation have to do with avoiding the selection of applicants who exhibit too marked extremes of temperament and mood—the depressed, melancholic, sullen, irritable and grouchy person, as well as the extremely cheerful, overoptimistic, exaggeratedly enthusiastic types. These extreme types are unusual and almost invariably make poor personnel risks.

4. Self-expression, including consideration of evidences of pronounced extroversion or introversion.
5. Sociability, including ability to work well with others.
6. Home factors.

In still further detail, Dr. Anderson suggests the following outline for the personality study:

I. *Facial Expression.*—Does the applicant look fearful, anxious, apprehensive, shy, timid, sad, gay, surly, hostile, suspicious, visionary, gullible, expressionless, intent, alert, eager, arrogant, cynical, fatigued, interested, indifferent, resistive, supercilious, etc., etc.?

II. *Movements.*—Are there movements of the head, of the face, of the body, of the hands, of the feet? Are there rhythmic quiverings of the mouth? Are there wrinklings of the forehead, peculiar facial expressions, peculiar attitudes of the body, nervous twitchings of the hands, licking of the lips, biting of the nails, idling with pencils and paper, etc.?

III. *General Observations.*—Does the employee speak voluntarily to the inverviewer of his own problems, interests, and ambitions? Does he talk freely and intelligently? Does he give a related story? Does he make a good first impression? Does he seem well developed and well nourished? Is his color good? Does he appear well dressed and neat? Is he careful about his clothes? Does he make a good contact? Does he appear to be full of problems of an emotional nature? Does he seek a listener and seem anxious to talk about his troubles? Does he appear self-centered? Does he crave sympathy, etc., etc.?

IV. *Speech.*—Is the voice well modulated, full, resonant, pleasing? Or is it pinched, small, strained? Or loud, harsh, irritating? Does he stammer, or slur words, or lisp, etc.?

V. *Mental Attitude toward Work.*—Give details of the attitude shown by individual toward the jobs he has held in the past, and his reasons for leaving them; his eagerness to secure other work, how definitely decided he is on the present job under consideration; his attitude toward the nature of work it calls for; his vocational interests and work ambition, etc.

VI. *Mental Attitude toward Authority and Associates.*—It is wise to make judgments of the applicant along these lines, inasmuch as the inability to take directions from those in charge, to work carefully under supervision, or to get along with one's associates is an important cause of resignations and lay-offs.

VII. *Mental Atttitude toward Home Relationships.*—Is there friction, or worry, or difficulty of a psychological or financial nature at home? If so, how do they affect the individual, and his attitude toward them?

VIII. *Mental Attitude toward Himself and His Own Personal Make-up.*—How does he feel about his own personal defects and disorders? Does he complain much? Does he overreact, taking the whole thing too seriously? Does he feel inferior, or ashamed, or shy, or timid, or superior and well satisfied with himself, etc.? What is his attitude toward his own failures or achievements?

IX. *Psychoneurotic States.*—Such people complain of undue fatigability or irritable weakness or inability to concentrate attention for a very long period of time, pessimistic moods, subjective disturbances of the nature of difficulty in breathing, profuse perspiration, trembling, shaking, disturbances in appetite, dizziness, diarrhea, etc. These cases pay more or less continuous attention to their bodily functions, their attitude being to no small extent fostered by the undue sympathy received, or by medical treatment on the physical level, which in many cases centers the patient's attention on his bodily functions.

X. *Psychotic States.*

XI. *Other Mental Conditions.*—Peculiar ideas or feeling of uncertainty or doubts, memory defects, and other undefinable miscellaneous conditions.

XII. *Recreation.*

XIII. *Summary* of the personality traits or characteristics (having specifically in mind the qualities or traits suited to the job in question).

While recognizing that the point of approach which has animated the above statement of method of personality study is one peculiarly concerned to discover mental shortcomings, I am convinced that this same method, modified where necessary, is capable of wide extension in business. Mental happiness in work is being increasingly sought for; and to secure it a technique of analysis such as is proposed above will have to be more and more widely used as part of the interview.

The evaluation of all the facts about the applicant in relation to those about the job is a matter of careful judgment in which experience can supply one of the best guides. If there are, as part of the selection process, definite tests used and a physical examination given, they, of course, must take place before a final evaluation and decision can be made. Should the decision to employ be favorable, it may be desirable in some cases to have the worker see the job in action or make a trial at it for an agreed period before asking him to make a decision. Test by actual job performance, after all, still remains the most reliable that is known.

The Use of Tests.—Whether or not it will pay to employ special psychological tests in addition to a careful interview depends upon the nature of the job, the character of the tests, their proved reliability, and the expense of administering them. And it may not be possible to know all this in the absence of a definite trial.

Their only point, of course, is in cases where their diagnostic value is good and the expense at least no greater than that of actual trial on the job.

Also, it should be emphasized that no one advocates placing sole reliance on the results of tests. They are always to be used as supplementary to all the other information, as partial evidence to be weighed in relation to all the facts.

Again, these tests and the method of scoring and interpreting them should be prepared by accredited professional psychologists. The first step for a company to take if it thinks it can make effective use of any type of special tests is to associate with itself such a trained psychologist. This is throughout a technical problem and up to a point all the technical detail must be worked out in close conjunction with such an expert over a considerable period of time. Usually, little can be done of any demonstrable value in less than a year or two of analysis and testing of tests in relation to specific jobs. For this reason the effort in this chapter will be only to convey a general picture of the testing problem from the managerial point of view. Specialized manuals and monographs must be studied for adequate technical discussion of the construction of tests, testing of tests, test scoring, and the like.[2]   The Psychological Corporation in New York City, the American Psychological Association, and the departments of psychology in the leading universities can usually supply reliable information about individual psychologists and about the relative soundness of the various standardized tests already widely known.

Too much importance can hardly be attached to the right selection of the expert to prepare the tests, since the field seems to have invited many consultants whose wares are not psychologically sound and who often promise more than can, in the present state of knowledge, be delivered.

Intelligence Tests.—Intelligence tests, as already pointed out, are tests of a quality of mental alertness.   The factor being studied has been further defined as follows:

> Intelligence is represented in behavior by the capacity of the individual to adjust himself to new situations, to solve new problems, to learn.   On the side of descriptive psychology, intelligence is exhibited especially by capacity for carrying on the higher mental operations, for abstract thought, for dealing with symbols, for generalizing, and for reasoning. If we analyze the types of operations which characterize intelligence, we discover an underlying principle which fits both the psychological and physiological conditions.   According to this principle, degrees of intelligence are determined by the general capacity of the psychophysical organism for the formation of new patterns among the elements of experience.[3]

It was tests to measure this capacity which were specially developed and widely used in the army during the World War. And the use of the same and similar tests to discover the measure of intelligence for business and industrial positions has been widely experimented with subsequently.   Whether or not a high, low, or medium score according to these tests is required at the given job, must be determined by experiment.   It is to be hoped that eventually it will be possible to say for most jobs that people with intelligence ratings in a given range will be likely to be best at those jobs; and some progress has been made

along these lines.   But the present use of such tests by themselves does not seem to throw very conclusive light on the
individual's suitability for many occupations.[4]

In other words, with just what other abilities, aptitudes, and
character traits intelligence correlates is still by no means
finally established.   In several instances, intelligence scores
have proved of help in classifying new workers in relation to
the rapidity of training for which they are adapted; and this
is highly useful.   And in other cases, it seems to have been shown
that workers with a too high or too low score do not fit permanently into certain jobs.   But reliance on such tests alone is
generally agreed to be fallacious; and only as the scores are
interpreted in relation to a variety of other data, like early home
conditions, educational background, and occupational experience,
can they be utilized to good effect and with any important
insight as to the accuracy of the final outcome.   In short, the
room for experiment and trial with this type of test is still great.

Two valuable estimates of the worth of intelligence tests
in industry have recently been made which, in a general way,
indicate the possibilities here.   They follow:[5]

A variety of objective and reliable tests, which probe primarily the
so-called higher mental abilities, are combined to form a test of intelligence.   Memory, reasoning, attention, imagination, and ability to use
elementary school information as an adult are combined in most tests.

Some tests are designed to be given individually.   The industrial cost
of these would be prohibitive.   Group tests which a regiment of men
can take simultaneously under one tester but which are practically as
valid have more industrial usefulness.

The first scores on two different intelligence tests cannot be compared
with fairness.   The scores should be reduced to a common denominator.
This common denominator is usually the average age of children who
make a similar score on the test.   This, roughly, is known as "mental
age."

. . . It certainly takes an expert interpreter to salve the wrath of the
forty-year-old man who is told his mental age is equal to that of the
average fourteen-year-old child.   Even that mental age score is above
the average of the general population, but it is not going to help matters
along by informing the testee that facts indicate that after about eight-

een years of age intelligence itself grows but little, while the knowledge for the intelligence to use accumulates in greater amounts each year. This results in a forty-year-old man with an intelligence equal to that of the fourteen-year-old high-school boy having a greater *effective intelligence,* in some cases! How effective his fourteen-year mental age is depends upon how well he has stored up information with which to use it.

With children under twelve years of age the ratio of their actual mental age to their birthday age yields the intelligence quotient, or I.Q. As yet there is no agreement regarding the birthday age to use in computing the I.Q. of an adult. For all practical industrial purposes, the raw score with a table for interpreting this in terms of mental age is all that is needed.

This section must not be passed over without emphasizing the foolhardiness of a policy of telling applicants or workers their scores on intelligence tests. The score should be interpreted for them in occupational terms and not mathematically. They should be told simply that "the test indicates that you shouldn't waste your time trying to be a doctor or a bank clerk. Those aren't the jobs you could earn most in. You should develop into an *expert* bench mechanic, a *real workman!*"

In any plant there is a close correlation between the size of the wage envelope and the size of intelligence scores. The exceptions to this rule reflect the importance of having tests on something besides intelligence to give a well-rounded and useful testing program. No other single test, however, or anything else, correlates so well with earnings.

There are probably several dozen different jobs that an applicant with an intelligence score of *x* could do. Of the 170,000 or more specialized tasks in our present industrial organization only a mere handful have had intelligence averages determined. A list of these, as prepared by Douglas Fryer, follows:

A mental age of 18.5 years or more for:
  Accountant.
  Business executive.
  College teacher.
  Editor.
  Lawyer.
  Engineer (mechanical, electrical, civil).
A mental age of 16 to 18.4 years for:
  Business man.
  Buyer.

Chemist.
Correspondent.
Dentist.
Draftsman.
Elementary-school teacher.
Factory superintendent.
Insurance salesman.
Journalist.
Minor business executive.
Office manager.
Physician.
Private secretary.

A mental age of 15 to 15.9 years for:
Bank clerk.
Bookkeeper.
Construction foreman.
Dictating machine operator.
Factory foreman.
File clerk.
Nurse.
Office clerk.
Photographer.
Postal clerk.
Radio operator.
Railroad clerk.
Shipping clerk.
Sign letterer.
Stenographer.
Stock clerk.
Traffic clerk.
Telegrapher.
Typist.
Wholesale salesman.

A mental age of 13.6 to 15 years for:
Automobile assembler.
Automobile mechanic.
Barber.
Bricklayer.
Butcher.
Carpenter.

Caterer.
Chauffeur.
Concrete worker.
Dressmaker.
Engineman.
Farmer.
General blacksmith.
General mechanic.
Gunsmith.
Handy man.
Horse trainer.
Lathe hand (production).
Laundryman.
Lineman.
Machinist.
Milliner.
Motorman.
Painter.
Pipe fitter.
Plumber.
Policeman.
Painter.
Riveter.
Sales clerk.
Stock checker.
Teamster.
Telephone operator.
Vaudeville actor.
Waiter.
A mental age of 11.5 to 13.5 years for:
Canvas worker.
Construction worker.
Domestic servant.
Factory worker.
Fireman (stationary).
Leather worker.
Lumberman.
Mason.
Porter.
Sailor

Shoemaker.
Sheet-metal worker.
Structural-steel worker.
Textile worker.
Watchman.
A mental age of 10 to 11.4 years for:
Fisherman.
Lifter.
Loader.
Unskilled labor.

There are occupations which do not require for their effective performance any specified capacity, but rather general ability or intelligence. A consideration of the average intelligence of various groups of workers reveals an occupational hierarchy. The unskilled laborers are inferior in intelligence to the semi-skilled or skilled workers. These in turn are surpassed by persons in technical, business, or clerical work. Members of the professions come at the top of the scale. The theory is that a person will in the long run attain about as high an occupational level in the hierarchy as his intelligence warrants. Hence these group averages are tantamount to the intellectual requirements of the occupations in question. It is thus possible to locate an individual applicant at somewhere near the occupational level for which he is best fitted, and with applicants of extreme intelligence the assignment to occupations at the opposite extreme is manifestly inadvisable. Similar hierarchies are found for the various jobs within a single organization and for different types of salespeople . . .

In occupations which show a correlation between proficiency and intelligence it is not necessarily desirable to employ persons with the maximum possible intelligence. Such individuals may learn readily and become effective workers soon after their induction, but in many instances it has been demonstrated that they do not remain long in the employ. With various types of office workers, cashiers, policemen, waitresses, and some of the lower grades of salesmanship, there has been found to be more instability or turnover among those of high intelligence than among those of average intelligence. While persons of very low intelligence may not have sufficient ability to learn effectively and perform their duties, those of very high intelligence may be too good for the job. It is not sufficiently exacting to hold their interest, their intellectual ability has insufficient outlet, and they become dissatisfied. This points is some instances to the necessity for an upper critical score. Applicants scoring above this amount are considered unsuitable material from the standpoint of permanancy. Where intelligence is related to vocational aptitude, it is often desirable to consider not maximum intelligence but optimum intelligence.

Special-abilities Tests.—Tests of special abilities, such as manual dexterity, mechanical aptitudes, and special motor coordinations for individual jobs, have been developed for a number of companies with promising results. The General Electric Company at Lynn, Mass., the Scovill Manufacturing Company at Waterbury, Conn., the Yellow Cab Company at Chicago, the Atlantic Refining Company, H. L. Doherty and Company, Cheney Brothers, Eastman Kodak Company, Aetna Insurance Company are among those which, pursuing quite different test methods, have secured results which are felt to aid materially in improving the selective process.[6]

Occupations which have thus far lent themselves to the successful use of special tests are those of motormen, taxi drivers, typists, clerical workers, metal-machine operators, mechanical engineers, apprentices in certain metal trades, certain inspection and assembling work, etc. Whether or not others could take over these tests bodily from the companies which developed them and apply them for selecting purposes without a good deal of adaptation is highly doubtful. Developed as they were in direct relation to specific needs, they have proved useful—especially in suggesting methods for discovering a good group of tests. But other companies will have to start experimentally at a point nearly as far back as those already using tests.

There will undoubtedly be further application of special-abilities tests as time goes on; and great benefit can be anticipated from them. But their development in relation to the jobs in each new company is a slow process. Cooperative research here in a group of companies doing similar work could undoubtedly speed up the experimenting and lessen the expense as well.

An excellent outline of the procedure here and of the difficulties to be encountered is given by Burtt[7] as follows:

In devising tests of special mental capacity for predicting vocational aptitude, there are two common methods of approach—reproducing the total mental situation involved in the job or analyzing the operation into its mental components and testing these components separately. In either instance it is necessary to make a preliminary analysis of the mental aspects of the job. It is also necessary to give the test or tests to workers and to correlate the score or scores with the criterion. To analyze the mental aspects of the job, it may be well to observe workers carefully, actually to try the job and observe one's own experiences, to discuss the requisites with foremen and executives with especial reference to the distinguishing features of efficient and inefficient workers, or to use as a starting-point a job analysis that has previously been systematically conducted.

In devising the test for total mental situation, it is wise to avoid undue complexity, because the apparatus is at the outset purely experimental and may later be scrapped. The test need not necessarily be a miniature of the job, because it is the subjective rather than the objective similarity that is important. It should, however, be technically foolproof and yield an objective score.

The next step is to give the test to subjects whose ability in the job is known. The testing may be done in a separate laboratory or in a screened portion of the factory. The former affords more quiet and allows more flexible and permanent equipment, while the latter is more natural and convenient for the subjects. The emotional factor, however, can usually be controlled by giving a "shock absorber" test preceding the crucial series.

After the test has been given to a group of workers, it is necessary to correlate the scores with the criterion. This may be done by appropriate formulæ which consider the differences between each subject's rank in the test and rank in the criterion, or which involve the product of each man's deviation from the average test score and his deviation from the average criterion score, or the data may be plotted with test scores on one axis and criterion scores on the other. In any instance the magnitude of the correlation coefficient indicates the validity of the test. It is also possible to work out a regression equation which expresses criterion in terms of test score and gives the best prediction that can be made of the man's ability on the job with that particular test.

The test for total mental situation has one serious limitation. If its correlation with the criterion proves to be small, the work has been practically wasted and it is necessary to start again. It is often difficult or embarrassing to have the same subjects return later for further examination.

Various examples of such tests were cited. The situation for hand-feed dial-machine operators was reproduced by a rotating disc containing a hole through which steel balls were dropped by the subject. A test for motormen involved an endless belt with a track in the middle passing an opening in the apparatus. Numbers at various positions relative to the track had various significance and the subject reacted accordingly. Gun-pointers looked through an eye-piece and by a hand lever kept it trained on a moving target. Aerial observers were required to memorize certain patterns of illuminated points that were flashed on electrically. The validity of these and other tests that were cited was sufficiently high to warrant their practical use . . .

To simplify the administration, it is possible to work out for any given correlation a general table showing for various ranges of test scores the chances of attaining various degrees of occupational proficiency. We may arbitrarily call certain ranges of ability good, average, and poor, and then state the probability of a given applicant's being a good, average, or poor workman. The employment department can then decide where to draw the line for a given set of tests on the basis of how large a chance it wishes to take in hiring applicants. This line is the critical score.

Trade Tests.—Trade tests are tests of trade knowledge and proficiency. They may be oral, picture or performance on miniature, or actual apparatus. Their use is limited to actual crafts for which it is possible to isolate a body of information known to the fully qualified craftsman but not to the apprentice, and another body of facts known to the apprentice but not to the novice. Thus, an actual identification of the relative amount of trade knowledge and skill possessed by an applicant may be secured.

How far such tests, following, in general, the line of development begun during the World War, are in actual use it is impossible to say. But the best opinion seems to be that relatively little use is made of them in selecting craftsmen. This is probably due to the expense of devising and administering them in each separate factory in comparison with what is popularly thought to be the quicker method of putting a man on the job he claims he can do and seeing if he qualifies.

Ideally, if there were greater uniformity and standardization of terminology in crafts over wide areas of the country, it should be possible to administer such tests economically. But, in fact, this lack of uniformity is one of the important stumbling blocks.

Special Interests.—Experimental work is now being done to see if people's interests in various sorts of life activities supply a clear index of vocational or occupational fitness. Thus far, these efforts have been made more in relation to professional work than in the ordinary run of business, mercantile, and industrial jobs.[8]

A useful summary of the present situation regarding the value of tests of interests is given by Burtt as follows:[9]

Occupational success depends on other things than ability alone, and interest is one of them. There is some indication that interests are rather permanent, and hence it is necessary to reckon with them in the employment situation rather than to rely on their changing to meet conditions. There is also some relation between interest and ability. Whether the ability motivates the interest or *vice versa* has not been determined. In either instance, however, interests are to some extent diagnostic of what the person will ultimately do in the occupation.

Several methods have been used to determine systematically a person's interests. A questionnaire may be devised dealing with previous occupational, with avocational, or with social interests, any of which may be of practical significance. Instead of answering questions the procedure is sometimes varied by having the subject check a list of items according to whether he likes or dislikes them. Information tests are sometimes used as a measure of interest on the theory that a person who is interested in a certain field will go out of his way to obtain more information about it and will remain "set" for anything pertaining to it, so that he will in the long run be able to give a better account of himself in an information test involving items in this field. Still more indirect methods have been attempted. In what is ostensibly a memory test, in which some items appealing to a certain interest are mingled with other normal items, it is assumed that relatively more of the former will be retained by a person with that particular interest. In a test involving cancellation of irrelevant words in a text, it is assumed that if the content of the text appeals especially to the person's interest he will become engrossed in it and mark relatively fewer of the irrelevant words.

These methods have been evaluated by administering the measurements or tests to certain occupational groups or to groups known to have some fundamental difference in interest and determining which items serve most clearly to differentiate the groups. It was possible from a list of items regarding which the subjects expressed their like or dislike to select a set which would differentiate fairly well the engineering type of individual from the salesman type. In quite similar fashion it proved possible to obtain differential items for the socially inclined as compared with the mechanically inclined. The information test as a measure of interest proved of some value in discriminating different degrees of success in selling. There were indications that the successful salesman was an individual who had accepted social responsibilities. The more indirect methods of measuring interests have been tried to only a slight extent, but the correlations with estimated interest were somewhat encouraging. The whole matter of measuring interest and using such measurements in a practical way is still very much in the experimental stage, but satisfactory progress is being made.

Personality Tests.—The study of personality as a picture of the total effectiveness of the individual is being pursued experimentally from a variety of angles. Such special modifying factors as temperament and character, for example, have been studied in this connection. But to what extent these findings are available for ready adaptation to general use in business it is as yet impossible to say. Tests of so-called "extroversion" and "introversion" have been devised which undoubtedly throw some light on extreme cases of either type of personality. But since many jobs require and most people possess qualities which are partly classifiable as introvert and partly as extrovert, these tests do not seem, as yet at least, to offer great assistance.

Tests of Working Capacity: Rating Scales.—Rating scales represent a method of comparative estimate of objectively unmeasurable qualities which presumably in the aggregate give a close picture of total working effectiveness. A good deal of experimental work has been done in this field and some promising results have been obtained.[10]

The rating scale has been found to serve two valuable purposes. It gives an improved, comparable, and somewhat explicit basis for judging special working capacities and attitudes. And it supplies a splendid educational weapon in enabling the personnel executive to discuss with the person rated his particular deficiencies and the ways of overcoming them.   This is, perhaps, its most valuable use.

A number of different methods of rating have been employed. The man-to-man rating involves a comparison of an individual with a related number of workers who supply a standard in point of the agreed qualities.   The numerical rating gives either a percentage or point-system estimate of an individual in relation to the qualities to be rated.   The linear scale makes it possible to check the estimate on a line for each quality with reference to such words as "excellent," "good," "fair," "poor."   The graphic rating uses the linear scale but places, under the line for each characteristic, adjectives more closely descriptive of the relative degrees of the possession of the quality from a maximum to a minimum.   With these qualities checked at a point on each line, it is possible to make a graphic "profile" picture of the individual's total rating which is easy to read and informing.   Of this method, Bingham and Freyd say:[11]

The graphic rating method is at present the most popular.   By the use of this method judges agree closely among themselves in rating the same men, and judgments are consistent when repeated after a long interval.   It is simple and easy to grasp, easily filled out and scored, frees the rater from direct quantitative terms, and makes the degree of the ability concrete.   Finally, it has been found to be more interesting to use, as well as convenient and reliable.

These writers also make the following helpful summary as to methods to be followed in devising rating scales:[12]

The tendency in the evaluation of graphic rating scales has been toward the adoption of the practices recommended below.   The superiority of these practices has not in all cases been demonstrated experimentally, and much research is still needed in order to develop the most reliable as well as the most convenient forms of scales.

It will help the rater if each scale is prefaced by a description of the ability in question.

It is important that this description be in terms of behavior rather than of mental qualities.   The more concretely the ability is expressed the greater is the expectation that the various raters will be judging the same thing.

Be sure that the ability is not a composite of several abilities that vary independently.

Decide definitely upon the extremes of ability which will probably occur among the persons to be rated.

The end phrases should not be so extreme in meaning that their use is completely avoided by raters . . .

Place in the center of the scale the phrase describing the neutral or average or typical degree of the ability . . .

Usually not more than five nor less than three descriptive phrases are used to mark the steps on the scale.

If there are five phrases, make the intermediate ones closer in meaning to the central one that to the extremes but maintain an equal amount of linear space between phrases. This has the effect of spreading the distribution. The same end may be accomplished by making the intervals on the scale larger between the central phrase and the intermediate ones than between the intermediate ones and the extremes.

The phrases used should have the same meaning to all raters. Slang is occasionally effective, but there must be no doubt about its meaning. Special terms and phrases in use in the occupation may be freely substituted for more general terms.

Avoid such terms as *average, very, extremely, excellent, good, fair,* or *poor*. It is better to use adjectives which in themselves express varying degrees of the ability. Thus, in place of *extremely neat* one may say *fastidious,* or in place of *very careless in dress* one may say *slovenly.*

Make the descriptive phrases short, concise, and apt.

Have the phrases set in small type with plenty of white space between them.

Have the two extreme phrases set flush with the ends of the line.

Allow no breaks or divisions in the rating line. Where the line is divided vertically into five or ten parts, accuracy of rating is sacrificed for convenience in scoring.

The line should not be much more than 5 inches in length, otherwise it cannot be easily grasped as a whole.

The favorable extremes of a series of scales should be placed alternately to the right and to the left. Or, better yet, the scales may be arranged in an apparently haphazard way so far as the position of the favorable extreme is concerned, but in half the instances it should be at the left end of the line. This arrangement breaks a motor tendency to check at one side of the page.　It helps to reduce the halo effect, resulting in more discriminating judgments.

Regardless of the type of rating scale which is used, experience dictates certain precautions.

Ratings on each person should be obtained from at least three competent judges who are thoroughly acquainted with his abilities.　This is not always possible; but the cautious investigator will frankly recognize that anything short of this minimum gives him a measure with only very meagre reliability.

To get the most representative measure of each ability in each person the ratings of the judges should be averaged, or if two out of three of them agree, the judgment of the majority should be accepted.

The raters should be carefully trained in the use of the scale.　The investigator should go over it with them in detail to make sure that they understand its operation and the pitfalls they are to avoid.

Most raters are at first unaccustomed to think of men analytically. They tend to think in terms of general impressions, prejudices, or indefinite descriptive phrases.　Some information will have to be given them about the statistics of distribution of abilities and the quantitative relationship of differences in abilities.

The raters should be warned to avoid being influenced in their judgments on any one ability by a general set or attitude they may have formed toward the person whom they are rating.　This tendency is lessened if the raters consider all the persons to be rated with regard to the first ability, then the second ability, and so on.

Another influence to be guarded against is closeness of friendship with the person rated . . .

. . . Supervisors tend to rate old employees high as compared with new employees.　Three reasons are given for this: (1) The supervisor will not admit that being under his direction has brought no improvement in the employee.　(2) The supervisor unconsciously identifies himself with older employees who are perhaps more like him than new employees.　(3) The supervisor has become used to the older employees and overlooks their weaknesses . . .

The scale should be placed in the hands of the raters and should be discussed with them several weeks before the ratings are called for, to allow them time to observe the subjects with reference to the abilities to be rated.　Needless to say, the behavior of the subjects will be more typical and characteristic if they do not know during this time that they are being rated.

The following are the most important points which should be brought to the attention of the rater, regardless of the type of scale in use:

1. If you have any question about the operation of the scale, be sure to have it answered before you make your ratings.

2. Be certain that you understand what is meant by each listed ability.

3. Do not begin to rate until you have observed every employee from the point of view of the abilities on the scale.

4. Do not begin to rate the employees until you have considered all of them with regard to the abilities on the scale.

5. Consider one ability at a time and rate all the persons on that ability before proceeding to the next ability.

6. Try to free your rating on any one ability from the influence of the other abilities of the person, or of any general impression or attitude in regard to him.

7. Remember that extremes of ability are rare. Measurements of abilities have generally shown that most people are grouped about the average and that fewer perons have the higher or lower degrees of ability. Do not, therefore, consider all the persons to be either very high or very low in the ability.

8. When judging a person, call to mind concrete instances of the type of behavior in question.

9. Behavior on the job or when making business contacts is more significant for present purposes than behavior in purely social gatherings.

10. Try to be uninfluenced by the time you have worked with the person or the closeness of your friendship with him.

In conclusion, rating scales offer a potentially helpful tool for executives to use with other executives, foremen, and rank-and-file workers, both from the point of view of appraisal of value for purposes of increases in pay, promotions, and personal reeducation. But the difficulties and dangers in their use have to be carefully observed and it is unwise to use them without full observance of all the technical points which experience has shown to be valuable.

Placement.—Assuming that the interviewer's evaluation of all available tests and of the interview are favorable, the actual placing of the individual at work is a procedure which can go far toward making or marring the cooperative attitude of the new worker. Detailed discussion of all the interesting methods now in use to facilitate the placement process is not in place here.[13] But it is important to stress the point that all those who come into contact with new workers should realize the value of helping to create a *favorable first impression* in the mind of the impressionable new worker. This should be a matter of definite concern to the employment department, involving if necessary specific educational work with foremen and fellow-workers. To get each new employee embarked on his career with a company in the friendliest and most informed manner is highly important if the care and expense involved in making the selection are not to be lost at subsequent stages of the new employee's personal contacts.

The Follow-up of the Placement.—The method of following up applicants who have been actually placed in jobs does not, as yet at least, lend itself to systematic psychological statement. But its crucial importance as an aid to the interviewer no less than to the new worker cannot be overemphasized. When the first follow-up should be made, how many such visits there should be, just how misplacements should be handled, the content of the interview with the worker at this point—these are all vital matters on which no standard practice is discoverable. But the intelligent interviewer can make this an occasion which can greatly facilitate satisfactory placement both of the worker in question and of other applicants whom he has subsequently to place, if he will analyze carefully why and how he went wrong.

Conclusion.—The tenor of this chapter has been deliberately tentative and cautious about the use of tests. A company embarking on the use of any test procedure should realize that it takes time, patience, skill, and money to get worthwhile results. Personally, I entertain high hopes about the possibility of reducing waste and unhappiness by improved selection based on carefully designed tests. The present favorable results are but a pale suggestion of what we may expect in the next quarter century. But these results will come only if companies determine to experiment with test procedures under scientific guidance and with real willingness to see through to the end the process of finding good tests.

CHAPTER XVI

THE TECHNIQUE OF TRAINING

The practical aids which are brought to the task of training by a knowledge of psychology are among its most impressive contributions. What is known about the character of the learning process, the inner nature of training and of education in general, the methods of good pedagogy—all offer specific helpful suggestions which can yield economies in time and effort, greatly enhanced efficiency, and a sense of mastery in the learner.

First, to distinguish between education and training—the one being general, the other more applied. Education can be defined as the progressive utilization *of the experience of one's self and of others in the direction of securing the more satisfactory adjustment and relation of one's self to the surrounding world.* This conception helps to keep to the fore the vital idea that education is or should be a continuing process which is not necessarily tied up at all with the usual methods of formal schooling. The emphasis upon progressively successful adjustment to one's environment should be in the executive leader's mind as an objective for his relation to his staff exactly as much as it should be in the mind of a school teacher.

But more immediately the executive's interest centers upon training. For training is *the acquiring of an ability to exercise a given skill.* This skill may be some manual dexterity, or it may equally well be a skill in utilizing ideas, dealing with people, assimilating an attitude, or developing an appreciation. One may be trained, for example, to think of people as human beings like oneself or to enjoy good books or to conduct a group conference—all of which are mastered in much the same way that a manual skill is acquired. In all of these skills the same learning elements are entailed. The learner, as we saw in Chap. VI, must do the learning. He it is who must live his way by practice into his new skill. "There is no learning without learning to use." And learning to use may be, depending on the nature of the problem, a comparatively isolated experience where the individual is relating himself to the elements of a job. Or it may be a broader attainment where, as we have seen before, the learning comes through the larger adjustment of the learner to a complex total situation or set of experiences through which he passes, as, for example, in the case where he is trying to learn how to become a conference leader or how to judge wisely as to the right kind of personnel policies to sponsor.

And in either case, the truth must not be lost sight of that the reasoning element in the learning process should be made to supplement and assist the motor and the trial-and-error elements. The characteristic of prior rehearsal of possible alternatives and exercise of judgment as to the wisest among them—which is the essence of reasoning—should be encouraged as the constant attendant of the slower, more painful method of motor, that is, physical experience of numerous trials, till the successful solution is discovered. The best trainer will necessarily subject learners to novel situations with which they must cope; but he will also encourage in the learner imaginative thinking about how he can cope with them most quickly and sagaciously without the inevitable necessity for motor experience.

The Transfer of Training.—The extent to which training and learning in one field can be carried over to facilitate learning in another should be understood, since trainers have tended to labor under a misconception here. All recent studies seem to point conclusively to the truth that all that can be transferred when one changes his field of study are *the attitude and method of attack upon the subject*. One who has learned how to study and how to learn economically can apply this knowledge in numerous fields. But the specific skills have largely to be learned afresh each time. This points to the added importance of helping to understand how to learn.

The Objectives in Training.—Obviously, the results or objectives determined upon govern, in the first instance, who is to be trained and in what they are to be trained. In industry, there are executives, major and minor, there are foremen, office workers, sales people, rank-and-file shop workers, all of whom are possible subjects for training.

Also, there are different instructional problems for the newcomers and for those who have been employed some time. There is the training to fit people better for the job they have; and that designed to fit them for a better job—training for upgrading. Again, there is training for job fitness and training for organization fitness; and each of these entails separate objectives and methods.

First arises this question: For whom is this training to be given and to attain what end? This point disposed of, attention can then be turned to securing and preparing subject matter which will fit the case and to deciding upon those training methods best designed to yield successful learning.

Ideally, of course, a well-organized corporation might, over a period of years, undertake training for all its different functional groups, for upgrading, and for organization as well as job fitness. And, within certain limits, the same psychological principles will obtain in all cases. The purpose of this chapter will be to deal with these principles more than the specific differences between, for example, foreman training and job instruction. The executive trainer should then find it easy to apply these truths to his particular problem.

Qualifying Factors.—Most of the training problems will have this in common, that it is adults who are the learners. And the problems of adult training are today recognized as slightly different in character from those of child instruction. Perhaps the first point should be to remember that, in the main, the trainer *has to work with the people he has.* Improved selection of new employees may, over a period of time, gradually alter for the better the caliber of material he faces in this respect. But the executive groups and the great body of employees have to be taken as they are. This means, usually, numbers of people with varied amounts of schooling, wide divergences in native intelligence, differing interest in and aptitude for further training efforts. It means, also, in most cases, a distrust of any formal educational programs, due to pride, fear, laziness, or indifference. Adults are naturally reluctant to be shown up, to be ridiculed, to have their customary routine of habits, attitudes, and opinions disturbed. Their experience with formal schooling has often not been a happy or fruitful one; they may have lost confidence in themselves, lost ambition, and have become impregnated with the prevailing view that "you can't teach an old dog new tricks."

All adult training programs have to overcome the hurdles which these conditions present. But experience shows clearly that if they are recognized and reckoned with they can be overcome. In the first place, the trainer should realize and help his people to realize that modern psychologists agree that up to forty-five years of age the speed of the learning process is affected by age to a very slight extent. Summing up numerous and extensive studies, Professor Thorndike of Columbia University has recently concluded that "age in itself is a minor factor in either success or failure. Capacity, interest, energy, and time are the essentials."[1] This conclusion should be given wide circulation as an aid in building up the initial confidence of adult learners.

If this disturbing notion that adults cannot learn readily can be dispelled, the next job is to see that the learning process itself is made interesting, related to the learners' needs and problems, freed from any atmosphere of "talking down" or of ridicule from fellow learners or others, and organized to let the individual know when he is making real progress.

An element as vital as any is the classifying by previous education and intelligence levels of those who are to be trained— a principle which should have wide application to different kinds of groups. This grouping for instructional purposes should take account of "school grade reached, plus a measure of the shortness of the time to attain that grade, plus some reasonable intelligence test."[2] Thus, the speed of progress and the method of instruction can be far better adapted to the individual needs of each one. Part of the group can then start out from their more advanced standing while the others can start more slowly as a homogeneous group having the same handicaps in capacity and schooling.

The other important factor in helping to make adult educational efforts successful is *the desire of the learners themselves.* Their initial enthusiasm and the inspiration which they receive are pivotal features. They must feel some incentive either in the subjective rewards which will accrue in their own larger grasp and power or in their own enhanced usefulness and income-producing ability—or, best of all, of course, in both.

If, then, these several qualifying and preliminary difficulties are intelligently reckoned with so that throughout the organization there develops a sentiment that training for everyone is a natural, wholesome, and productive activity, the stage is set for continued and repeated efforts which should keep training from becoming sporadic and superficial.

The Training Methods.—The selection of training methods refers to two separable problems—that of the methods of presenting the material and conducting the group, and that of the methods of developing and unfolding the material in detail.

The methods of presentation that may be employed include the demonstration, the lecture, the recitation, the working out of a project, the analysis of a case or problem, a group discussion under the leadership of the trainer, or some combination of these. There is apparently no one best way; but if the true nature of the learning process is appreciated by the teacher, he will be likely to place a minimum of reliance upon lectures or any other form of relatively passive learning. A word about the limits upon each of these methods may be helpful.

A demonstration is one of the best ways of beginning the learning process, whether at some kinds of machine operating or of selling or other activities. Usually, it is wise to preface the demonstration by some explanation of what is about to be done and why and how. The demonstration helps the visually-minded learners and those whose powers of abstraction are undeveloped.   But it must be closely related to and promptly followed by practice by the student himself; and if any fundamental grasp of the subject matter is to be given, there must also be supplied, sooner or later, the more theoretical background knowledge.

The lecture enables the teacher to present new matter in a highly selected, orderly, and logical manner.   Much related reading can be digested by the lecturer, and ideas not yet in print can be presented.   Also, the presentation can aid greatly in imparting to the learner some of the teacher's enthusiasm and vision.   Undoubtedly, occasional short summing-up talks can help the student toward better orientation and can stimulate him to renewed efforts of his own.   On the other hand, much lecturing involves the presentation of material available in books which should be studied by the student himself.   The matter on which it takes an hour to lecture can usually be better presented in print that can be read in 20 minutes.   The learner is too passive under most lecturing to obtain any other result than the usual "in one ear and out the other."   It leads him to believe that what he has heard about he knows and thus leads to a perpetuation of the vicious notion that one can learn without learning how to use.   Broadly speaking, the printing press and the mimeographing process should have rendered the lecture all but obsolete in education decades ago.

The recitation by itself is in danger of degenerating into a mere verbal exercise in memorizing what someone else has thought on a subject.   Where the training problem is, in the first instance, one of having to give the student definite information as a tool— as it may, perhaps, be in some mathematical or technical field where formulæ and terminology have to be mastered—the recitation reaches its greatest usefulness.   But in those more frequently met instances where the training also implies ability to use information in action, the recitation is clearly an inadequate medium.   There are other ways of assuring that each member of a training group is mentally involved in the instruction that is going forward, which are not quite so parrot-like in character.   There is a further risk that under recitations both teacher and students will gage success by good recitations rather than by *bona fide* intellectual and motor proficiency in action.

The project method means that the student is assigned a task or project to perform or carry out. Suppose that in a foreman-training course the leader requests a foreman to find out how inspectors are trained in the other shops in the locality; that is an example of project. To be useful, this method requires prior information by the student of methods of investigation and of the kind of results which he is, in general, expected to find. It requires careful supervision; but if that is assured, the student can usually gain much from this kind of experience. It is often difficult to supply enough projects to go around in a large group and to assure enough supervision. But projects have the merit of requiring active self-instruction.

The case method may involve the discussion in class of a case already read in advance; or it may mean merely the written submission by the student of a case and its solution for comment by the instructor. If the case really illustrates the matter under consideration, if it really presents all the necessary relevant facts (which it is extremely difficult to do on industrial problems), if the student has some background as to principles and related experience, then his analysis and solution of the case can be an effective training experience. The trouble is that it is so difficult to satisfy all these requirements. The consideration of cases orally before groups can often overcome some of these deficiencies and become a splendid method. It is, however, important to foster a sense of due humility in the student as to the relative value of his solution as compared with the one actually reached and used by the executive in action. The danger is that he will have a false sense of simplicity about the nature of the problem and think that he can solve it without realizing his ignorance of many complicating factors. But if cases are being discussed in groups where actual experience is represented, this danger is greatly lessened.

The other danger is that cases will be discussed without adequate knowledge of any general principles under which the case may fall. Then the level of constructive consideration can rise no higher than the experience of the most experienced member of the group. Suppose that a board of directors has before it a group-insurance plan for adoption—which is, in reality, a case problem. If no one has any more information on the question than the facts supplied by the salesman for the insurance company who is preparing to sell the group policy, it is obvious that the discussion of the merits of the plan will not be sufficiently enlightened to insure a wise decision.

In most such matters that relate to personnel policies, the procedure and method are to be evaluated in the light of a corporation's basic objectives and motives; so that a knowledge of these should form the background for any case study of proposed new methods. To ignore consideration of the general principles and assumptions which underlie and validate every procedure is to lessen the usefulness of case discussions to the point of nullification.

Discussion under Leadership.—The method of conference discussion is the one that promises best results for certain kinds of training. The requirements for its successful use are (1) a very well-informed leader who can help to supply all the necessary facts on a problem; (2) clear recognition by all that they are confronting a real case, problem, project, or controversial situation; (3) careful stimulation of all members to assure their participation and growth as the discussion proceeds; (4) rigorous holding of the group to the subject and to the reaching of a solution to its problem; (5) eventual agreement (or, in the absence of this possibility, explicitly stated disagreement) on the assumptions which underlie the discussion.

On this last point, for example, it would be all but idle to foster discussion in a foremen's conference of new ways to handle the labor problem, if the head executives of the organization hold the conviction and assumption that no new ways of handling labor are necessary or desirable.

Discussion properly organized and adequately informed has the advantage of assuring active thinking effort on the part of all who participate. It can broaden individual knowledge, experience, and conviction; it can foster freedom in individual thought and expression; it can "get somewhere," *if the leader has a clear notion of the direction in which he wants to go.* And it is a medium sufficiently flexible to be adapted to a wide variety of learning groups.

Indeed, it is possible when this conference idea is recognized, to use all kinds of existing conferences as living mediums of instruction even while they proceed under the normal guise of being only established, necessary, and routine business bodies. Thus, training can proceed by a relatively painless, natural, but deliberate use of committee or conference methods.

The very conception of the discussion method helps to minimize the classroom atmosphere and cultivate one of adult inquiry, interchange, and deliberation. It is thus peculiarly calculated to appeal to the self-respect of adults who might rebel at being set down in front of a teacher.

Presentation of Material to Be Learned.—Whatever method is in use for the general conduct of training, there are a few simple pedagogical principles which should be applied in presenting and following through on the subject matter itself. Since an extended discussion of these points fills the textbooks on the art of teaching, I must content myself with a very condensed statement.

The subject matter should be determined upon in close relation to a knowledge of the requirements of the activity for which training is being undertaken. The information supplied by job analyses and by difficulty analyses is an essential prerequisite in job training. Where the matter for instruction relates to foremen's work, to company policies and methods, the assembling of data can be aided by submitting tentative drafts of lesson material in advance to the executives whose work is involved; and their cooperation, both in giving new facts and in agreeing upon the accuracy of the course subject matter, is thus better assured. To have all such instruction material relate in some approximate way to the actual conditions of each company seems one of the surest ways of arousing interest in it and securing the best educational results.

The teacher should commence his presentation with matter or problems which the student knows and understands. Learning becomes a relating of a new element in experience to the existing background of the content of the learner's experience.

Start, then, from the known; and proceed to that element in the matter to be learned which, in point of difficulty and ease of assimilation, can be most readily grafted onto the known.

The right sequence for the order of learning the elements of a subject is not necessarily the order in which the elements operate in action. In job instruction, for example, the order in which job elements are taught is frequently not the order in which they are performed. One proceeds from what is, from the student's point of view, the simple to the more complex.

The new element should be presented as a problem or difficulty which the student really senses. The matter in hand must seem to him to be of consequence, to relate vitally to his own needs, experience, and progress. This truth supplies a vital reason why in job training the effort is usually made to have the training take place on goods which will actually go into the production output and, therefore, have to measure up to standard in quality and workmanship.

The student should be supplied with or directed to fact data which throw light on the problem.

Each lesson or conference should begin by having the student understand the relation of the last session to the present one; and it should end by having the relation made clear of the present lesson to the new matter for the next lesson.

Some measure of his progress should be supplied to the student at intervals varying with his age and maturity.

Definite effort should be made by the teacher to sustain the student over the discouraging periods which are graphically pictured on all learning curves as the "plateaus," where progress seems temporarily to cease.

The Teacher's Task.—All of this suggests the rôle of the teacher in the learning process. And every executive would do well to have in mind a clear notion of just what the teacher's relation to the learning activity is, if he purposes to let a training point of view color and actuate his own executive contacts.

The teacher presents the problem or poses the difficulty or makes articulate for the learner a difficulty which he is already facing.

He directs the way to facts relevant to the solution of the problem.

He suggests approaches to the solution. He may do this by demonstration, by verbal hints, by recommending reading. Or, in certain training problems where changes in attitude are desired, he plunges the student into situations and experiences in which the latter is bound to learn (or fail) in finding his way out.

He inspires the student and helps him to sustain confidence in himself.

He avoids a teacher-student relationship in favor of a guide-and-leader kind of attitude. His attitude is not one of superiority but one of a cooperator in a joint search for truth.

Finally, the teacher will find his whole educational contact of immense value in helping to identify and encourage workers who will qualify for special attention and advancement. This important task of identifying executive timber and offering to such individuals further help is one of the fruitful justifications of all good corporate training work.

H. G. Kenagy[3] has made such an excellent and helpful summary of some of the more technical aspects of the teacher's job that I quote it in full:

I shall assume that, as a preliminary matter, the particular job has been analyzed for its teaching content and I know what must be taught in terms of the knowledge and skills required and the personal characteristics either necessary or desirable for success. My objectives are therefore clear. It seems to me that the first point in good technique is: Arrange the instructional matter and teaching plan to correspond with the order in which problems arise in doing the job because, of course, I would use the project method of teaching.

Second, from a study of the tasks to be done and the things to be learned in connection with each problem, I would arrange and teach them in the order of learning difficulty. I would know, and record on my training plan, the proper point or step in the teaching process at which each element of knowledge should be taught, because I would recognize that a fact is learned with least effort when the need for that fact has risen in the process of solving a problem.

Third, in teaching each element of manual, or even lingual, skill (for it applies in teaching selling), I would demonstrate under job conditions just how the thing should be done, and repeat the demonstration until the student was ready to try it for himself. I would judge his readiness by the questions which he had asked in response to my invitation, and by his answers to my questions. I would have the essential points of each step in mind and on paper so that guesswork would be eliminated.

Fourth, I would let the beginner try, correct his mistakes one at a time by redemonstration and further explanation, and continue this process until the student had reduced the acts or series of acts to a habit.

Fifth, I would measure the individual student's learning ability as accurately as possible and endeavor to teach in each lesson only as much as the student could grasp. I would teach slowly or rapidly, depending on the student, and I would make sure, by drill and examination, that each element was learned before passing to the next.

Sixth, I would maintain, at all costs, a personal interest in the beginner's progress and an attitude born of patience with an understanding of his human tendencies to make mistakes and to do as little work as possible.

Finally, I would keep an experimental, inquiring attitude toward my teaching methods, introducing new bits of technique suggested by others or by my own experience, and carefully recording the results secured. Thus I would contribute my share to the advancement of knowledge regarding the technique of training on the job.

Other helpful cautionary hints are contained in a group of questions asked a few years ago by Professor Hanus.[4] Anyone in a teaching post would do well to ask himself at periodic intervals what his honest answers would be to them:

I. In my teaching, are my aims, ultimate and immediate, clear in my own mind?

Ultimate aims—What ought the students to get out of every course I teach?

Immediate aims—What point or points should be made today in order to make progress toward the realization of my ultimate aims?

II. Do I avoid talking too much or too little?

There must be as much learning as teaching. The teacher should stimulate relevant inquiry and discussion, and participate in them; but the teacher must remember that students learn only *by their own efforts.* The teacher is guide, not purveyor.

III. Do I make appropriate use of the students' previous experience and instructions?

New facts or principles (experiences) are assimilated only when they are related to past related experiences.

IV. Do I make good use of illustrative material?

Much of this material should be collected by students as well as by the teacher.

V. Am I sure that my students react vigorously to my instruction? Are they passive or alert during the class exercises? Do they ask pertinent questions? Do I get pointed answers or discussions in response to my questions? Do they discuss my expositions or points of view among themselves?

VI. Are most of my students usually interested in the classroom work?

The secret of interest is their own activity. Keep most of the class busy most of the time. If classes are not interested the fault is with the teacher.

VII. Do I habitually read the best contemporary literature in my field?

As soon as the teacher stops growing he should stop teaching.

He must be both a reader and an observer.

VIII. What tests do I employ to assure myself that my students are achieving the results at which I aim?

Such tests must themselves be constantly tested.

Who Does the Training?—I have repeatedly suggested that the wise executive takes a training attitude into all of his work that involves personal contact with subordinates. This change from a military attitude of commanding to an instructional attitude of guiding, unfolding, and developing people's capacities is one of the profound and radical innovations of our generation. And its application has only begun. Indeed, the value of this attitude supplies one big reason for fostering a plan for training executives themselves—a plan which will primarily help to inculcate in them this training attitude and the general methods necessary to employ in following it out in action.   In a profound sense *all* executives are trainers, and as such, their conscious use of the training attitude and of good teaching methods is a matter of greatest concern.

Here, again, as in morale instruction, the personnel executive is the head training executive *par excellence.*   And in an organization of more than three or four hundred people he would have under his direction a training director who would be a technically equipped educator capable of developing in detail the programs of training, including the large and necessary job of training the trainers.

That, perhaps, is, logically at least, the first training job in large organizations—*to be sure that the people now carrying training responsibilities are using the best pedagogical methods known.*

After that, the problem is one of extending the training program throughout the organization to other groups as rapidly as the need for it and the demand for it become evident.

Training for Organization Fitness.—Specific mention should be made of the second important half of an organization's training problem—namely, training for organization fitness. What has been said about the methods of building morale might well be repeated from this point of view, since organization fitness refers to the qualities in the individual which make morale easier to build up.

To train in this larger field of personal attitude and enthusiasm thus implies consideration of a number of points already stressed. There must be recognition of the possibility of intergroup conflicts within an organization and of the ways of integrating those conflicts.   There must be recognition of the importance of clarifying and making explicit the purposes and   objectives of the organization.   And there must be recognition of the necessary part to be played by the right kind of leader or leaders in focusing and carrying forward the process of integrating company spirit out of individual diversities.

It is, indeed, not a repetition of previous points but an underscoring of an entire point of view when I pull together these several threads of thought from other chapters and point out that considerations of conflicts of purpose and the aims of leaders are at the very core of the executive's problem as a mobilizer and trainer of human energy. Attack, in the first instance, upon any problems of method instead of upon these issues of what are, in reality, matters of business and social philosophy and outlook will have negligible value. If the executive and the board of directors are *thinking straight and candidly* on these basic issues of outlook and objective, all the rest will follow in due course.

Teaching How to Study.—The act of studying is itself an art which can be acquired and improved. Especially with adults whose habits of study have long since been forgotten if they were ever acquired, the value of definite tuition in the technique of study should not be ignored. A few simple rules can be set down which a good teacher can inculcate in a way to bring the student to greatly increased proficiency when confronted by the printed page.

There is, first, the importance of having the student get the right attitude toward books. As far as the kind of books used in most industrial training is concerned, these will usually be *records of human experience*, compressed for convenience between the covers of a book. As such, they are *data for new learning*, just as much as the demonstrations or the ideas of the instructor. They mobilize quickly and economically for the inexperienced the accumulated facts, activities, opinions, and conclusions of the writer. The learner must be brought to realize that books are thus not dead things but live and vital resources, *if they are books that have been chosen with care and are by people who have gained a right to a public hearing.*

On the other hand, the student must be warned against the tyranny of the printed page. Nothing is true merely because it is in print. And the printed word as such supplies no proof of anything. It is solely data and evidence on one or another phase of a question; and the reader's *critical* consideration and evaluation of it is the important requirement. Good studying is examination of the ideas of others in an open-minded but query-ing frame of mind. Is his evidence sufficient to lead to his conclusions?   Are his conclusions in line with my own in the light of my own experience?   These are the questions which the intelligent reader will constantly ask of his author.   Not only does this attitude make his understanding of what he reads greater; but also it keeps his mind awake and interested.

If, then, the student can be brought to look on the book he is taking up as a window through which he is about to view new experience, if he can be made *to anticipate pleasantly* the act of reading, and if, finally, he is not preparing to swallow every word as gospel truth, his preliminary attitude will be a favorable one for good results.

His preliminary physical situation is also important.   He must be free of distractions; he must be comfortably seated—but not too comfortably.   He should not be too fatigued nor too overfed when he tries to study; and he should have the light properly located in relation to the printed page—that is, it should come over his left shoulder.

His reading of an assignment should take place as far as possible at one sitting and be gone through *as a whole*.   After one straightaway reading he should ask himself, "What is the author trying to say?"   If he can frame this in his own words in writing in a notebook, he has probably grasped the idea.   If he cannot do this, he should read the entire chapter or section a second time and then repeat to himself the same question.   When the major thesis has thus been discovered, it is time enough to go back and outline and analyze the argument and its supporting data, examples, and conclusions.   Enough of this material should then be *reduced to writing by the student in his own words*, so that by reference to his notes thereafter he can quickly recover to his mind the content of his reading.   This note taking is a vital part of the learning process, as it helps to introduce the motor element which facilitates the permanent retention of the new ideas.   If it is not successful at first, this is often because the student has a defective sense of what *is* the main thesis and what *are* the main arguments in the author's case.   A teacher who will go over such notes for a student for two or three lessons can often help him in this respect and make both his note taking and his reading attitude more discerning. But at best there will be great individual differences in the quickness with which the reader discovers what an author is trying to say.

An added point of value can be secured under those desirable conditions where the student owns the book that he is reading. He can then underline and check in the margin the sentences and new ideas which he wants especially to refer to again. This adds greatly to the permanent value of the book as a reference tool. For to know where to look for the idea you want is the next thing in value to having it on the tip of your tongue.

Comprehension is also increased if the reader will faithfully look up and *write down* the meaning of every word he encounters with which he is unfamiliar. It is unavoidable that, to a certain extent, written English should be somewhat more formal than the spoken word. And the reader who is to get maximum value out of his labors should strive to increase his vocabulary both of literary and of technical words which he is likely to encounter again.

Reading can prove such a tremendously illuminating, broadening, and enjoyable activity that every help should be given by the teacher to removing the barriers between the inexperienced book user and the contents of the book. And, of course, not the least of the responsibilities of the teacher is to be, as someone has said, "a walking bibliography." In large plants, moreover, a good company librarian should be able to add her assistance in this difficult process of selecting suitable books and being sure that the reader finds what is in them for him.

CHAPTER XVII

AROUSING INTEREST AND SUPPLYING INCENTIVES

Industry has made use for years of much human effort where the existence or non-existence of interest on the part of the worker was of no special concern to executives. The fact that workmanship was often as good as it was or that individuals did not more often register a strong protest at the dwarfing or cramping of their natures was no proof that all was well. It was rather a tribute to the adaptability of human nature—and to the fact that people once involved in a routine seek either to find some interest in it or to compensate for its lack by interesting activities in other directions.

Now the truth is being realized that individuals who pursue an activity over a long period of time chiefly because of outside compulsion are neither accomplishing their best productively nor aiding in the growth of personality. The outcome of such routinized performance has again and again been shown to be indifferent workmanship and stultified individuality.

Today, we are reaping in the indifference and unresponsiveness of workers the results of the nineteenth-century neglect of the problem of interest and incentives. But the last few years have, happily, brought an increasing concern over the problem and it has been approached by executives from a number of distinct points of view, each of which has a certain contribution to make in helping to lead on to a balanced understanding of the problem as a whole. It will, therefore, be helpful to pass these points of view briefly in review.

In other words, the purpose of this chapter is primarily to consider the psychological background and sources of interest and incentives and only secondarily to discuss actual methods of arousing interest or supplying incentives. For once a few general principles are in mind, the detailed applications which can be made in store, office, and factory are legion in number. Indeed, a mere recitation of existing devices in these two fields would occupy many pages. For there has already been much experimentation, some of which is amateurish just because it is not soundly based on its psychological side.

The first of these current points of view about the dangers of monotony in work may, therefore, be truly denoted as the old-fashioned view, which still lingers on among older executives. It holds that most work, and especially that of the manual workers, is a curse and a drudgery. It holds that the worker's interest is not wanted or needed, because machinery is more and more preponderant in production. It holds that interest is difficult if not impossible to secure—largely, it would seem, because it has not been much in evidence in the past. This is the discouraged view, and the executives who voice it naturally are not interested in doing anything positive that might prove themselves wrong.

A more subtle approach to the problem is one which says that much work is inevitably automatic and that the thing to do is to reduce it to automatic, habitual activities, which leave the workers' minds free to range over the universe at their pleasure. The important thing in this view is to be sure that the workers have cheerful and optimistic daydreams or reveries in mind rather than "pessimistic reveries." For pessimistic reveries, which imply unwholesome centering of attention on maladjustments at home or at work, lead to discouragement, unhappiness, and even more serious mental aberrations. The idea here is to encourage pleasant daydreams by providing all the surrounding conditions which assure a wholesome content to the flow of consciousness. The corrective effort is not directed at the work but at the mental outlook of each individual worker.

Related to this is the idea that the dullness of work can be offset by attractive noon-hour activities—band concerts, dances, ball games, radio, reading rooms—and by interesting evening diversions—glee clubs, dramatics, bowling contests, etc. Here, again, the corrective effort is not at all directed at the work as such but at compensatory activity outside.

Again, some executives believe that the problem can be solved by offering financial incentives which will distract the workers' minds from the vacuity of monotonous effort by centering attention on the reward and the effort to secure it. Although they do not quite say so, those who hold this view propose to bribe the worker into drudgery by a money stake in the outcome.

More constructive is the attack that would shorten hours, encourage transfers, increase the amount of automatically fed machinery, alternate factory and farm work opportunities— in short, lessen the duration of the strain of monotony or remove it by new mechanical installations. Particularly in this latter direction, much is inevitably being accomplished through the great improvements in machinery.

A final view—which aims to take modern knowledge of human nature most fully into account—holds that *the aim should be to arouse real interest in the hour-by-hour work process itself as one vital means of having this important segment of the waking life yield a positive satisfaction to individuals and become a real medium for expressing, enriching, and developing personality.*

This objective is admittedly not widely held among executives as yet. And the difficulties of achieving it in action are not to be minimized. But nothing short of this aim would seem to be a worthy goal in the light of our knowledge of the conditions under which people work and progress best. Surely, if one views the present situation historically, one would have to admit that it is only in the relatively few years since power machinery has been introduced that this complete disassociation of labor and interest in labor has become quite so prevalent. And there is no *a priori* reason why, with the application of intelligence to the problem, it may not be possible to combine in work the values of fruitful effort and enjoyable activity. Indeed, the sincere attempts thus far made by some executives along these lines indicate, in a most hopeful way, that the real thing needed is the will to create conditions that bring interest. And the evidence is that the creation of such conditions is not going to be so difficult as was at first supposed. In fact, the technical conditions of work today point more hopefully than ever before to the likelihood of this restoration of natural and genuine interest. Far from its being true that increased mechanization is requiring uninterested, routinized labor, it is demanding mental activity from the manual worker of a kind that greatly predisposes to a condition of interest.

It is interesting to note that another recent student of this problem confirms this view and suggests that factory machine work can be traced through three successive steps as follow:[1]

"First, they supplied more power to the skilled worker. They increased his output, but left his job substantially unchanged.

Second, they subdivided the manufacturing process, allowing unskilled or semi-skilled workers to feed them, remove the output, and carry on the few repetitive motions which their tending required. This is the robot stage.

Third, they replaced the unskilled worker with their own steel fingers, doing the feeding, processing, packaging, themselves. The skilled man comes back into the picture as inspector, repairer, adjuster of delicate controls. His job is interesting, non-repetitive; requires intelligence. The robot has largely disappeared."

Also, experience is conclusive that it is worthwhile for executives to try to obtain interest in industry. It has cash value for organizations because it encourages and implies in its members an attitude which is indispensable for all-around morale—an attitude of sustained attention and creative absorption in the task. It is psychologically demonstrable that people who are interested make better and happier individuals. A managerial objective of arousing interest can certainly pay dividends by encouraging conditions which promote the development of producers and of citizens.

The Nature of Interest.—The psychological reason why this is true will be most readily seen if one understands clearly what the true nature of interest is. *Interest is an attitude of continuing attention induced where the individual finds that the activity gives him a sense of self-expression.* Interest is present where the person doing and the thing being done merge into an absorbing and sustained performance of some accomplishment. The person acting and the thing acted upon become, for the time, a living, dynamic unity of human experience.   The one interested has no reservations about the value of the action; he has only the exhilaration of creative experience.

Interest may thus be achieved in the most varied ways. And it is obviously a very individual thing.   It is a matter of a temporarily successful relation of person to immediate evironment.   As the person grows in capacity or changes in purposes or aptitudes, the activity in which interest will be found changes.

In a word, it is always a problem of adjusting a relationship of person to activity.   This means that it is a recurring problem for the individual; which makes it also a recurring problem for the executive who is concerned to keep individuals interested. Naturally, this fact complicates the problem, but there is no good reason to suppose that it makes it insoluble.

"Monotony" is the name for the condition where the activity is not sustaining attention in this exhilarating way and is not felt to be self-expressive.   Hence, what is monotonous to one person may not be so for another; and what may not be monotonous to a person at one time may become so for him later on. *Interest and monotony do not inhere in any particular type of working activity as such.*   They inhere in a relationship of the worker to a particular piece of work.

This understanding of the psychological elements of the problem is important, as it suggests the point of attack.   It is an attack which must be particularized upon individuals and their suitability for specific tasks.   Translated into these terms, it is a matter that foremen, personnel managers, and all executives can work at constructively.   In part, their efforts can be in the establishing of certain prerequisite corporate policies that will predispose people to becoming interested; and, in part, they can be in the setting up of a variety of devices and schemes for putting people into surroundings where self-expression can truly take place.

Prerequisites to an Interest Program.—The company which has become convinced that the interest of its employees is a valuable business asset will find it necessary to pay attention at the start to several matters.   For it is clear that self-expressive action is likely to occur only where certain possible prior mental concerns and preoccupations have been disposed of. The following points should, therefore, be carefully provided for: (1) The company must carry on the process of selection of employees with the greatest care, so that each individual's aptitudes and talents are utilized in a way which is as close as possible to their native or trained abilities and aptitudes. (2) It must be able to assure some reasonable security of tenure in employment, so that the individual will not be ridden by preoccupying fears of unemployment. (3) It must assure that the worker who does become interested and, therefore, inevitably does work with better application gets some tangible benefit as a result. (4) It must assure that the entire working relationship is on a basis that commends itself to the workers' sense of justice and fairness.

The difficulty has been that interest-arousing programs have ignored these basic elements, have been worked at sporadically, and have, perhaps, unconsciously become exploitive in the sense of getting for the company all the gains accruing from the absorption of the worker in his task. Only temporarily can success be attained for a program thus defective in conception. Fundamentally and over a period of time, interest will persist only as the individual's sense of self-expression comes *throughout the entire range of his motives* and not merely in his immediate manipulative activity. If he discovers—as he inevitably will—that his interest in his job is resulting in his being merely a money-making agent for others, he will lose interest. If he finds that this absorption penalizes him in terms of fatigue, insecure employment, narrowness of outlook, or any other drawback, he will lose interest. Too great emphasis cannot be placed on this idea that *true and permanent interest—with all the values which it can bring—is a growth resulting from a whole setting of favorable and fair working terms and surroundings.* It requires a program of supporting aids which cannot be applied by halves.

The Psychological Bases of Interest.—Given the prerequisite conditions just named, the planning of an interest program must take account of its psychological roots. Interest, because it comes in the course of self-expressive action, requires the presence of the mental elements which always in human experience have gone to make up well-integrated activity. This means that the one interested must share in the experience of (1) knowledge, (2) skill, (3) a sense of approval, (4) a feeling of status, (5) a sense of progress, and (6) an assurance of reward.

Briefly, the relation of these factors to interest is as follows: Knowledge of material, machinery, process, and product is one essential mental accompaniment of true self-expressive activity in work, because the absence of it—to say nothing of ignorance of company policies and prospects—means that work is taking place on the level of muscle power only. Which means that the self-expression is on the muscle level only. Self-expression in any fundamental sense has always, as one necessary aspect, this intellectual awareness of the setting and *rationale* of one's activity. This close relation of knowledge to interest is a basic psychological truth.

Knowledge also helps to increase the likelihood of creating interest in respect to new and as yet uninteresting parts of an activity or to new fields of activity. Professor William James has wisely called attention to this truth when he says:[2]

Any object not interesting in itself may become interesting through becoming associated with an object in which an interest already exists. The two associated objects grow, as it were, together; the interesting portion sheds its quality over the whole; and thus things not interesting in their own right borrow an interest which becomes as real and as strong as that of any natively interesting thing. The odd circumstance is that the borrowing does not impoverish the source, the objects taken together being more interesting, perhaps, than the originally interesting portion was by itself.

Nor can there be prolonged interest if one is a failure in the technical side of one's activity. Generally speaking, poor work and listlessness go hand in hand; proficiency and keen interest arise together. To bring workers quickly to the point of good workmanship by intensive job training is a necessary element in a situation which is to be favorable to the creation of interest.

Also, most people do not become self-expressive in a social vacuum. The virtues and satisfactions of the hermit have a most restricted appeal. People tend to register happily in those channels where other people will see, appreciate, and approve. So basic is this urge to win the approval of those whose esteem we crave that it must be provided for in fostering interest.

Tied up closely with the desire for approval is the yearning for status in one's own eyes no less than in the eyes of the surrounding community. If there is felt to be no status in the work being done, interest will be slow in coming. This sense of status is a complex thing, tied up by social conventions with certain types of work and with one's own estimate of the significance of the work upon which one is engaged. But that work which is to be interesting must seem to have in the worker's eye some status and dignity, is a necessary element in the interest-sustaining environment.

Again, and especially for people who are not too old, their sense of self-realization and interest is tied up with a sense of "getting somewhere," of developing their powers and increasing their range. This urge to progress, wherever it exists, is obviously a highly valuable stimulus; and some provision to satisfy it is a highly important factor.

Finally, continued and zealous interest cannot, except in rare cases, be expected if there is no reward in promotion or compensation or reputation ever seen to accrue out of the labors of the worker. Interest, effort, and reward are normally intertwined closely in human motivation; and executives must remember that the hard work of the interested subordinate will continue only as long as he can justifiably nourish some hope of reward. There is a familiar cartoon of the donkey being lured to fresh exertion by a bag of hay just beyond his reach in front of his head. And there is real danger that managers will create an analogous situation for workers if the reward from incentives is not clearly provided, and will thus foredoom their incentive efforts to failure.

Devices Which Conduce to Interest.—It is not necessary here to repeat what I have said elsewhere[3] as to the ways and means of providing these several appeals in a specific program. Many companies have, in the last 15 years, developed successfully a great variety of devices which assure to the worker that knowledge, skill, group approval, status, sense of progress, and reward which, combined in one well-conceived organization plan, conduce to an attitude of interest.

What is more important in this connection is to discuss how the trend to increased mechanization is of itself helping to make the carrying out of such a program an encouraging possibility. For if executives will see the essential hopefulness in the present situation, the larger half of the battle will be won. A close scrutiny of technological processes shows unmistakably that the newer machinery, instead of requiring "hands" to operate, requires people who can do real head work. Machines which formerly required hand feeding of a highly routine sort are rapidly being mechanized to the point where instead of being hand fed they are being machine fed. This means that the work which remains for people to do must be increasingly centered on the building and setting up of very complex machines, on machine operation, maintenance, and repair—on tasks which require mechanical ability and ingenuity of a much higher order than hand feeding ever required. This tendency is particularly noteworthy in textiles, machine tools, boots and shoes, printing, steel, and mining. And it is conspicuous in the elimination of heavy lifting work in all industries because of the use of mechanical hoists, conveyors, and the like. In the industries where the moving platform takes the work past the worker for gradual assembly—typified in the mass production of automobiles—this tendency is far less noticeable. But there the chance for transfer at relatively unskilled jobs is great, and the simplification of hand processing is sure to lead again to further mechanization of simple operations.

In short, the tendency is markedly in the direction of requiring people with real brains to attend intelligently to the operation of highly elaborate machines in order to assure their smooth and efficient operation. This means inevitably that more and more work is of a sort which predisposes to the creation of interest in the operator or supervisor. A man who supervises a battery of automatic punch presses or cares for the operation of thirty automatic looms has a work problem which definitely challenges interest if the other supporting conditions of knowledge, skill, approval, and the like are also provided.

These considerations lead to hopeful conclusions. And instead of looking with alarm at the increasing mechanization of process, I for one welcome it as evidence that men are by way of becoming the real masters of machinery and not its slaves. Executives who will thus understand how current trends can be capitalized upon will be in a position as never before to create a body of interested fellow workers in their rank and file.

Difficulties in the Way.—I do not want, however, to convey an impression of false simplicity or ease about the difficulties of arousing interest. There remain numerous kinds of work— elevator operating, much assembling work, unskilled office jobs, some inspection work, much work in new industries which has not yet become sufficiently standardized to reach the point of complete mechanization—where the intrinsic nature of the task makes the provision of supporting conditions of interest a big challenge to ingenuity. In the aggregate, these types of work engage tens of thousands of people, and at some of them it may be possible to mitigate the drudgery only by compensatory rewards not in the work itself.

Also, there will apparently always be certain work which would be monotonous to people of high intelligence but which provides an adequate mental challenge and outlet to those of low or even slightly subnormal mentality. Today, we use people from fourteen to twenty years of age at many kinds of jobs that are conclusively "blind-alley" jobs from the point of view of their personalities—jobs which would be done with interest, dignity, and enjoyment by rightly selected men or women in their later years when the tide of energy and ambition has normally tended to ebb.

Again, it has to be remembered that every job—mental as well as physical, from the president down to the office boy—has its periods of uninteresting routine, which do not and cannot enlist interest to the maximum at every single moment of the working day. One does not seek the impossible in this connection or expect industry to conduct itself as a four-ring circus. Every adult should realize that up to a point work is work and that whether it is interesting or not a certain amount of it has to be done. Nevertheless, my contention is that there is so much that can be done to stimulate more interest at so many tasks, that the fact that perfection cannot be attained should not deter managers from making a beginning. In reality, industry has hardly faced the problem.

The Nature of Incentives.—Many executives have expressed the belief and acted on the assumption that the provision of incentives will of itself create a condition of interest. That the two subjects are closely connected is true; but that incentives alone will bestir workers to harder work and to an attitude of interest is clearly not the case. Incentives, by leading to increased application to a job, may—other conditions being right—carry an uninterested worker over into a condition of mastery where an attitude of interest may grow. Or when interest is present, incentives may help to sustain and increase it. Or they may occasionally help to restore interest temporarily. But it is important to see the psychological distinction between the two. The special definition of an incentive which will here be adhered to helps to make this difference clear.

An incentive is an external stimulus which prompts the individual to an activity by attracting and satisfying some part of his nature. It is an outside appeal to a part of one's nature which can become effective without necessarily involving the intellectual and emotional drive of the whole personality. A piece-work system of payment, for example, may supply the incentive to a worker to earn as much as he can. But he can easily at the same time possess a mental attitude which says, "I'll get all the money I can out of this job, but it's a blank blank company to work for and I'll drive as good a bargain with 'em as I can."

This does not mean that incentives are without value; quite the contrary. But it is important to see the results that they are calculated to produce and not to expect too much of them

in point of changed attitude. Experience shows that even by
themselves they supply an excellent means for increasing output,
securing a more sustained application of energy, and eliminating
waste; and as long as they are kept to their proper task and
intelligently administered, they are a highly useful and necessary
instrument.

The conclusion reached by the National Metal Trades
Association[4] after an extensive recent study concerning the value
of an incentive plan contains a sound emphasis when it says
that its success "lies not in the assumption that it causes employes
to work harder, but rather upon the fact that it induces employes,
consciously or unconsciously, to work better, with less waste
motion and waste time."

Prerequisites to the Use of Incentives.—To work effectively,
any incentive plan should be built on carefully laid foundations.
There are, as in the case of interest, certain predisposing favorable
conditions which must be satisfied if the total situation is to be
such that the psychological motives to which appeal is being made
will really operate.

Preliminary work should, therefore, be undertaken, experience
shows, along the following lines: First, the task to be undertaken
should be carefully defined. The statement of work content
should usually be in terms as definite as possible regarding
quantity, quality, method of work, amount of waste, seconds,
wear and tear on equipment, and, perhaps, other factors. There
has to be some clearly defined base from which effort starts—
some "par," "bogey," "scratch," or standard, to surpass which
the incentive is introduced.

One danger in the careless use of incentives—that people may
exert themselves beyond their strength—can usually be guarded
against if definite knowledge is at hand regarding a reasonable
performance and if maximum limits are set. Indeed, only
with these facts can a normal standard operate and amounts
above that set for reward by incentives.

Second, there must be good instruction, demonstration, and
training in the right methods to be used. To offer incentives
and to leave to chance the determination and use of a good

standard method of performance, is to lose much of the desired gain. Every worker should have the benefit of all that experience and analytical study have taught about the most efficient method of procedure. Otherwise, the incentive will become for the slower workers a source of discouragement.

Third, there must be devised methods of measuring the several elements in the work for the improvement of which the incentive is being introduced. To offer incentives and have no accurate measure as to when quality, cost, amount of waste, or some other factor is, in fact, being improved is, of course, to deprive the plan of most of its value.

Fourth,[5] there must be records compiled, made clear, and made public regarding individual and group accomplishment. Since experience shows that the publication of the records of work will of itself supply an incentive, even when no more tangible inducement is proposed, it is tremendously important that the recording problem be intelligently handled. The well-known work of Robert B. Wolf in supplying a variety of accurate control records of production results in the paper-making industry offers a surprisingly convincing example on this point—evidence which the experience of others who have followed his suggestions has completely corroborated.

Fifth, the confidence of the workers in the entire integrity of the management's use of the incentive plan must be assured. This includes assurance on such vital points as that the plan will not be used for undue speeding up of working pace, will not lead to employees' working themselves out of a job by high productivity, will not take for the management all or a too great fraction of the gain from improved results. Again and again, incentive plans otherwise sound have been wrecked because one or another of these three points was not handled in a way that made the workers feel that their legitimate rights were being safe-guarded. The best plans have always given explicit protection on these items and left the workers' minds free to feel that they could throw themselves into their work without fear of hurtful results.

Elliott D. Smith has called attention to the difficulties of the rate-cutting problem, for example, by pointing out that there are occasions when rate cutting may, in their own interest, have to be put to the employees as a necessary exception to the usual rule. He says:[6]

> The thing which is most dangerous and most to be guarded against in this long-term rate thinking is cutting or not cutting the rate. Each is equally hazardous under certain conditions. If employees have no confidence in the permanency of a rate, they do not work to full capacity. Sometimes, conceivably, harm is also done by not cutting a rate, for competitors may make it necessary to give up the work of a certain department, as occurred in the Dennison Company, making it necessary to put forty people out of employment.

Sixth, as a further guarantee that the workers will continue to have complete confidence in the management's operation of incentive measures, it is highly *desirable that the employees themselves be a party to the installation and administration of the measures.* Admittedly, this practice is not universal today. But the testimony of some of the most successful plans is that it is a helpful feature. As the description of one plan well says:

> All questions arising out of the working of the plan must be dealt with by the management and the workers' committee together. If no committee exists, one should be formed. The committee will examine the basis of the system, check the calculation of the bonus, discuss any suggested changes in point values, etc.

Principles in the Application of Incentives.—The experience with applying incentives is now so extensive that a few simple principles can be set down as a guide to follow in the inception of any scheme, once the above prerequisites are provided.

First, the granting of the incentive must be in direct and obvious relation to the results obtained. The whole sense of the fairness of the plan depends upon recognition's coming in accurate relation to performance with every trace of arbitrariness removed.

Second, any good incentive plan will necessarily be preceded by the installation of a well-organized procedure for managerial control of work in process. Standardization of shop or office practice throughout the entire mechanism of flow of work, supplying of material, maintaining machine performance, and the like, is essential if conditions at the job are to remain uniform enough for production standards to be achieved by the worker and amounts above those standards to be possible of attainment. Incentives cannot be introduced successfully if machines are always breaking down, materials not to be found promptly, tools missing, deliveries from previous processes or departments irregular in time and quality.   And all of these things happen in plants where the control of the production process has not been scientifically organized and maintained by the management. Management must be responsible for supplying standardized conditions in all these respects.

Third, there is no point in introducing an incentive plan if it costs more to operate than is gained in increased production. This applies, of course, especially to financial incentives.   As Elliott D. Smith has wisely pointed out:[7]

> Often conditions are such that the exact knowledge of daily output necessary for direct payment by results cannot be obtained without disproportionate expense.   This has been most conspicuously true of the expense of inspecting after each operation and of figuring quality ratings in those few places where direct quality incentives have been attempted.   There are many places where the difficulty or the expense of standardization and of exact measurement of results is so great that time payments in one form or another are far better than any form of piece payment.

Fourth, it is impossible to contrive an incentive plan that will of itself supply all the stimulus needed.   "Valuable as financial incentives are," says Mr. Smith, "their limitation must not be overlooked.   Primary among these is the fact that they do not reach the invaluable voluntary cooperation and effort which each workman can, but cannot be forced to, give."   And the same holds true of so-called "non-financial incentives."   No one form can possibly appeal to all the possible elements in human nature which might be made the basis for an appeal. But if it is remembered that people are appealed to by assurances of approval, security, good workmanship, reward, and the like, a combination of incentive devices can frequently be supplied.

Fifth, the incentive itself must be clearly understood; the way in which it will be applied to the individual case must be clearly known by the workers; the reward offered must come with reasonable promptness after the task is performed.

Sixth, it should be recognized that the use of incentives may call out effort in such a way that the energy cost per unit of product is too high. Professor Poffenberger has called attention to this possibility as follows:[3]

Measured in the customary terms of *output*, incentives are effective. Are they equally so when measured in terms of efficiency, that is, output divided by cost? As far as I have been able to discover, the cost of an incentive device has never been directly measured in terms of energy units. One study made in our own laboratory suggests that most careful measurements of the effects of incentives should be made. Physical work was carried on both with incentive and without incentive, in such a way that the worker in every case continued work until he was exhausted. A rest period then followed, which was succeeded by a second work period. Now the effects (or cost) of the first work period were measured in terms of the amount of recovery that took place during the rest period. The greater the cost of the first work period the less could the worker do in the second work period after the rest. It was found that work with incentive gave a higher output during the first work period but that also the amount of work after rest was less. That is to say, the gain in output from the incentive was not all "velvet," but some of it at least had to be charged off against the increased cost. This study is merely suggestive of what may be found in more direct study. There is something to be said in favor of the use of incentives in everyday work, where the rate of work is suspected of being below the optimum. In fact, where time rate prevails, the use of incentives is probably safe. Where piece rates are in operation, it is not so certain that rates of work or output do not sometimes go beyond the maximum, with the result that the cost per unit of useful work becomes excessively high. In any case, a thoroughly efficient system of work would demand knowledge concerning the exact increase to be attributed to an incentive, or to one incentive as compared with another. This can be done, not in terms of increase in output, but in terms of cost per unit of output.

If these six general considerations are held in view, there is an almost infinite number of applications that human ingenuity can hit upon to realize them in action. A few of the better tested of these may be mentioned.

Suggested Incentive Devices.—Confining the enumeration, first, to incentives that involve no financial payment, we find that use is made of medals, scrolls, distinguished service badges, and the like. The American Telephone and Telegraph Company has an impressive plan of distinguished service awards which are given annually with dignified public recognition for conspicuous faithfulness under hazardous conditions. The Pennsylvania Railroad has a plan which works along similar lines. The New York Building Congress gives a certificate of workmanship annually to a worker in each of the major crafts of the building trades for distinctive performance in craftsmanship.

A few companies operate their promotion plan in a way to supply a definite incentive. By giving publicity regarding vacancies higher up, by publishing promotion charts, by inviting candidates to volunteer for possible advancement, they capitalize on this feature.

More and more companies are finding it stimulating to publish on bulletin boards, by special department charts, by huge graphic clocks or thermometers, and by other similar methods, the production records of individuals, groups, departments, and the plant as a whole. Many variants of this idea are worked. Records are published on costs, quantity, power used, quality, idle machine time, waste, volume of shipments, volume of sales, monthly earnings, etc. And on every hand the experience is the same, that knowledge by the workers of what they have done spurs them to equal or surpass previous records. Of course, this stimulus cannot go on forever with equal effectiveness. And some companies have found it valuable to institute short-time campaigns specializing from time to time on various factors.

A typical case out of dozens that might be cited is supplied from the experience of the Westinghouse Lamp Company as follows:[9]

. . . the delicate nature of the processes and the fragility of the materials used result in a great deal of breakage and a rather high percentage of rejections on the final tests under the best conditions. It is not hard to imagine how much worse it would be with the ordinary run of girls who had been selected without care or discrimination. Even so these losses or "shrinkage," as it is called, formerly ran as high as 5 per cent. This has now been reduced by one-third. It has not been done by nagging or severe discipline. It could never have been accomplished in that way.

The mode of attack on this problem of spoilage has been by exciting that universal instinct which loves sportsmanlike competition. This consists of organizing contests, in which cash prizes are offered, between departments for the greatest improvement in the amount of spoilage.

As these contests must cover a period of about 3 months, it has been quite a proposition to sustain a lively interest in them for that length of time.

In the first place, prizes are given to every department so that none will feel entirely left out, and as a reward for the extra effort. Each department also appoints its own committee to decide before the contest starts how the money is to be used when awarded. In some cases the members with the highest individual records of improvement have the money divided among them, and in others, the committee decides to spend it on a departmental picnic or similar group jollification. Each department decides this matter for itself.

A chart is posted in each department which shows the status of the contestants, and in order to link them with the most interesting and thrilling sporting event of the day, each department was represented last summer as a channel swimmer.

In addition to this, every department has a contest of its own in which the units, or groups, compete. Smaller prizes are given in these contests. The same pictorial method of showing the standing of the contestants is used but frequently with variations. For instance, they might represent an aeroplane race or an around the world race.

Besides these, some departments have hourly contests for the best records, which have had remarkable results. Sometimes a group around a machine, where each girl is responsible for a particular detail of the work, maintains perfect records with no spoilage for several consecutive hours. Before these contests were started such performance was practically never attained.

In contract work where special jobs are taken on under conditions of competitive bidding, there are numerous instances where managers have gone before a group of workers and pointed out that a job could be obtained and more continuous work assured if the men could get the job finished by a certain time or at a certain cost. Usually, these proposals are taken up by the workers and the whole arrangement becomes a definite incentive of a valuable sort. Admittedly, this type of proposition is susceptible to abuse by managers, but where it is honestly undertaken and the terms are reasonable, all may benefit by it.

Suggestion systems wisely administered can supply a wholesome incentive. But there are several factors in the running of the system which have to be carefully thought through. Probably the most important is the adequacy of the award for the suggestion. A system of flat payments of $5, $10, or $20 for suggestions, regardless of their value to the company, is insufficient and inflexible. As Henry S. Dennison wisely says:[10]

. . . there is a minimum below which it is no incentive whatever and a maximum above which it starts up so many other influences that its effect as an incentive to active and energetic work is smothered. The greatest good per dollar lies in the middle ranges.

Also, the act of granting the awards must be made sufficiently impressive so that everyone feels that the whole plan has real company backing and real prestige among one's fellow workers. Various kinds of publicity and an annual banquet are among the methods employed. For it usually proves necessary for managers to do something to stimulate sustained interest in the suggestion system. And for this reason, it may be well to have definite suggestion campaigns recurring at specified intervals.[11]

A well-conceived training program where much emphasis is put upon training for upgrading or improvement in individual equipment looking to promotion can also supply a good incentive.

Knowledge about the company and its products and their uses can supply an incentive if it is effectively put over to workers. And where this knowledge extends to taking the workers into the management's confidence on the state of business, future prospects, dividend possibilities, etc., the information may have a most stimulating effect. This is, of course, most true where employees also have a financial stake in the business through bonuses, profit sharing, or stock ownership.

One citation, from among many that might be made, calls attention to what can be done here with the offering of facts in the effort to secure greater employee effort. Discussing relations with his shop committee, Mr. Suddard of the Hamilton Watch Company says:[12]

. . . we have played as square as we know how, and have placed all the information at our command in the hands of the committee. In other words, we have taken the whole story to the organization. No trump cards are held back.

One of the important means of getting all the facts to the men in such shape that they can readily absorb them has been graphic charts. We have gone to considerable trouble to draw up the charts in intelligible form.

And in this connection it may be worth noting here that at the outset we made overall charts. That is, they concerned our business more or less as a whole. Then, as the years went on and the employees became used to having the facts presented to them, as they became accustomed to interpreting the various values, we began breaking down these overall figures by departments and by types of controllable expense.

For example, we started out by plotting only one figure, the cost per man per hour. Then we added an overall sufficiency curve. Next, as the explanations became complicated we broke it up by departments.

And now our graphic performance sheets show a clear picture of the ups and downs of such items as non-productive labor, store supplies, defective work, total direct expense, standard hours, cost per standard hour, efficiency, and so on.

These graphic presentations do not have to stand entirely by themselves, for with them are presented all the supporting data. No committee meeting goes by without a full consideration and discussion of the graphic story of the period's accomplishments.

In a word, everything we do under this plan is directed toward giving employees all the facts about the business. Do this and the results will take care of themselves is our belief—and experience.

One significant figure, which is representative of overall controllable costs, was reduced 50 per cent before the first year under this plan was over. And the second year saw this figure cut in two again. This is somewhat typical of the results we have had since we took the employees into our full confidence.

Finally, there are some types of business where the appeal of the work as public service requiring a high sense of responsibility on the part of all workers can be clearly brought home. The incentive thus offered for safe operation, for example, in all kinds of public transit lines has proved to be substantial. And by an enlightened no-accident drive, many railroad companies, as well as others not usually spoken of as public servants, have done remarkable things in reducing accidents to employees and the general public as well. The important point here is that the employees' consciousness of public responsibility shall be appealed to by constant, recurring, and attention-impelling publicity in house organs, bulletins, committee meetings, special awards, and the like.

In fact, all the incentives that have these varying appeals to group approval, self-pride, self-development, and group consciousness are splendid and invaluable aids to morale, to interest, enthusiasm, and organization progress. They have shown conclusively in action that the pay-envelope appeal is not the only effective one but rather one to be supplemented in a great variety of ways. They show that it is not a question of financial or non-financial incentives but rather of adapting each to its best uses.

The Financial Incentives.—Now as to financial incentives, a reasonable division can be made as between short-time and long-time incentives. In the former class, we find the most important to be piece-work payment, payment of flat weekly sums plus piece rates or bonuses, payment for specific tasks plus bonuses, differential piece rates, and numerous more or less complex variants on these.[12] And these may again be divided into individual- and group-incentive plans. Also, a distinction has to be observed as between incentives for rank and file and those for executives.

Without pretending to consider the details of these plans, it is in place here to point out some of the psychological considerations which arise to affect the value of incentives, particularly for the rank and file.

First, the question of the base rate of pay per hour, day, or week on which the rest of the plan is built is a moot one. In practice, some base rates are below the market rate, some at the market rate, some a little above it. What is wise procedure is a point that cannot be settled in the abstract, since so much depends upon the amounts which are, in fact, added in order to make up the total weekly payment. But it does seem clear that any plan to be successful should provide that the sum of the base rate and the incentive payment will be appreciably above the market rate of the locality for that kind of work. To elaborate a plan to provide a reward for extra effort which is only little if any above the local market rate for that type of work is psychologically valueless.

Second, agreement is general that the method of computing the gains to the worker should be simple enough for him to be able to figure them out for himself with reasonable ease. He must be able to keep his own score or at least to learn what it is at the end of each day.

Third, the worker must not be penalized for failures to earn which are due to deficiencies in management. This seems to argue for some type of guaranteed day or week rate. Nothing will prove more fatal over a period of time than an incentive plan which penalizes the worker for failures to earn for which he personally is in no sense responsible.

Fourth, the standards set should be attainable by the average worker. It has a poor effect if standards are so high that week after week workers do not rank more than 80 per cent of the standard. It is much sounder, as a matter of motivation, when they are able to point with pride to the fact that they have performed 125 per cent of the standard in a given period.

Group Incentives.—Where work conditions admit, there is much to be said for the use of a group-production standard with a group incentive. The appeal that it makes to a variety of human motives is valid, useful, and psychologically superior to that of an individual incentive. In the study of the National

Metal Trades Association, the advantages and drawbacks of group incentives are well summarized as follows:[14]

The advantages of gang incentives are said to be

1. Group system eliminates necessity for numerous individual rates, piece prices, or standards.

2. Makes possible recognition of long service, loyalty, etc., by changing basic day rate.

3. Unaffected by changes in labor markets, as standards are in terms of hours instead of money.

4. Permits transfer of men from department to department without changing rates.

5. Simplifies factory cost system.

6. Tends to reduce scrap and defective workmanship.

7. Spirit of teamwork developed reduces labor turnover and induces skilled men to instruct and assist beginners.

8. Permits assigning most difficult jobs to old and skilled men without complaints.

The disadvantages are said to be

1. Arbitrary fixing of hourly rates tends to disrupt gang morale.
2. Productive effort less than under individual incentive system.
3. Not easily understood by employees.
4. Payroll computation rather complex.
5. Danger of injustice to individuals.

Actual experience shows, however, that under intelligent administration, the benefits of group incentives far outweigh the difficulties; and the recent rapid extension of this form of payment indicates its popular appeal no less than its scientific soundness.

At least one company has applied the group-incentive idea to its entire factory force as one group, thus involving the so-called "indirect" as well as direct labor groups in an appeal to help maintain and increase the output of the plant as a whole in relation to a predefined standard of total production. The benefits claimed for this plan are interesting to consider, especially as it has been in successful operation since 1917. Summarizing them, the author of the plan says:[15]

The men work at their optimum speed and find much satisfaction in always doing their best without the necessity for a watchful foreman constantly supervising them.

The slack worker generally improves, but if he is incorrigible he leaves.

Men prefer to be in a collective system. If they stand out they get no help and they cannot earn the full reward of their effort even under piece rates because they do not get the necessary assistance.

The elimination of the slacker means a better tone in the factory and automatically increases output because a productive worker takes the place of an indifferent one.

The men appreciate the advantage of everyone's having a good all-round bonus rather than a few workers' receiving exceptionally high wages.

As the standards are fixed by the work previously done, the men cannot possibly lose by the system, and the fairness of the basis encourages them to put their best into their work.

It is a great satisfaction to know that the bonus is not jeopardized even when the firm is losing financially.

The impossibility of cutting times or rates gives them a sense of satisfaction and security.

The men make suggestions and recommendations for improving the facilities and amenities of the factory.

The men take greater interest in the management of the factory and appreciate manufacturing difficulties much more than before.

From a psychological point of view, there is much to commend the group incentive idea. It helps in a remarkable way to develop team spirit throughout an organization and supplies a mechanism of measure and reward much more direct and related to individual effort than those long-time measures in which the factors which affect profits are often so largely outside the control of those involved only in the production side of the business.

Long-time Incentives.—Agreement is general that, as immediate incentives to greater output, the more long-range rewards of annual bonuses, profit-sharing plans, and stock distribution to employees are not effective. Their value lies in other quarters —in the sense of cooperation evoked, in the sense of permanent relation to the company which tends to grow up, in the proprietary feeling in the corporate welfare which may develop with the years, all of which may have, in the aggregate, a profound influence for good on the basic attitude of workers toward their company.

There are, however, certain special problems to be confronted if these incentives to morale are not to act as a boomerang. For example, if common stock has been widely distributed among employees and then its value per share depreciates greatly, the ill effects of this have been known in certain companies almost completely to undo the benefits which seemed on the way to being enjoyed. A profit-sharing plan, also, in a plant where profits continue at a negligible level is not calculated to act as much of an incentive.

The following characterization of these provisions as incentives made by Mr. Dennison is an accurate estimate of the positive and negative aspects of their value:[16]

For the stock incentive (and there again I limit that to a not easily salable or actually transferable stock in the company the man is working for) we have, of course, a much weaker spur than the cash, so weak that in the early years—for at least two or three—we need expect no visible results to exist, perhaps none at all. To receive some non-convertible stock at the end of the year is obviously not an intense spur to hop around and do a great deal better job. To the man with imagination enough to see that it is actually good and amounts to so much in cash, it has some additional advantages; but to the average run of man it cannot be looked to as an active spur in many years. It has, however, this advantage—it has an accumulating spur which is a steady one.

If the incentive plan gives stock each year you can at least be sure of one thing—the man has the last year's incentive still on hand. As it is non-salable he cannot get rid of it, and this year's incentive adds to it. You have (and this, of course, is again in accordance with our own experience) an incentive which practically begins at zero, starts very slowly, but always grows in the depth and strength of its power.

The cash incentive requires repeated doses. A single dose of last year is done for when it gives out. If you have no more next year the effect is gone. The stock incentive has a persistent effect. It arouses the complex of motives which are very powerful—what we call the sense of proprietorship or ownership—something fairly deep in human nature. Having stock in the company, being a proprietor—even to a small extent —has a distinct and decided effect upon people by its own virtue.

As I have already said, there are not two kinds of incentives, one wholly cash and one wholly stock. As a matter of fact, most stock incentives depend at least upon the cash dividend to give cogency and value to the stock itself.

The experience of the Dennison Manufacturing Company, from which these observations are largely drawn, is not unique. Professor Feis, in evaluating the stock-sale plan of the Procter & Gamble Company, says:[17]

The plan does offer, it is true, an indirect incentive to increase net earnings in the hope of increased dividends on company stock and an increase in the market value of the stock. The workmen are alive to these considerations, and they have given rise to watchfulness and effort in the company's interests.

On these indirect incentives, on the protection given in bad periods, upon the general opportunity given to save, the company relies, as sufficient to establish in the minds of the men the value of the plan to them; and on the whole it is established, and the workmen regard the opportunity to participate as one of the distinct advantages of being in the employment of Procter & Gamble. To be a "profit sharer" sets a man off among the men in the plant and among the general body of industrial laborers in Cincinnati, especially if he has been in the plan for a long stretch of years. In many cases it places a man in his own eyes as a "man of property." A growing number of men in the Procter & Gamble plants see open to them a road to acquisition not found before. . . . With savings running into several thousands, the property line between these industrial workers and the middle class in the community is partly broken down. But up to the present only a fifth of the men in the production plants have reached that position.

Again, the house organ of the Philadelphia Rapid Transit Company says on this point:[18]

Mitten Management has found that the best results in industry are always attained when the workers participate in profits earned by increased efficiency and are themselves stockholders in their companies. This policy not only insures the investment against loss by strikes and poor workmanship but also helps to establish a better order of society through labor's becoming capital.

And the opinion of many other companies employing one or another similar long-time incentive is that it does tend to supply an incentive for the development of that invaluable, responsible attitude of self-respect and interest in company welfare.

Incentives for Executives.—Of late, much attention is being paid to the matter of executives' incentives along these same lines. And the values which it has been hoped that they would create have, in almost every case, been secured.

Perhaps the most elaborate and far-reaching plan of executives' incentives is that of the General Motors Corporation. In addition to a salary bonus plan awarded on a basis of ratings on performance, personal characteristics, cooperation, general intelligence and specialized knowledge, executive ability, and future value to the corporation, there was created a Managers Securities Company composed of eighty senior and junior executives. This plan made a strong stockholding unit among the executives and also has given these men financial rewards commensurate with the responsibility they were carrying. In his description and advocacy of the plan, John J. Raskob, then vice-president of the company, has said:[19]

It seems to me imperatively necessary to put the managers of the large modern corporations into something of the position of owners and to create in those corporations a body of important stockholders in various walks of life to whom the managers must answer. Those corporations which today are best managed have in them large—although not necessarily controlling—stock interests that can ask the why of a bad year and give a slap on the back for a good year.

Howard Coonley, President of the Walworth Company, discussing the successful experience of his company with executive incentives, says:[20]

There are hundreds of different methods of executive incentive which will be successful. There is none that is ideal. A variety of incentives planned to meet the individual situation is much the best solution. Often a method may be followed successfully for years and become obsolete. Like every other phase of business activity, styles change. Incentives must be studied and kept up to date just as much as processes and designs.

Gorton James well summarizes a wide study of executives' incentives in the following words:[21]

The experience of American companies with profit sharing for administrative officers, although frequently clothed in secrecy, apparently has been encouraging. It has the same fundamental basis as pay in terms of physical output for the direct workers, or as pay based on departmental unit costs for foremen. The obvious measure of achievement for administrative officers lies in profits, and pay based on them has the same qualities of incentive as any other system of wages that varies with the achievement. Of course the reward is not so prompt as in the other instances mentioned, but it is not so essential that it should be. One executive explained that he had been working harder than he had ever worked before, knowing that it was a bad year and that profits would be small or non-existent, but also realizing that the efforts which he and his colleagues were exerting that year would come back to them in their participation of increased profits in following years. Other business executives, who receive this type of compensation, out of their own experiences have corroborated this testimony as to its effectiveness.

In most cases of larger corporations, so far as can be judged from information available, profit sharing of the nature discussed in this chapter is handled through special contracts with individual executives. Where it has been applied to groups of officers, especially in the smaller organizations, there has been added the element of the incentive for cooperation among the members of the group; but with this element have been introduced two destructive tendencies, one of selfishness within the group and the other of jealousy without. In some instances, however, where there has been firm leadership to nullify these latter tendencies and where the natural boundaries of such groups have been recognized in the scope of the plan, the addition of the incentive for cooperation, by making profit sharing a group affair, has proved of genuine, long-time value. Applied, in either form—as individual contracts or as a group plan—profit sharing may be said to be a useful aid in securing lasting interest by its officers in the success of an organization and thus making for continuity of management.

Difficulties with Incentives.—The continued use of incentives is not without its special problems. The one suggested above by Mr. Coonley is most important, namely, that the incentive has to be varied in order to get new attention and fresh interest.

In the second place, in order to keep the incentive constant, it is often necessary to increase the stimulus of the incentive, either quantitatively or qualitatively. Experience is conclusive that incentive plans do have to be watched to see that people are not becoming too habituated to them and, therefore, are not finding a spur in them.

Thirdly, they must be conceived so as to protect the quality of production. If the emphasis is all on volume, the best results will not come.

Fourth, the slower workers must be taken care of in such a way that the incentives will encourage and not dishearten them. This is peculiarly true in group plans. Some provision for special training is the only way to overcome this difficulty. If that fails, resort must usually be had to transfer to a type of work where the worker can show a better performance.

Fifth, in emphasis of a point already made, no one incentive is the best. Financial incentives are not necessarily to be preferred to non-financial. Both have their place and experience shows that the non-financial methods deserve much greater recognition than they have yet received. The non-acquisitive motives in human nature are very strong despite the fact that industry has so largely worked on the acquisitive motives. The more executives understand about the complexity of motivation the more sure they are to utilize plans which provide a place for approval, for a sense of personal significance, progress, and growth.

Conclusion.—The effort to arouse interest in work is far from a hopeless task. The chief need is that managers should realize what can be done and appreciate how much more valuable interested workers are than those who are indifferent. The inevitable trend to mechanization can be capitalized to give to the operators of the elaborate new machines scope for interest-arousing experience.

The provision of incentives is only one means, but an important one, for arousing and sustaining interest and improving output.

The appeal must be to a sufficient variety of human motives so that the whole personality will be summoned into action. Various incentives call out different ones of these motives. A wise program of interest-arousing methods plus a varied combination of incentives can do much to restore a relationship between the worker and his work which will make it a medium of increased earning power, growth, and self-expression.

CHAPTER XVIII

THE NEW DISCIPLINE

. . . the new discipline means domination of the corporate will, carefully enlightened and fostered.

—John Lee.

Good discipline is essential for the orderly conduct of any organization where any considerable number of people are working together. No one who has ever had executive responsibility would deny this. The only questions which modern psychology raises are as to what "good" discipline is and how it can best be assured.

To answer these questions, one must first be clear as to what end result is sought. The objective, I take it, is general and willing adherence to a certain minimum of reasonable rules or regulations which are necessary to assure promptness and regularity in attendance, honesty in the use and disposition of company property and time, freedom from gross insubordination to the reasonable requests of designated leaders, elimination of fighting, drunkenness, and gross immorality among employees while on the premises, avoidance of conduct which involves hazard to life and limb of fellow employees as well as to the property of the company. Among normal people, these objectives are not usually thought of as unduly arbitrary or severe, and the necessity for ruling against offenders in these matters is, in fact, quite generally recognized. The problems that arise center around such points as just what matters are to be regulated, what cases fall under the rules, what extenuations are to be made in the individual case, and what penalties are to be imposed. For, despite the reasonableness of regulations, questions of individual adjustment do arise; and the more we know of the likelihood that individuals will depart from the normal the more we realize the likelihood of infringement and the necessity for special handling of individual aberrations. For example, sometimes people have not been properly instructed as to the rules; or they may become careless, reckless, stubborn, angry, or tired. Or, they may develop fixations of inferiority, persecution, and the like, as shown in Chap. IX, so that they become "problem cases"—all of which points to the need of going at the disciplinary function in a careful and constructive way with attention paid both to the general policies to be pursued and to the handling of personal maladjustments.

The Old Discipline.—Two widely different attitudes toward discipline are in action today—the autocratic and what I shall call, for want of a better word, the democratic. The autocratic is the policy with which most of us became familiar first in the schoolroom and have seen in later years in action in the shop, store, or office. It was the policy of commands superimposed on our wills from someone in superior position, a teacher or foreman. We were supposed "to do as we were told." "Theirs not to reason why, theirs but to do and die" was the note. Constant supervision by this superior was relied upon to maintain order and faithful application. Transgressions were guarded against by open or tacit threats of punishment in some form. The fear motive was the one principally appealed to, and submissiveness and docility were looked upon as cardinal virtues. Punishment when it came was swift, severe, firm, not to be appealed from.

The fact that this has been the kind of discipline historically sought in school and home, no less than in industry, has special significance. For it calls attention to the strong traditional and conventional hold which this conception has upon all of us, especially if our education took place largely in prewar days. And no attack on the problem is possible unless we see, first, what the shortcomings of this conception are; second, what the alternative to it is; and, third, the psychological methods necessary to get those who direct and those who are directed both to approach the problem of group control in the newer way.

The troubles with autocratic discipline are these: It does not take account of the desires of those commanded; it ignores the relation of willing, sustained action to knowledge and desire; it appeals solely to the fear motive and not at all to the great variety of other more positive and more creative motives; it requires constant supervision because it breeds an attitude which tries to "get away with" whatever it can when the commander is not present. In a word, the sources of power and influence over the group's behavior lie wholly *outside* the group and take account, little if at all, of the tremendous sources of power which lie *within* the group, once it becomes self-conscious, articulate, and possessed of a corporate sense.

The New Discipline.—Over against this still widely current conception is that of a group discipline where *the group comes as rapidly as it will to a condition of awareness of itself as a working entity and imposes by itself on itself those standards of individual and group behavior which it finds it necessary to impose in the interests of group effectiveness in carrying on its work.*

The emphasis here is twofold—on the element of growth through leadership into a condition of group self-responsibility, and on the ultimate creation of a sense of what self-imposed group restrictions are necessary for efficiency in action.

No doubt one reason why this newer view of self-discipline gains in acceptance so slowly is that executive and workers alike have, because of their background and training, no confidence in a group's ability to control itself. The psychologist realizes that this new state of mind is a growth, that it does not come spontaneously, that the notion of being commanded to which people are habituated gives way to the newer notion of orderly conduct growing out of the requirements of the work situation and of participation in group activity *only slowly as a result of actual experience.* No executive will be discouraged with his efforts at developing this new discipline who will realize that *the thought patterns of subexecutives and workers alike have to be reeducated before self-command can truly replace external command.* The whole tradition is against this new outlook, which means that the unique values of it have to be fully understood if one is to make the struggle to secure them. For the values are unmistakably there; and the experience of recent years, both in the newer educational procedures and within industry itself, proves conclusively that they are worth the effort to secure. The values to be gained are the exact opposite of those features characteristic of autocratic discipline.

The new discipline does take account of the desires of those in the group—not by blindly trying to satisfy those of every member but by seeking, through that process of integration previously defined (see Chap. XI), to bring a real unity of desire into being. The new view also aims to help the integrative process by supplying knowledge—knowledge of the essential conditions of orderliness under each special set of circumstances, knowledge of special dangers, hazards, responsibilities, etc., which are different for every group, different in a factory manufacturing gun powder from what they are in a banking office, but important just the same. The new view aims to build largely on motives of group approval, individual creativeness, and desire for status and growth. It aims to capitalize on those inner forces of thought and emotion combined which spontaneously give rise to individual application, group loyalty, and reasonable subordination of individual will to group achievement. It realizes that "power with" is more productive than "power over," because by evolving power in a group the creative interest of each member is evoked. Finally, it does *not* require the constant supervision of a taskmaster or driver. The evidence, for example, of all forms of group-incentive payment, as described in the previous chapter, is conclusive that, given the mechanisms and arrangements for group cooperation, the group is its own best supervisor, the best judge of the amount of regulation which there has to be in order to keep all of its members contributing dutifully to the performance of the group task.

In short, the new discipline, by definition and by actual experience, provides a total working situation in which a variety of positive motives helps each individual in a group to apply himself, to subordinate himself in a reasonable way, and to contribute to the group effort as a natural result of his normal desire to express himself in action.

I repeat that this happy condition is not the result of a week's effort within a corporate or departmental group. It is a slow growth, built up only as *executives and workers go through the actual experience of vesting explicitly and acknowledgedly in the hands of the group one responsibility after another and then helping it to fulfill that responsibility by advice and suggestion.* Indeed, on the whole, this growth is conditional, in most organizations, as much *on the change in outlook of executives directly above the rank and file,* such as foremen, department heads, gang bosses, and the like, as it is on changes in the rank and file itself. For what the group usually needs is the chance to assume self-direction, whereas the minor executive has to be reeducated to conduct himself as a leader and not as a boss—a change which comes hard with seasoned managers and foremen. This need has been well characterized in sound psychological terms in the following analysis of the way in which childish emotional patterns are likely to linger on in the motivation of adults and complicate their behavior as executives:[1]

If immaturity in work-relationships were confined to underlings the problem would be much simplified, but for every childish attitude in the private there is likely to be another in the captain, and the child in one has an unholy way of calling out the child in the other. I am thinking not so much of the classic man-who-cannot-command-others-because-he-cannot-command-himself—the man in whom the voice of authority is perpetually changing for the good reason that he is still emotionally adolescent—as of the father-child relationship. Suppose I as boss am not sufficiently mature to be happy without the responses a child theoretically owes the father—unquestioning recognition of authority, and love (or "loyalty") in exchange for protection. Put me in charge of a force of workers, and I cannot be trusted not to demand these responses from them. The experience of directing other people is strong drink; it warms the ego and puffs up one's sense of power. It is easy to slip into either of two alternatives: on the one hand, using that power as an end in itself, becoming a little Mussolini in whatever station God has called us to; or, on the other, using authority as a means of buying gratitude, becoming what we accurately call paternalistic, interfering with the lives of less important people "for their own good."

The experience of the Baltimore and Ohio Railroad in its cooperative activities with its shop employees in recent years— a plan later adopted, also, by the Canadian National Railways— supplies an instructive illustration of the basic values in this newer view of the whole disciplinary problem. Under this plan, the company managers work in the closest relations with the employees and their labor union through a "cooperative committee" to improve production, review grievances, and adjust all difficulties. And in commenting on the results of the plan after 4 years of existence, Otto Beyer, the consulting engineer for the employees, has this to say:[2]

I can testify from a wide range of experience as to the leadership which is released by such a change. I have seen foremen, superintendents, managers relieved of a vast and troublesome burden of grievances and the necessity of administering sullen discipline. And I have seen agitators, grievers, committeemen representing employees changed into useful, helpful, necessary members of the industrial administrative machine. I have seen workers in industry mobilize and bring to the attention of management thousands of constructive measures devised by these workers in their own environment all aimed at improving the conduct of the enterprise. I have observed how collectively they have stimulated management to improve its own conduct, how they introduced a positive stimulus for management to exert itself in behalf of still better performance. I have been struck by the readiness on the part of the workers to assume responsibilities for better individual as well as mass performance on their part. Where formerly foremen were needed to boss a gang and keep it properly disciplined, these individuals have tended to become the guides of their group. And what is perhaps most significant o all, the cooperative relationship has revealed all kinds of managerial talent, potential industrial leadership, all of which remains hidden most effectively under the usual scheme of things.

Definition of Good Discipline.—The question as to what is good discipline is, therefore, answered by saying that it is *that orderly conduct of affairs by the members of an organization who adhere to its necessary regulations because they desire to cooperate* *harmoniously in forwarding the ends which the group has in view and willingly recognize that to do this their own wishes must be brought into reasonable unison with the requirements of the group in action.*

If now, as I suggest, good discipline is achieved only by conscious educational effort, the next question is as to what provisions can be made which will cultivate in each individual the kind of responsible conduct required. Here, again, the experience of an increasing number of companies offers a clue as to the procedure to be supplied.

Arrangements to Support Good Discipline.—Perhaps the first requirement is one which, in the first instance, falls largely on the mangement itself. There should be competent organization from the managerial end to control the flow of work in process. The entire procedure of systematization, sometimes referred to as "scientific management," means and entails planning, laying out, scheduling, and routing of work, its assignment to individuals, clear-cut standards of correct performance as to process and as to amount and quality of output. And without the precision in work control which all this brings about, there inevitably arise hitches, delays, and confusion about individual and group responsibilities which create problems of an essentially disciplinary character. Basic in the effort to have a well-disciplined organization is the task of providing a well-organized and clearly functionalized structure and procedure of organization into which each individual knows where and how he fits. Miss Follett makes almost this same point when she insists that the function of order giving and, indeed, the orders themselves really grow out of the implications and necessities of each work situation, in any well-planned organization. In a sense, the situation produces its own orders and requirements, if it is well conceived in relation to the work of the rest of the supporting group. In short, the best way to be sure that disciplinary issues are not presented is to have every member of the organization know just what is expected of him and to have the members of his group and his supervisor no less than himself support him in seeing that it is done.

Second in importance is the provision that the whole disciplinary plan, including the statement of the necessary rules and the imposing of penalties, *should gradually be shared in by the employees in an organized way.* This requirement will not sound strange or extreme to executives who deal with labor unions and have arrangements with them under collective agreements for the handling of disciplinary problems; nor to those who have active plans of employee representation under which all such matters are normally brought up at joint conference meetings. Those with experience in either of these two forms of joint dealing know that disciplinary issues are settled more quickly, equitably, and agreeably thus, than under the old scheme of things where the individual foreman or superintendent retained in his own hands the sole right of discipline and of discharge as the ultimate penalty. Obviously, where there is no redress or appeal, to say nothing of there being no initial cooperation in the promulgation of rules, the reaction of the employee is not one of a developing self-responsibility for his own and his group's behavior. Actually, in those companies where problems of regular attendance, loss of materials and tools, individual slacking on the job, are put squarely up to the employee-representation plan, the results in practically all cases have been the same. These matters have been handled with a directness, sureness, and constructive benefit which has often left managers gasping with agreeable surprise.

The fact is that a number of corporations have gone farther than this and placed in an employee committee's hands the power of final review over discharge. Of course in such cases, this is the outcome of considerable employee education in group self-control; and it is of interest here not so much because it is a policy necessarily to be recommended for adoption by others, but because the experience is that the employees, once given this serious responsibility, tend to exercise it more severely than many executives would themselves think advisable.

The third requirement to support good discipline is care in assuring that all regulations adopted are (*a*) as explicit as possible; (*b*) as few and simple as possible; (*c*) as clear as possible as to penalties. And of course there should be the widest publicity of rules, through employee handbooks, bulletin boards, verbal explanations to new employees, and the like.

Consistency and fairness in the application of the rules to the individual case are necessary. This entails having an agreed procedure of appeal, chance for statement of all sides of a case, and a final decision by an agreed tribunal which is as impartial as possible.

The theory on which penalties should be devised and administered should be one of constructive correction and not of vindictiveness. Discharge is normally the most serious punishment which can be inflicted and its use must be reserved for the worst offenders and careful review of such cases should be allowed. In general, a plan of rewards for rules well complied with should be emphasized as contrasted with emphasis on the penalty features. In fact, the scheme of incentives suggested in the last chapter will usually act by itself as a stimulus to good discipline which is vastly more valuable than any penalty provisions.

Finally, as suggested above, the disciplinary plan should protect workers against a too drastic imposition of punishment by the employees' own group. Workers will rule against their fellows with a severity that most executives would not dare to show. And while this may have its good features, experience suggests that it can be overdone. The tempering of justice with mercy, patience, and understanding is required—especially in those difficult cases where individuals who have infringed the rules present some special problem of mental abnormality or personality maladjustment.

The new discipline depends, then, not alone upon a new attitude but upon specific procedures for adopting, interpreting, and applying rules and orders in a cooperative way. The machinery is as necessary as the spirit, and the fact that such machinery must be built experimentally in each instance only goes to emphasize the educational nature of the problem.

Finally, once the whole question of discipline has been attacked in the way suggested here, the head executives of a company will have much work to do in getting the right kind of cooperation from the minor officials who actually associate with the rank and file. For these men have to be brought to realize that they can get more satisfaction, more fun out of the job—and also be doing a better job—if they try to cultivate an autonomous, group self-discipline among their subordinates than if they remain high-handed and arbitrary bosses. They have to come to realize by experience that their hold over their staff is a stronger and longer one when it comes from leading and teaching than when it comes from bossing.

In short, this new discipline is something which can be appreciated, in which faith can be placed, from which results can be obtained, only when those in power themselves have faith enough in human nature to give it a chance to vindicate itself in the conduct of others in group relationships. The wisdom of cultivating this kind of method of control over and within a working group is thus something of which one becomes convinced in the doing. But there is, I have tried to show, enough successful prior experience with its use to give an executive confidence in making the trial for himself. He who would know must do!

CHAPTER XIX

INDUSTRIAL DEMOCRACY PSYCHOLOGICALLY VIEWED

Our great problem, for the next decade at least, is a problem of persons. A democracy does not involve the leveling of mankind so that none will lead. It means a system under which each individual is allowed fair and equal scope for developing his or her own personality and for bringing out all those qualities necessary for serving the community, and under such a system certain men and women would naturally lead. A democratic government would particularly need strong leaders with clear vision and sound judgment in business, as well as a realization of social needs, and it is in the growth and development of such leaders within our group that we have not progressed so much as we might and so much as it was anticipated.

—The Columbia Cauldron
(House Organ of Columbia Conserve Company).

What share in management should be given to workers who are inexperienced, or ignorant, or irresponsible, or who, if experienced, intelligent and reliable, still lack the qualities of poise and judgment necessary for the exercise of authority? . . . Authority in management must rest, as it does today, primarily with those skilled and experienced officers and workers who necessarily assume the responsibility for operating results, and secondarily with those who take the financial risks, whether they be private investors or the public as a whole.

Nevertheless, I conceive that, up to the point of weakening necessary discipline, *the ordinary workers should have power to check any abuses of authority.*

—Malcolm C. Rorty.

It will hardly be thought to demand argument that men work together better when they regard themselves as substantially equals. Indeed in so far as inequality is confessed and paraded, cooperative activity is certainly inhibited. Activity may go on: one working for another, or

280

another directing the one. But neither true cooperation nor maximum efficiency nor happy contentment exists . . .

Man has learned to share large purposes by sharing small purposes, to work together for great achievements by working together at commonplace tasks, to cooperate in later life by giving together in youth.

The present individualistic extreme threatens stability and defeats social justice; the socialistic extreme menaces maximum productivity, which must not only be maintained but even increased if the means for the good life are to be available for all. Somewhere between the two extremes lies . . . the *via media* which can be discovered only by intelligent social experimentation.

—T. V. Smith.

For the twentieth century, democracy is not only a theory of politics; it is confidently invading the realms of industry . . . the essential spirit of democracy is that of infectious creative energy. The economist, measuring the chief productive resources of a nation, places first free institutions . . . The great principle upon which the modern factory system is built is that where two men work together, the total result of their labor is something more than it would have been if they had worked separately. The proportion of this surplus product grows greater as a larger number of workmen are properly associated . . . We live in the age of association. The great man of modern days is the man who understands this preeminently creative power . . .

The main body of objection to this general tendency has to do with the vital importance of leadership. It is urged that the democratic form of business organization would not produce and afford full stimulus to higher forms of expert capacity and leadership. It is the most serious weakness of the democratic form of government that it has not yet learned sufficiently to trust the expert, the man who by heredity and training has the physical energy, intellectual grasp, and moral power effectively to handle groups and masses of men or to bring to light the hidden resources of nature. Administrative democracy is, in its early stages, a scheme of education rather than of efficiency. Its aim is first of all to bring on the whole mass of the people. The root of the matter is, democracy represents a strongly confirmed and ever spreading conviction that as the people are thus brought on, gradually laying hold on power proportionately to their newly elicited capacities, the average man proves equal to the political demands laid upon him, and makes a more alert and more loyal member of the community.

—Robert A. Woods.

Right conscience in a natural creature can be nothing but self-knowledge, by which man discovers his own nature and the good on which it is set; so that the margin of free choice and initiative for a man of understanding is exceedingly narrow; and grows narrower as the field of his competence grows wider and his science clearer . . .

—GEORGE SANTAYANA.

The central fact that we have to remember about the industrial system is the psychological fact that workers are human beings with wills of their own, and that, now they have become possessed through their organizations of great power in society, it is useless to say that this power ought not to exist. We must recognize their power and endeavour, by giving it full scope within an ordered social scheme, to harness it to the work of serving the best interests of society.

—G. D. H. COLE.

In proportion to the development of his individuality, each person becomes more valuable to himself, and is therefore capable of being more valuable to others. There is a greater fullness of life about his own existence, and when there is more life in the units there is more in the mass which is composed of them.

—JOHN STUART MILL.

The essential of progress is not the automatic conformity too often confused with democracy, but a development of thoughtful individuality in free men bound together by fellowship.

—NORMAN THOMAS.

The best guarantee of collective efficiency and power is liberation and use of the diversity of individual capacities in initiative, planning, foresight, vigor and endurance. Personality must be educated, and personality cannot be educated by confining its operations to technical and specialized things, or to the less important relationships of life. Full education comes only when there is a responsible share on the part of each person, in proportion to capacity, in shaping the aims and policies of the social groups to which he belongs. This fact fixes the significance of democracy.

—JOHN DEWEY.

The phrase "industrial democracy" is growing in popular use. What does it mean? Today it is applied by managers to a great variety of organizational policies and structures quite diverse in character. And the question is whether a study of human nature and its essential characteristics suggests anything at all definite about the kind of industrial and economic organization which would in its working constitute a wholesome and happy medium for people's living. Can a psychological criterion be set up which helps to indicate anything of the value and utility of industrial democracy; and which also suggests any more definite notion of its inner meaning?

To answer these questions requires several steps. It is important to know the kind of experiments now covered by the name "industrial democracy." It is interesting to see why this type of experiment is gaining in favor. What if any consensus of outlook about the nature of human beings grows out of a study of psychology? Does this knowledge suggest any particular kind of policy or procedure in industrial government as better because psychologically sounder than any other? And, finally, to what several additional tests must any form of organization submit itself to prove its social worth?

Present Connotations of Industrial Democracy.—Looseness in the application of such a beguiling phrase as industrial democracy is, perhaps, inevitable. The problem is serious only because, under present conditions, many managers have come to feel that if what they are doing may be characterized as democratic, then they are on firm ground and making progress in line with the temper of the times. A sound intuition has told them that the democratic idea is in the ascendant, that sentiments already vital in the political world are gaining ground in the economic arena. Hence, it is worthwhile to be sure that in applying the phrase industrial democracy, executives are not by way of fooling themselves and others as to the value and virtue of their efforts at reorganization.

Newer Forms in Industrial Government.—In the recent experience and literature of industrial government, democracy is identified, for example, with the so-called "federal plan" of employee representation, used by a number of companies, in which the form of the federal government of the United States is adapted for use in one company. The executives constitute the cabinet, the foremen constitute a senate, and the rank and file a house of representatives.[1]

Collective bargaining of the kind usually employed between employers or employers' associations and labor unions is frequently referred to as industrial democracy.

Various forms of intramural employee-representation plans are often spoken of, especially by managers, as instances of industrial democracy.

One might, with some reason, apply the phrase to companies where employees are the owners of a considerable fraction of the stock of the company or are buying it up out of profits on special and advantageous terms.[2]

In the few cases where one or two employees have been placed on corporate boards of directors, that, too, has been cited as an instance of industrial democracy.

One can, of course, see certain common influences at work in all such efforts. But their variety does raise the question, *What does industrial democracy really mean?* Can this tendency in a democratic direction be characterized in some definite way which would make it possible to evaluate democratic procedures and, also, to direct it in a scientific and human way? Is there some principle which can be applied to suggest when an executive is on the right track from this democratic point of view?

The Political Analogy.—It is interesting that while this democratic impulse is gaining favor in industry, the public sentiment as to the value of political democracy is, in certain quarters, increasingly sceptical and even cynical. Arguments are abroad which in conflicting fashion aver that political democracy is a failure, that good government is impossible under democratic control, that true political democracy has never been tried, that self-government is a ridiculous objective. Throughout this undercurrent of contradictory criticism, one notes an unfortunate confusion between ends and means, between political objectives and governmental forms. Much of the adverse comment is really directed against *forms* of control which have proved unsuccessful.

The fundamental conception present in the writings of all the profound prophets of the democratic way of life—that democracy is a process and a spirit and not a form, that it is a dynamic experience of self-education and not a complete prescription of final structural plans, that self-government is better than good government in the sense that the personal growth of citizens is more valuable than technical expertness in operation —this essentially spiritual and psychological outlook upon democracy has tended to be forgotten. The quotations at the beginning of this chapter are introduced to suggest what the true emphasis of democracy's interpreters has been.

There exist, then, at the moment these two apparently contradictory forces in politics and industry. The pessimism in politics has seemingly grown out of a mistaken notion as to how to evaluate what is wanted in civic life and how to dramatize the democratic idea into workable forms. The optimistic bias in industry grows out of a groping and sometimes uncritical sentiment that self-government in economic life offers a way out of some of its most serious difficulties. If only the development of the democratic tendency in industry can in advance be controlled by those considerations which people have tended to forget in evaluating political democratic life, there is good reason to believe that this growth of economic democracy can help the entire community to a more healthy, experimental, and educational view of the essential soundness of the democratic outlook in all affairs. The hope that this may come about lies partly in the fact that industrial experiments, concerned as they are with matters closest to the purse strings, with matters of bread and butter and shelter, will, as they progress, be guarded from the worst mistakes of misapplied democratic notions by sheer Yankee shrewdness, by the necessities of a high productivity. Extreme decentralization of authority and control, for example, or a foolish extension of the "one man one vote" idea to decisions on all sorts of complex issues, or universal suffrage in the selection of big executives and staff heads—industry is, in the main, likely to be protected from these follies in a way and for reasons that did not apply so closely in civic matters. In short, unwise application of a mistaken idea of what democracy requires in conducting an organization is far less likely in industry than it was in political experiments, for the good reason that considerations of profit and productivity necessarily help everyone to keep realistic.

Broadly speaking, the processes which have laid political democracy open to the accusation of inefficiency are to be explained on one of two counts: Either the structural plan was not intelligently conceived as a technical instrument, or the leadership employed was defective in not educating the constituency to the responsibilities of its job. Industry can learn from both these shortcomings.

The political experiments with democracy, therefore, neither prove nor disprove in any final way the case for democracy in industry. They rather provide a presumption in favor of the general idea, because of the undeniable fact that, over a period of centuries, the tendency to place ultimate control over their own affairs in the hands of the rank and file of a people has, in fact, progressed and extended throughout the civilized world. Is there, perhaps, something in human nature which has made such a tendency inevitable?

The Needs of Human Nature.—The picture of human nature which this book has tried scientifically to build up emphasizes the need in every individual's life of adjusting a complex and contradictory group of impulses and habits to the requirements and delights of associated and corporate enterprises. A fairly definitely known body of inborn traits is early and progressively modified and organized into patterns of habits which people tend to repeat as often as they can but which they break and re-form as they find conflicts and obstructions when old habits are baulked. What we call the "claims of society," as well as people's internal conflicting desires, require more or less use of reasoning in the deliberate, conscious choice of alternatives. These choices are conditioned by many factors, including the purposes held in view at the moment. These purposes grow and change with changes in each total situation. In general, however, the purposes which individuals and groups adhere to over a period are those that seem to them to contribute to self-realization, to growth, to a freer range of choices, and a wiser experience of satisfaction in choices.

Human nature is not static in this adjusting process, for the process is never complete. The will to live of itself supplies people with the dynamic and eternal drive for better adjustments and fuller satisfactions. In short, no ends can ultimately be conceived as final beyond the end of more and more active living and being. One end of living is more living; one end of activity is still more activity. And that is why aims suggested by such words as "growth," "opportunity for self-expression," "self-realization," "emergence" are significant in human experience as major objectives.

All this characterization of human nature carries with it two important truths. First, people have necessarily to do *their own* experimenting as to what satisfies and brings better adjustment, their own choosing to see which of the fruits of life are sweet. Second, people have by nature to function in the vital affairs of living in larger and smaller associated groups, and they find positive satisfaction in the fact of association and of group efforts. In other words, human beings are progressively embarked upon a career of self-discovery, upon trying their powers and learning their grasp and reach. And they are embarked upon this career not as isolated or separable individuals, but as a network of interlocking and interfunctioning groups. Group experience is native to life, is itself pleasurable, is educational, is the medium in and through which self-realization comes by a process of reciprocal give and take. The relative value of the altruistic and egoistic emphasis in the individual life are, therefore, never absolute. No man *can* live to himself alone. It is only a question of the degree of his choice to be consciously group-minded and group-loyal.

The Idea of Democracy.—If, then, human nature is this kind of groping, yeasty, dynamic thing, struggling to self-knowledge, command and fuller experience, if it lives and grows in and through the experience of association, the kind of organization it needs for itself must reflect and be adjustable to these peculiar characteristics. The kind of organization suggested must, in its most general outline, *be one allowing room for self-choice, self-discovery, experiment, the testing of untried powers.* And it must be one in which group needs and claims and responsibilities balance and so far as possible harmonize with the claims of individual personality and its unfolding.

The case for democracy on its psychological side lies precisely here. "Democracy" however confusedly expressed has, as the human mind has become clearer about itself, been the word to connote that principle in group control and that motive in individual development, which have put upon associated human beings themselves the ultimate decisions about their destinies and affairs. Democracy has been the sentiment that significant and central in the determination of issues and practices in life, must come the claims of individual personalities and their flowering. The democratic idea is that for the best results in all the necessary forms of human association the acts of association must be made contributory to the fact of growth in personality.

The historic democratic rallying cry of liberty, equality, and fraternity may have been conceived philosophically. The important thing to realize is that it gets its stronger validation today from psychology, from the science which is trying to tell what people are and how they function best. The notion of liberty, psychologically viewed, has reference to the conditions necessary for the growth of responsibility, power, and insight in the individual.

The notion of equality, thus viewed, has reference to the necessity for opportunity for the unfolding of every individual's peculiar talents. It implies the necessity for recognizing and establishing that atmosphere in the group mentally and economically which will assure to each individual his chance to be what he can be.

The notion of fraternity, psychologically considered, has reference to the affectional conditions under which both liberty and equality are best assured. More than an intellectual conviction and more than mere institutional arrangements are required to keep people true to the assuring of conditions in which personality thrives. The quality of personal relationship, of regard, and of human interest which is implied in the word "fraternity" is an indispensable asset in human attitudes. The requirements of association, putting as they do an increasing burden of understanding and cooperation upon humankind, are made easier where a fraternal spirit prevails. The brotherly spirit supplies a needed lubricant, working in which the friction of the whole elaborate, organizational machine is greatly reduced.[3]

Psychologically viewed, therefore, the idea of democracy remains one of the biggest, most comprehensive, most penetrating and wise conceptions which the human mind has formulated. Its daring, its grasp of deep-rooted realities, its prophetic quality —these are equalled only by the astounding accuracy with which it goes to the heart of the problem of the nature of personality and the nature of the outreaching quality of life itself. The fact that as an idea it, of course, requires embodiment in institutional expression in organizations which may have varying degrees of effectiveness, should not distract attention from its underlying truth. And, on the other hand, the fact that its embodiment requires a certain kind of education, a certain kind of leadership, a widely held attitude of faith in human nature, can be ignored only at the peril of endangering the very democratic institutions which may be in process of becoming.

The conclusion is that the democratic idea is marching on because it is working in harmony with the major forces in human nature. There is, it should be emphasized, no inevitable, overriding, predestined quality to the idea. Democracy will be an achievement of the human spirit. It may conceivably come to nothing in the face of stupidity, selfishness, inertia, hatred, or prejudice. But, on the other hand, there is that in human nature which responds deeply to the idea and to the creative challenge which it presents. The conflicts, bafflements, obstructions, and disappointments of life will continue always to yield unrest in humanity and will thus spur it on in directions which seem to offer a lessening of the fetters and repressions to which human flesh is heir. And that direction, if one reads the human organism aright, is democratic in its spirit and method. Again and again, mankind has emerged from conditions of too great hardship and of too great luxury, from conditions of too great tyranny and of too great individual license, in order stubbornly to carry on its search for a way of life which balanced the claims of sense and spirit, of assertiveness and submissiveness, of obedience and independence. And that, it would seem, is exactly what it is trying to do in economic life today.

Whether or not it is to be successful depends on the factors already mentioned—on education, leadership, and faith. And it further depends on people's realizing the necessary limitations under which any given civilization labors in its efforts to give personality its chance to develop. Indeed, any conception of personality which conceived its fuller realization in terms unrelated to the basic conditions necessary to carrying on life would be superficial and transitory.

The idea of democracy in industry to be valid in this broader sense must take into account and be held in balance and perspective by the requirements of productivity, perpetuation of the race, and profit. Economic institutions which reckon without these three claims are doomed, however democratic they may seem from the point of view of seeming to assure individual growth. The population of our country must, it may fairly be assumed, be assured the basic necessities of food, clothes, and shelter. Any scheme of control, however nominally democratic, which by some mischance seriously cut down the total necessary productivity, would be digging its own grave. Also, the assumption is reasonably tenable that the population should be perpetuated. Any social measures or standards which interfered with the replacing of ourselves by another generation would be nihilistic, no matter how democratically they might have been adopted.

Similarly as to profits, if a distinction is made between profiteering and the earning of enough surplus income to supply needed new capital for necessary replacement and expansion, the latter will continue to be essential in a large-scale, machine civilization. Any measures which did away with profits in this special sense would again be suicidal, however popular the vote for their abolition.

It is in the light of considerations like these that democracy must work. Education in the necessity of applying these criteria in concrete decisions must sooner or later be provided. It is leadership that will help to make these limiting factors real to people that must be supplied.

Democracy in Action.—It is a sound impulse which realizes that democracy becomes no more real and living in providing scope for personality than its institutional embodiments allow. It is a process transmitted and utilized only as organizations in the various arenas of social life act in democratic ways. And industry is no exception. To become democratic, industry must embody in its ways of working the idea that people and their fuller life count preponderantly.

Industrial democracy is thus not, in the first instance, a form of organization. Nor is it merely an objective to be stated in abstract psychological terms. It begins to exist when there is combined a psychologically sound objective with an adequate organized setting. It is not any one specific arrangement; it has no one formula of organization, election, or voting. It may become articulate in quite diverse forms. And it may usefully exist, in partial form, at different levels in the economic structure. A factory or store organization may be democratically organized—and beneficially so. The idea may be applied to a corporation or an industry yet it should be remembered that until the democratic idea and point of view actuates, for example, the credit system or the banking policies of a country, the economic life will, in a serious way, be devoid of the larger implications of democracy in industry. To amplify this point would carry the discussion too far afield. It is rather the purpose only to suggest the pervasive influence which the democratic idea may have, once it gets fair headway in the economic world.

In the light of these complex possibilities, a definition of industrial democracy becomes increasingly difficult. But it may help to clarify the issues if we define it as *that state of economic*

institutions in which they are guided and controlled in ways cal-
culated to allow all members of the economic community an
opportunity to help formulate its objectives and, also, to realize for
themselves in and through their economic life a sense of personal
growth, development, and realization. It is that form of an organization which in a given time and place does, in fact, assure the
growth of free personalities among its members. Industrial
democracy will imply self-protection of individual and group
interests, self-assumption of individual and group cooperative
responsibilities, together with self-determination by persons and
functional groups of the ends they believe worth striving for.

In the light of this definition, many forms, methods, and
procedures will be found to be working educationally in a
democratic direction. And, in so far, they are good. But more
penetrating questions must be asked about such efforts. Are
the particular methods the best educational ones? Are additional methods being tried when one set of procedures has been
well established or has failed? Is the dynamic, progressive,
ever changing character of the problem of embodying democracy
fully realized by those directing the educational process? Are
those being educated having some control over the method and
manner of the process? Are they a conscious and, to some
degree, a willing party to the evolutionary process going forward?

Many organizations, both within economic life and without,
are and will increasingly satisfy in part the requirement of acting
as a training school for more democracy. The danger may be
that the good is interfering with the appearance of the better.
The touchstone by which to judge is in reality the constantly
progressive character of the instruction and of the recognition
of the claims of personal growth and achievement. Thus
judged, many corporations experimenting in this field may seem
lacking in courage and in pace. Especially on these counts
may their experimenting be at fault.

Every organization which is trying what it believes to be a
democratic experiment is thus pursuing at least two purposes—
one, the immediate purpose for which its members become
associated; the other, the education of its members in a demo-

cratic direction. Such an underlying duality of purposes is a wholesome corrective to the older view that associated groups had only the single purpose of their obvious and immediate objective.

One can, in short, view with interest many liberal experiments in industrial government today. Perhaps the most determining factors in disclosing their soundness are, first, knowledge of the motives that actuate their trial; and, second, evidence embodied in procedures to indicate the astuteness with which the educational emphasis is being combined with the necessary striving after immediate ends. Where the motive is explicitly educational for all the personalities involved and explicitly in the direction of a progressively broadened control in self-direction, the soundness and effectiveness of "industrial democracy" experiments are undoubtedly increased. Yet it is of the essence of the social process that experiments and new procedures set up for one purpose prove, as time goes on, to be contributing to the carrying on of other purposes. And in industry it is thus true that many new methods in personnel management may prove to be unconsciously contributing to a state of mind and body which will, in fact, greatly facilitate the spread of the democratic idea.

Tests of democratic soundness have, therefore, to be applied with utmost care. It certainly is not possible to look with equal favor on all activities of a "personnel" character in industry, even though some of them may undoubtedly and unwittingly be by way of yielding fruits of an educational sort which will be good. Those organizational experiments which promise to help society most in its search for "democratic" techniques are those which are explicitly and intelligently being directed to building an organizational form *in which aims of personality development for all and self-realization for all are really controlling factors in shaping choices. The intention to bring a larger and larger number in each corporate group progressively into a position of sharing in basic decisions on purpose, policy, and method is essential to the soundest progress.* Growth is conditional upon the assumption of personal responsibility, upon the exercise of personal choice. The area over which that choice should be exercised can never be finally stated, as it grows with capacity. And that is one more reason why the process of arriving at group decisions must be flexibly conceived by leaders with an eye on the development of the group.

How essential it is for this intention to be conscious is further seen when one realizes that its existence in an individual indicates, also, the presence of a growing sense of faith in the possibilities of human nature. And in action that faith plus that intention are together calculated to yield good results, if to them are added (as in every activity of life) a sufficient injection of intelligent deliberation about methods of action.

Are All Purposes Equally Good?—The attempt to characterize democracy inevitably raises one further point to which, even if no final answer can be supplied, consideration must be given. How do we know that claims for self-realization will not be so individualistic that a universalizing of this objective would lead in a fundamentally anarchistic direction? Will attempts to enrich personality require a kind of individualism in personal standards and organized efforts which will defeat the necessities of cooperative group living? Is there, speaking institutionally, a necessary disparity between self-government and good government?

Adequate answer to these questions might well require another complete volume. Two brief paragraphs must suffice.

First, the hope of personality development is tied up integrally with the hope of group and community development. People are so made mentally that their efforts at realization may be as individual and unique as they want, and they will still, in the main and under normal conditions, be contributing to the social process. Indeed, with some few reservations, the more individual and distinctive the manner in which they endeavor to express themselves the richer life is made for all. Personality development generalized as an objective leads not to anarchy but to a richly variegated life, in which quality in the individual life and significance in the social contribution become two ways of looking at the same thing. And the reason for this is that the forces normally controlling in healthy human beings are forces whose release makes for their own and others' fuller life. The aspect of native "sinfulness" so emphasized in certain earlier views of human nature certainly cannot be ignored; but its relative importance is far less than was supposed. And the redemptive influences of social pressure and yearning for approval can be counted on far more than has usually been realized. Some other redemptive force may additionally be required to give, even in normal people, the balance of social outlook demanded of them for the best communal living. If and where such a force is necessary, that may be the distinctive field in which religion should and will function. But that there is a relatively large share of "natural" living which is also good social living, is the point to be stressed.

Second, we are not without guides from previous human experience as to what channels of activity give permanent self-satisfaction. The testing process as to what experience is satisfying does, in a real sense, begin anew with every individual. But along with that testing process goes and should go the educational process *which gives every individual some inkling of what the consensus of human experience has been as to what activities have been found satisfying.* Here, again, history psychologically viewed shows some approximate uniformity in the forms of experience which people have sought out and enjoyed.

It suggests that they want to create, to appreciate, to give and have affection, and in order to do all three they find they have to exercise self-control. No final or single objectives can be stated. But the range of human activities will normally tend to fall into ways of action in creation, into acts yielding esthetic satisfactions, into affectional enjoyments, and into the disciplines of self-control. And the differing outlets of expression which different personalities find in these several fields of human activity will tend to be good and contributory to fullness of life, provided the choices are made in some reasonably rational way in the light of what human experience has historically found good.

In other words, self-realization is not an anarchistic and anti-social objective. The self is realized in and through experiences which are socially valuable to just the extent that the individual makes critical and discriminating use of the broadly moral, ethical and esthetic experiences and judgments of the past in which he has been instructed.

Conclusion.—We are then in a position to give at least a general answer to our question as to when a given democratic experiment is relatively sound. It is sound when it has the intention of giving due weight to the claims of self-realization of the members of an organization while serving the immediate claims of the organization's explicit purpose and, also, while it conceives of that necessary self-realization as entailing in action the exercise of self-control, the outplay of creativity, the exercise of affection, and a keen awareness of sensuous appreciations.

A psychological approach to problems of industrial government is distinctly enlightening and heartening. The democratic trend, where now observable, seems sound and in need only of more conscious and deliberate direction and acceleration.

Human nature is not exalted or deified as it has been presented in this book. We have been mindful of its origins and its limitations. But it does offer us the only material with which we have to work. As such, it has far greater potentialities than, in our inertia, fatigue, or discouragement, we sometimes believe.

The way ahead to a more mature and effectual control of human behavior in the interest of human beings themselves and of their own richer life lies in and through the use of psychological knowledge in progressively more democratic institutions. And such knowledge must be used not alone by the acknowledged leaders of organizations but by the members themselves. They too, all the way down the line, have to come to a fuller self knowledge, which will be the basis of a wider exercise of new power and of a deeper experience of satisfaction in living.

Industrial democracy psychologically viewed is a valid and valuable conception and objective. But to progress toward it will require that a new aristocracy emerge, recruited out of every group in society—an aristocracy of leaders possessing character, intellect, faith, and goodwill.

> "The common problem, yours, mine, everyone's,
> Is—not to fancy what were fair in life
> Provided it could be—but, finding first
> What may be, then find how to make it fair
> Up to our means: a very different thing!"

FOOTNOTES TO CHAPTERS

Chapter II

[1] HUXLEY, JULIAN, "Essays in Popular Science."

[2] THURSTONE, L. L., "The Nature of Intelligence," pp. 166–167.

[3] See, for example, HAGGARD, H. G., "What You Should Know about Health and Disease."

[4] See a good summary, THOMSON, M. K., "The Springs of Human Action."

[5] See, for example, WOODWORTH, R. S., "Psychology, a Study of Mental Life," Chaps. II, III.

[6] ROBINSON, JAMES HARVEY, "The Mind in the Making."

Chapter III

[1] A number of books which in the accuracy of their scientific vocabulary and nomenclature are now out of date are nevertheless useful from the descriptive and interpretive point of view, and as interpretations they can still be profitably read. See TEAD, ORDWAY, "Instincts in Industry," Boston, 1918; PARKER, CARLETON H., "The Casual Laborer and Other Essays," New York, 1919; MAROT, HELEN, "The Creative Impulse in Industry," New York, 1918.

[2] An excellent statement of this point of view is to be found in "What's on the Worker's Mind" and "The Mainsprings of Men" by Whiting Williams.

Chapter IV

[1] From BRIERLEY, S. S., "An Introduction to Psychology," pp. 83, 84–85; 86. Reprinted in "Source Book of Social Psychology."

[2] See DEWEY, JOHN, "The Public and Its Problems."

[3] For further details, see WATSON, JOHN B., "Psychology from the Standpoint of the Behaviorist," pp. 227–228.

Chapter V

[1] Paraphrased from DEWEY, JOHN, "Human Nature and Conduct," pp. 40, 41. This entire discussion of habit leans heavily on this source for its inspiration. The contribution of Dewey's work to clear thinking in psychology is tremendous.

[2] See JAMES, WILLIAM, "Psychology, a Briefer Course," Chap. X

[3] "Human Nature and Conduct," *op. cit.*, p. 193.

⁴ This interesting subject is helpfully discussed, for example, in "Being Well Born," by M. F. Guyer.

⁵ WOODWORTH, R. S., "Psychology, a Study of Mental Life," p. 177 The sections on the sensory equipment and the feelings draw heavily on this source.

⁶ FOLSOM, J. K., "The Conditioned Response and Personality," *Industrial Psychology*, December, 1926.

⁷ HOCKING, W. E., "Human Nature and Its Remaking," p. 148.

Chapter VI

¹ See THOMPSON, F. W., "Principles and Technique of Teaching," p. 37.
² *Op. cit.*, p. 353.
³ THORNDIKE, E. L., Quoted in "Source Book of Social Psychology," by Kimball Young, p. 140.
⁴ See YOUNG, p. 131.

Chapter VII

¹ See his "The Art of Thought."
² "Human Nature and Conduct," p. 193.   Subsequent sentences in this paragraph quote or paraphrase further from this volume.
³ See ROBINSON, E. S., ed., "Readings in General Psychology."
 CARR, HARVEY, article on "Types of Rational Problems."
⁴ HOCKING, W. E., "Human Nature and Its Remaking."
⁵ If anyone wants to realize the real range of topics comprised in "knowing one's subject" on this matter, let him examine the book, "How to Get Ahead Financially," by William A. Schnedler.

Chapter VIII

¹ McDOUGALL, WILLIAM, "Introduction to Social Psychology," paraphrased from p. 186.
² DEWEY, JOHN, "Reconstruction in Philosophy," p. 177.
³ CHARTERS, W. W., in the *American Magazine*, 1924.

Chapter IX

¹ See PARKER, CARLETON H., "The Casual Laborer and Other Essays."
² HOUSER, J. DAVID, "What the Employer Thinks."
³ See SMITH, E. D., Psychology for Executives, Chap. VII.
⁴ See SMITH, E. D., "Psychology for Executives."
⁵ See HART, BERNARD, "The Psychology of Insanity," for an excellent popular account of the subjects in this entire chapter.
⁶ For a fuller and excellent discussion of this subject, see ANDERSON, V. V., "Psychiatry in Industry."

Chapter X

[1] HEADLEY, L. A., "How to Study in College," p. 57.

[2] LAING, B. W., "A Study in Moral Problems," p. 218.

[3] LINDEMAN, E. C., "Industrial Technique and Social Ethics," *The Survey*, August, 1923.

[4] See FOLLETT, M. P., "Creative Experience."

[5] A further analysis of the conflict idea, not identical in conclusion with the above but of value as specifying a number of important and frequently met kinds of conflict, follows:

"In summary, therefore, let me repeat that there are but seven major types of conflict: (1) the pseudo-conflict of misunderstanding; (2) the intentional conflict of dishonesty; (3) the irrational conflict of emotional bias. The remainder form a series of rational conflicts, the first of which (4) is the conflict based upon the conclusion drawn from different facts, the second (5) disagreement as to what the facts are, the third (6) disagreement caused by defects in the generalizing process, and fourth (7) conflicts caused by differences in interpretation. Each has its appropriate remedy. It is our duty as rational beings, when we find ourselves in conflict with a fellow being, not to dissipate our energy in useless brainstorms but rationally to classify the conflict as to type, attach the proper label, and apply the proper remedy." S. A. Courtis, in *School and Society*, p. 709, June 5, 1926. See, also, the suggestions in "The Social Worker as Prophet," E. C. Lindeman, *The Survey*, June 15, 1924.

Chapter XI

[1] YOUNG, OWEN D., in his Dedication Address, Harvard Graduate School of Business Administration, see *Harvard Business Review*, p. 392, July, 1927.

[2] Excerpts from the review of his book "Icarus, or The Future of Science," in the *New Republic*, Oct. 22, 1924.

[3] DEWEY, JOHN, "Reconstruction in Philosophy," p. 209.

Chapter XII

[1] From NICHOLAS MURRAY, BUTLER, "Enthusiasm," address delivered at the 173rd Commencement of Columbia University, June 1, 1927.

[2] CHARTERS, W. W., *Amer. Management Assoc., Ann. Convention Ser.* 69, 1927.

[3] For further suggestions on this subject, see the references for Chaps. XII to XIV on p. 306.

[4] For a fuller discussion of the machinery of coordination, see Tead and Metcalf, "Personnel Administration," Chap. XXV.

[5] WHITE, AGNES B., "Does Leadership or the Machine Determine Productions?" *Industrial Psychology*, May, 1928.

[6] Navy Education Study Courses, *Personnel Management* 7, p. 6, Washington, D. C., 1923.

Chapter XIII

[1] HOCKING, WILLIAM E., "Morale and Its Enemies," p. 150.

[2] See, in this connection, an excellent series of articles by Glenn L. Gardiner, in *Industrial Psychology*, during 1928.

Chapter XIV

[1] "Dynamic Psychology."

[2] In TEAD and METCALF, "Personnel Administration," we have, in Chap. XXV, discussed this problem from the point of view of securing functional representation in a corporate organization.

[3] In *The Columbia Cauldron*, May, 1928.

[4] This problem is considered in more detail in Tead and Metcalf, "Personnel Administration," Chap. XXV.

Chapter XV

[1] See his "Psychiatry in Industry," Chap. VII; see, also, for a full and valuable discussion of this whole problem as it affects salesmen KENAGY, H. G., and C. S. YOAKUM, "The Selection and Training of Salesmen," Chaps. X–XIII.

[2] See in addition to other works referred to; BENGE, E. J., "How to Prepare and Validate an Employee Test;" *Amer. Management Assoc., Proceedings Inst. Management* 9.

[3] FREEMAN, F. L., "Mental Tests: Their History and Applications," p. 491.

[4] See an excellent summary of the use of such tests for typists: FREYD, MAX, "Selection of Typists," *Jour. Personnel Res.* 12, Vol. V, p. 490.

[5] LAIRD, D. A., "The Psychology of Selecting Men," 2d ed., pp. 283–287; BURTT, H. E., "Principles of Employment Psychology," p. 292–293.

[6] See O'CONNOR, JOHNSON, "Born That Way;" POND, MILLICENT, "Selective Placement of Metal Workers," *Jour. Personnel Res.* 9, 10 Vol. V, SNOW, A. J., "Psychology in Business Relations," Chap. XXX; see, also, ANDERSON, L. D., "Minnesota Mechanical Ability Test," *Personnel Jour.* 6, Vol. VI, p. 473; SHELLOW, S. M., and W. J. McCARTER, "Who Is a Good Motorman?" *Personnel Jour.* 5, Vol. VI, p. 338.

[7] BURTT, H. E., *op. cit.*, pp. 223–225.

[8] See GRIFFITTS, C. H., "Fundamentals of Vocational Psychology," pp. 332–334; also, STRONG, E. K. (1) Also STRONG, E. K., *Jour. Personnel Res.*, Vol. V, "An Interest Test for Personnel Managers;" pp. 194–203; "Interest Analysis of Personnel Managers;" pp. 235–242; also COWDERY, K. M., "Measurement of Professional Abilities," *Jour. Personnel Res.*, Vol. V, pp. 131–141.

[9] BURTT, H. E., *op. cit.*, pp. 314–16.

¹⁰ See in, this connection, the following: ELLERD, H. G., "Rating Supervisors," *Amer. Management Assoc. Production Executives Ser.* 42; STEARNS, W. D. and others, "Measuring and Grading the Supervisory Forces," *Amer. Management Assoc. Ann. Convention Ser.* 26.

¹¹ BINGHAM, W. V. and M. FREYD, "Procedures in Employment Psychology," p. 135.

¹² *Ibid.*, pp. 135–140.

¹³ For details see Tead and Metcalf's "Personnel Administration," pp. 70–71.

Chapter XVI

¹ THORNDIKE, E. L., and others, "Adult Learning," p. 179.

² THORNDIKE, E. L., *op. cit.*, p. 178.

³ KENAGY, H. G., "The Technique of Training on the Job," *Amer. Management Assoc., Ann. Convention Ser.* 74, 1928.

⁴ HANUS, PAUL, H., *Taylor Soc. Bull.* 6, Vol. X, p. 282, December, 1925.

Chapter XVII

¹ CHASE, STUART, "Men and Machines," in *The New Republic,* March 6, 1929.

² "Talks to Teachers," p. 94.

³ In TEAD and METCALF, "Personnel Administration, Its Principles and Practice," New York, 1926, we have reviewed in detail (Chap. XIV) numerous methods and devices being used to arouse interest. That chapter may profitably be read in this connection, since it supplements, in a factual way, the psychological background which is here provided.

⁴ "Methods of Wage Payment," Committee on Industrial Relations, *Nat. Metal Trade Assoc.,* Chicago, 1928.

⁵ For the suggestion regarding these four points I am indebted to Walter N. Polakov, "General Theory of Incentives and Its Application," *Amer. Management Assoc., Production Executives' Ser.* 25, 1925.

⁶ *The Human Factor,* 31, Vol. II, July 15, 1926.

⁷ SMITH, ELLIOTT D., "Financial Incentives," *Taylor Soc. Bull.* 3, Vol. XII, p. 429, June, 1927. The first four of the above principles are suggested by Mr. Smith's thoughtful discussion.

⁸ POFFENBERGER, A. T., an unpublished lecture before the Bureau of Personnel Administration, Nov. 15, 1928, on "The Measurement of Human Work."

⁹ WESTBROOK, FRANCIS, A., "Maintaining an Efficient Force of 1,500 Girl Operators," *Industrial Management* 6, Vol. LXXIV, p. 336, December, 1927.

¹⁰ DENNISON, HENRY S., "Incentives for Executives," *Amer. Management Assoc., Ann. Convention Ser.* 71, p. 10, New York, 1928.

¹¹ A valuable summary of recent experience with suggestion systems is to be found in Z. C. Dickinson, "Suggestions for Employees," *Univ. Mich. Business Studies* 3, Vol. I, August, 1927.

[12] SUDDARD, T. W., "Sharing Information with Employees Improves Product and Cuts Costs," *Manufacturing Ind.* 2, Vol. XV, p. 94, February, 1928.

[13] The American Management Association has, in pamphlet form, an extensive series of excellent and informing recent addresses and research studies on incentive plans, which any company embarking in this field will find to offer most valuable guidance. See their *Production Executives' Series.*

See, also, BLOOMFIELD, DANIEL, Ed., "Financial Incentives for Executives and Employees," for an extensive enumeration of specific methods.

[14] "Methods of Wage Payment," *op. cit.*, p. 51.

[15] ATKINSON, HENRY, "Cooperative Production," *U. S. Dept. Labor Monthly Rev.*, The Priestman-Atkinson System, London, 1927.

[16] "Incentives for Executives," *op. cit.*, pp. 7–8.

[17] FEIS, HERBERT, "Labor Relations," pp. 46–47.

[18] *Service Talks* 4, Vol. IX, Feb. 28, 1928.

[19] "Our New Industrial Set-up," *Mag. Business* 1, Vol. LIV, p. 24, July, 1922.

[20] *Printers' Ink*, p. 42, Feb. 23, 1928.

[21] "Profit Sharing and Stock Ownership for Employees," pp. 118–119.

Chapter XVIII

[1] SMITH, GEDDES, "The Adult: His Work," *Survey* 1, Vol. LX, p. 34, Apr. 1, 1928.

[2] From an unpublished address before the Bureau of Personnel Administration, New York, Mar. 1, 1928.

Chapter XIX

[1] See LEITCH, JOHN, "Man to Man," for a description of this procedure in action.

[2] As, for example, in the Dennison Manufacturing Company, the Columbia Conserve Company, the American Cast Iron and Pipe Company, Henry A. Dix and Company, the Philadelphia Rapid Transit Company, and a few others.

[3] For further elaboration of the point of view in these three paragraphs, see T. V. SMITH, "The Democratic Way of Life" and "The American Idea of Equality."

SELECTED REFERENCES

These references are deliberately confined to books despite the fact that the periodical literature in the field is voluminous. Most of it, however, is inaccessible except in so far as one has access to such journals as

Industrial Psychology (now discontinued)
The Journal of Applied Psychology
The Personnel Journal
The Psychological Abstracts
The Taylor Society Bulletin

The listing of book titles aims to be selective and brief, for which reason a book is only listed once, despite the fact that many of them have chapters relating to several chapters in this book.

CHAPTER I

ALLPORT, F. H., "Social Psychology."
EWER, B. C., "Applied Psychology."
HART, J. K., "Inside Experience."
LEWISOHN, S. A., "The New Leadership in Industry."
METCALF, H. C., ED., "Psychological Foundations of Management."
METCALF, H. C., ED., "Scientific Foundations of Business Administration."
MYERS, C. S., "Industrial Psychology."
OVERSTREET, H. A., "Influencing Human Behavior."
PARKER, C. H., "The Casual Laborer and Other Essays."
POFFENBERGER, A. T., "Applied Psychology."
SMITH, E. D., "Psychology for Executives."
WILLIAMS, WHITING, "The Mainsprings of Men."
———, "What's on the Worker's Mind?"

CHAPTERS II TO VIII

DEWEY, J., "Human Nature and Conduct."
———, "How We Think."
EDMAN, I., "Human Traits and Their Social Significance."
ELLIS, R. S., "The Psychology of Individual Differences."
JAMES, W., "Psychology, Briefer Course."

KOFFKA, K., "The Growth of the Mind."
McCLURE, M. T., "How to Think in Business."
McDOUGALL, W., "Introduction to Social Psychology."
MARTIN, E. D., "The Behavior of Crowds."
OGDEN, C. K., "The Meaning of Psychology."
THOMSON, M. K., "The Springs of Human Action."
VALENTINE, P. F., "The Psychology of Personality."
WALLAS, G., "The Art of Thought."
WATSON, J. B., "Psychology from the Standpoint of a Behaviorist."
WOODWORTH, R. S., "Psychology, A Study of Mental Life."

CHAPTER IX

ANDERSON, V. V., "Psychiatry in Industry."
BRILL, A. A., "Psychoanalysis: Its Theories and Practical Application."
FERENZI, S., "Contributions to Psychoanalysis."
HART, B., "The Psychology of Insanity."
PFISTER, O., "The Psychoanalytic Method."
TANSLEY, A. G., "The New Psychology and Its Relation to Life."

CHAPTERS X AND XI

FOLLETT, M. P., "Creative Experience."
LINDEMAN, E. C., "Social Discovery."

CHAPTERS XII TO XIV

ANDREWS, L. C., "Manpower."
BURTON, E. R., "Employee Representation."
CRAIG, D. R. and W. W. CHARTERS, "Personal Leadership in Industry."
CUSHMAN, F., "Foremanship and Supervision."
DIEMER, H., "Foremanship Training."
ELLIOTT, H. S., "The Process of Group Thinking."
Federal Board for Vocational Education, "The Training of Foreman Conference Leaders."
GARDINER, G. L., "Practical Foremanship."
HOUSER, J. D., "What the Employer Thinks."
HUNT, E. E., "Conferences, Committees and Conventions."
Inquiry, The, "Creative Discussion."
Research Bureau for Retail Training, "The Conference Method."
SCHELL, E. H., "The Technique of Executive Control."
SHEFFIELD, A. D., "Joining in Public Discussion."
———, "Training for Group Experience."

CHAPTER XV

BINGHAM, W. V. and M. FREYD, "Procedures in Employment Psychology."
BURTT, H. E., "Principles of Employment Psychology."

GRIFFITTS, C. H., "Fundamentals of Vocational Psychology."
HOOPINGARNER, N. L., "Personality and Business Analysis."
KENAGY, H. C. and C. S. YOAKUM, "Selection and Training of Salesmen."
KITSON, H. D., "The Psychology of Vocational Adjustment."
KORNHAUSER, A. W. and F. A. KINGSBURY, "Psychological Tests in Business."
LAIRD, D. A., "The Psychology of Selecting Men."
LINK, H. C., "Employment Psychology."
MANSON, G. E., "Bibliography of Analysis and Measurement of Human Personality up to 1926."
MOORE, B. V., "The Personal Interview, An Annotated Bibliography."
O'CONNOR, J., "Born That Way."
PEAR, T. H., "Fitness for Work."
SCOTT, W. D. and R. C. CLOTHIER, "Personnel Management."
SNOW, A. W., "Psychology in Business Relations."
TEAD, O., and H. C. METCALF, "Personnel Administration, Its Principles and Practice."
WIGGAM, A. E., "Exploring Your Mind."

CHAPTER XVI

ALLEN, C. R., "The Instructor, the Man and the Boss."
DEWEY, J., "Democracy and Education."
GATES, A. J., "Psychology for Students of Education."
GREENE, J. H., "Organized Training in Business."
JAMES, W., "Talks to Teachers on Psychology."
MELLEN, G. F., "Foreman Training."
THORNDIKE, E. C. and OTHERS, "Adult Learning."

CHAPTERS XVII TO XVIII

CHASE, S., "Men and Machines."
HOBSON, J. A., "Incentives in the New Industrial Order."
FISHER, B., "The Mental Causes of Accidents."

CHAPTER XIX

DEWEY, J., "Reconstruction in Philosophy."
———, "The Public and Its Problems."
LAING, B. M., "A Study in Moral Problems."
MASON, J. W. T., "Creative Freedom."
SANTAYANA, G., "Dialogues in Limbo."
SHELDON, O., "The Philosophy of Management."
SMITH, T. V., "The Democratic Way of Life."
———, "The American Philosophy of Equality."
WHITEHEAD, A. N., "Science and the Modern World."

INDEX